Angels, Bulldogs & Dragons

The 355th Fighter Group In World War II

Angels Bulldogs & Dragons

By
Bill Marshall

Champlin Fighter Museum

Copyright © 1984 by Bill Marshall

Published by Champlin Fighter Museum
Falcon Field, 4636 Fighter Aces Drive, Mesa, Arizona 85205

All rights reserved. No part of this book may be reproduced in any manner whatsoever without written permission from the publisher, except by reviewers who may quote brief passages to be printed in a magazine or newspaper.

Library of Congress Catalog Number
International Standard Book Number 0-912173-02-5
Printed and bound in the United States of America.

Library of Congress Cataloging in Publication Data

Marshall, Bill, 1945-
   Angels, Bulldogs and Dragons.

1. World War, 1939-1945 — Aerial operations, American.
2. United States. Army Air Forces. Fighter Group,
355th — History. I. Title. II. Title: Angels, Bulldogs, and Dragons.
D790.M335   1984   940.54'4973   85-5738
ISBN 0-912173-02-5

CONTENTS

	Page
FOREWORD (Graham)	V
INTRODUCTION	VI
ACKNOWLEDGEMENTS	VII
GLOSSARY	VIII
THE FAMILY TREE	X
COMBAT OPERATIONS DIARY, 1943	1
SUMMARY OF COMBAT OPERATIONS, 1943	7
COMBAT OPERATIONS DIARY, 1944	16
SUMMARY OF COMBAT OPERATIONS, 1944	86
COMBAT OPERATIONS DIARY, 1945	87
SUMMARY OF COMBAT OPERATIONS, WW II	117
POST VE-DAY	119
THE SECOND SCOUTING FORCE	120
POSTSCRIPT (Hovde)	122
APPENDIX A: CLAIMS	123
TABLE A CLAIMS	124
TABLE B AWARDS	134
TABLE C ACES	139
APPENDIX B: "FIRST, FASTEST & MOSTEST"	140
APPENDIX C: CAMPAIGNS of the 355th	141
APPENDIX D: UNIT CITATIONS	142
APPENDIX E: COMMANDING OFFICERS	143
APPENDIX F: LOSSES	144
APPENDIX G: ABOVE & BEYOND	153
APPENDIX H: THE LAST SHUTTLE	156
APPENDIX I: "ONE MISSION"	162

FOREWORD

"The most important branch of aviation is pursuit, which fights for and gains control of the air."
Brigadier General William Mitchell

The 355th Fighter Group was manned, trained and functioned similarly to many other fighter groups in World War II. No specially qualified people were assigned to it, nor was unusual training nor unique equipment furnished. But the 355th's outstanding combat record set it apart from similar units. Its achievements resulted from outstanding leadership in the air, loyalty and dedication of the non-flying personnel, and the spirit of the pilots.

This book has been carefully researched and methodically documented. Unlike many similar and interesting books about World War II fighter units, it was not written by a member of the group, and thus the subjectivity which inevitably creeps into such volumes has been avoided. The story of the 355th, as described in "Angels, Bulldogs and Dragons," is not bright and shiny from beginning to end. Mistakes were made. On occasion, missions were far from 100 percent successful. Human errors of judgement and execution occurred. Aircraft and pilots were lost. However, the group's overall performance placed it at the top of its class.

Today, the 355th Tactical Training Wing is an active unit of the United States Air Force's Tactical Air Command, following a superb record in Vietnam. From the original 355th Fighter Group, which was deactivated, reactivated, transferred and re-equipped several times, has been handed down the proud record of the World War II years, as related by Bill Marshall. I am certain the present 355th is aware and proud of its heritage and the accomplishments of the officers and men of the World War II organization.

Gordon M. Graham
Lieutenant General, USAF (Ret)

INTRODUCTION

The 355th Fighter Group was a combat organization that completed operations at the end of World War II as one of the very best American fighter groups. As the 355th Tactical Fighter Wing it carried on the traditions established during the Second World War, was acknowledged as one of the Airforce's top groups in Viet Nam and emerged as a fighting unit with one of the richest traditions in the annals of airpower.

"Angels, Bulldogs and Dragons" is a book in diary form, of the early history of the 355th and only attempts to capture the contributions of the group during combat operations in World War II. The history of the 355thTFW must be left for another time.

As the sixth operational fighter group in the 8th Air Force, the 355th did not begin its career with any particular distinction as far as victories over the Luftwaffe, and was in the middle of the pack until March of 1944. In the author's opinion, the spark that propelled the group into prominence was the February field order from 8th Air Force Command which instructed all fighter groups to "seek and destroy the German air force in the air and on the ground". The authority to go to the deck in search of the Lufwaffe enabled the 355th to combine the structured and restraining duty as bomber escorts with agressive pursuit of German aircraft after relief from escort tasks, and not have the two roles in conflict. The result was not only wholesale destruction of German aircraft on the ground but also massive destruction to road, rail and barge transportation. The latter fighter mission may have contributed as much to the collapse of Germany's ability to resist defeat in the West as the defeat of the Luftwaffe fighter arm.

While the 355th emerged as one of the best fighter groups in the Army Air Force as far as ratios of victories to losses in aerial combat, it absolutely excelled in perhaps the most dangerous fighter mission of all, namely the strafing of heavily defended airfields in the heart of Germany. The 355th pioneered and executed proven strategies to limit losses on strafing missions but still paid a terrible price. The group completed combat operations with the third highest total losses of all 8th Air Force fighter groups, mostly due to German flak.

This book is dedicated to the "Steeple Morden Strafers", the ground crews, the unsung support personnel and most of all to those who did not make it back. My hat is off to each and every one.

ACKNOWLEDGEMENTS

"Angels, Bulldogs and Dragons" is the result of thirty plus years active interest and four years of hard work. The seed of this project started growing shortly after the passing of the author's best friend and father, Bert Wilder Marshall, Jr. While sorting out his various high school, college and career scrapbooks and photos, the author decided to reorganize and restore the collection to a more permanent form suitable for donation to the American Fighter Aces Association.

Because the author wanted to include the photos of some of his father's best friends such as Billy Hovde, Royce Priest, Gordon Graham, Chuck Lenfest and Henry Brown, each was contacted and solicited for a few photos. The response was so overwhelming that the author was able to piece together a pretty decent photo collection of both the 354th and 358th Fighter Squadrons and was motivated to expand the project beyond a photo album of Bert Marshall's career. The result is now in your hands and, needless to say, it would not have been possible without the enthusiastic support of many veterans, surviving spouses and other interested people who contributed in so many ways.

Particular comment and acknowledgment must be made in reference to Garry Fry and Jeffery Ethell and their superb effort in "Escort to Berlin." Their book on the 4th Fighter Group provided the model for my own work. My hat is off to both for setting an example for all serious historians to shoot for.

The following members of the 355th Fighter Group contributed photos, information and time: Robert Allison, Charles Badavas, Robert Baldwin, Phillip Barnhart, Robert Barnhouse, Henry Bille, William Boulet, Morton Braun, Patrick Brennan, John Brooks, Henry Brown, Chester Butcher, Jeff Caldwell, Al Channing, Roe Claar, William Cullerton, William Cummings, Arthur De Costa, Robert Delhamer, Carl Decklar, Ward Douglass, James Duffy, Bill Dumas, John Elder, Francis Eshelman, Norman Fortier, Roscoe Fussell, Donald Galer, Robert Garlich, William Gilchrist, Myron Glantz, Victor Gore, Gordon Graham, Howard Greenwell, Walter Gresham, Walter Griswold, Larry Hart, Charles Hauver, Fred Haviland, Charles Hecht, Mason Hendrickson, William Hovde, Thomas Hubbard, Robert Hulderman, Carl Hull, Victor Iglesias, Norbert Jackson, Joe Kerch, Robert Kidwell, Harold Knight, Walter Koral, Walter Kossack, William Kubetin, Henry Kucheman, Robert Kuhnert, Robert Kurtz, Charles Lamer, Charles Lenfest, Danny Lewis, Walter MacFarlane, Harold Macurdy, John McGarity, Mac McGuinn, Phillip McHugh, Edward McNeff, Joe Mellen, Lee Mendenhall, Leslie Minchew, Anthony Mocerino, John Molnar, Ray Morris, Julius Moseley, Raymond Myers, Burdette Newcity, Richard Nyman, Robert Patelunas, Warren Peglar, Emil Perry, Noble Peterson, Harrison Price, Royce Priest, Scott Prothro, Fred Ramsdell, Fred Roberts, Ken Robinson, Charles Rosenblatt, Albert Santos, Morton Schmucker, Jerome Seidl, Ray Shewfelt, Floyd Shultz, Stanley Silva, Burton Sims, Emil Sluga, Albert Starr, Everett Stewart, Edward Szaniawski, James Tavares, Floyd Taylor, Gerald Thompson, Gale Torrey, Duran Vickery, Roy Vose, Douglas Warden, John Weidmann, Henry Wertz, Alvin White, Robert White, Robert Whitlow, Marvin Whitten, John Wilkerson, Glynn Williams, Brady Williamson, Jesse Williamson, Marion Wing, Robert Woody, Gil Wright, and John Wytko.

The widows of other deceased 355th veterans who contributed to this project are Mrs. William Gertzen, Mrs. Clarence Graham, Mrs. Garlyn Hoffman, Mrs. Ruth Kinnard, Mrs. Norman (Olson) Kresler, and Mrs. Everett Stewart.

Veteran aces historians who contributed so much time, photos, and advice include Bob Bennett, Marvin Bradburn, Harley Copic, Jeffrey Ethell, Chuck Francis, Garry Fry, Bill Hess, George Shiller, Barrett Tillman, and Ray Toliver.

Personnel from the Air Force Museum and the Albert Simpson Historical Research Center really lent a helping hand. Particular thanks go to Charles Worman, Judy Endicott, and Lynn Gamma for efforts "above and beyond".

Special thanks are extended to Bob Barnhouse, Marvin Bradburn, Henry Brown, Chet Butcher, Hank Bille, Jeff Ethell, Carl Decklar, Bill Dumas, Garry Fry, Don Galer, Adolph Galland, Gordon Graham, Bill Hess, Larry Hart, Fred Haviland, Billy Hovde, Ruth Kinnard, Hank Kucheman, Chuck Lenfest, Danny Lewis, Les Minchew, Pete Pompetti, Royce Priest (a man other than my father to whom I may owe my very existence!), Fred Ramsdell, Ken Robinson, Burt Sims, George Shiller, Ray Toliver, Gale Torrey, John Weidmann, and Glynn Williams.

My love to the special women who made this project possible: Mrs. Emmie Christy, who spent so much time helping me put this together, Mrs. Jane Marshall, who put me on this earth and provided so much love and support to both my father and myself, and especially my wife and best friend Dawn, for having the patience to see this through the tough times.

Bill Marshall
March 1984

GLOSSARY

Abort - turn back from a mission due to potential or actual mechanical problems
Ace - designation given to fighter pilot for destroying five or more enemy aircraft in the air. The Eighth Air Force designated pilots who destroyed five or more aircraft in any combination of air or the ground as aces but recinded the designation after the war
A/C - aircraft
A/D - airdrome
Area Support - name used to describe a fighter mission whose purpose was to provide cover for a particular area rather than close escort along the bomber track
Baby - slang for droppable fuel tanks attached to fighters to increase their range
Bandits - enemy aircraft
Big Friend - name for friendly bombers such as B-17s and B-24s
Bogies - unidentified aircraft
Briefing - detailed instructions given to combat crews or pilots prior to a mission
Chandelle - reversal of course by a climbing turn
CHATTANOOGA - code name for a strafing mission against rail targets
Circus - early code name for bomber escort mission
C.O. - Commanding Officer
Contrails - vapor trails behind engines of high flying aircraft
Combat Box - a combat formation of bombers, usually three or more bomber groups
Deck - the ground or a reference altitude very close to the ground
Deflection Shot - firing at an aircraft from an angle other than from directly behind or in front
DSC - Distinguished Service Cross. Second highest combat award.
DFC - Distinguished Flying Cross. Fourth highest combat award.
DO - Dornier (German aircraft)
Dryrun - rehearsal or practice
Element - the basic fighter unit of two aircraft
E.T.A. - Estimated Time of Arrival
E.T.O. - European Theater of Operations
Feather - slang for the mechanical rotation of the propeller blades of a failed engine to minimize wind resistance
Flak - slang for antiaircraft fire. Short for Flieger Abwehr Kanonen.
Flight - formation of two Elements or four fighters
Fort - nickname for B-17 Flying Fortress
F.O. - Field Order from higher command providing mission details and instructions
FG - abbreviation for Fighter Group
FS - abbreviation for Fighter Squadron
F/O - Flight Officer
Frisians - Islands off the Germans North Sea coast
Front - the line of division between two air masses
FW - Focke Wulf (German Aircraft)
Gaggle - collection or assemblage of loose flying enemy fighters
Group - three or four squadrons
HE - Heinkel (German aircraft)
IP - abbreviation for Initial Point, the point where the bomb run starts
JACKPOT - code name for strafing mission against German airfields
JG - Jagdgeschwader or German Fighter Regiment
Jerry - slang for German fighter pilot
JU - Junkers (German aircraft)
Jug - slang for Republic P47 Thunderbolt, also known as "T-Bolt"
KIA - Killed in Action

KIFA - Killed in Flying Accident
Lib - slang for Consolidated B-24 Liberator
Mae West - slang for inflatable life vest
ME - Messerschmitt (German aircraft)
MIA - Missing in Action
Milk Run - slang for an easy or frequently repeated mission
NYR - Not Yet Returned
OD - olive drab color
Ops - short for operations
O'clock - reference direction. Twelve o'clock represented a point directly in front, while six o'clock indicated a position directly behind the aircraft
POW - Prisoner of War
Prop Wash - turbulent air behind an aircraft caused by combination of propeller and wing tip vortex
PRU - Photo Reconnaissance Unit
Ramrod or Rodeo - bomber escort mission
R/T - slang for communications radio onboard aircraft. Short for Radio/Telephone
R/V - abbreviation for rendezvous
Split-S - to half roll into the inverted position and pull the stick back to dive vertically
Type 16 control - mission flown under radar observation from England. Codes included names such as Colgate or Nuthouse
Vector - direction to a specific point.
Wingman - second aircraft and pilot in a two ship element. Responsible for protecting his leader (and vice versa) in combat.

THE FAMILY TREE

The 355th Fighter Group was both constituted and activated on November 12, 1942, but traced its roots all the way back to the First Pursuit Group of World War I.

The First Pursuit Group was activated in May, 1918 and included the famous 94th Squadron of "Hat in the Ring" fame. Several notable combat veterans of the First included Captain Edward Rickenbacker and Lieutenant Frank Luke, Jr. Both pilots were awarded the Congressional Medal of Honor.

The 31st Pursuit Group was formed by personnel of the First and activated on February 1, 1940. In turn, the 49th, 50th, 52nd and 58th Pursuit Groups were formed by personnel of the 31st Group in 1941. The 50th Pursuit Group was activated January 15, 1941, at Selfridge Field, Michigan.

On March 20, 1942, the 50th Pursuit Group moved to Orlando to become the key group for the Army Air Force School of Applied Tactics. The primary mission of the AAFSAT was to train personnel in fighter tactics under simulated combat conditions, flying P-40s, P-47s and P-51s.

On November 12, 1942, the 355th Fighter Group was formed with 50th Group personnel. The 354th, 357th and 358th Fighter Squadrons comprised the basic combat elements of the group.

The 355th Fighter Group trained for combat operations in Orlando, Florida before moving to Philadelphia, Pennsylvania. Prior to moving overseas the group flew P-47s from Philadelphia, Pennsylvania; Richmond, Virginia and Millville, New Jersey. On July 1, 1943, the 355th boarded with the 352nd Fighter Group and several others combat organizations to sail for England.

The 355th was assigned to the mighty Eighth Air Force and stationed at Steeple Morden, England, just north of London and close to Cambridge, England.

Following intense training for a couple of months in fighter tactics as well as indoctrination to combat operations, the 355th was alerted for its first mission on September 9, 1943.

Angels, Bulldogs & Dragons

The 355th Fighter Group In World War II

COMBAT OPERATIONS DIARY
1943

September 9

The 355th Fighter Group was finally placed on operational status on this day.

Field Order 129. Major Phillip Tukey, on temporary loan from the 56th Fighter Group, led the group on a ramrod. The mission was delayed until 1816 and shortly after takeoff and assembly, the group was recalled for good. All pilots returned by 1846.

September 12

Tom Lea, from Life Magazine, was still on the base collecting sketches for paintings to be done when he returned to the States. Sam Goldstein, veteran of several bomber missions as a free-lance photographer, was also taking pictures of 355th activities. Flight Officer Henry Brown, future top ace of the group, joined the 354th Squadron.

September 14

F.O. 130. Major Tukey led the group on a rodeo at the head of the 357th Fighter Squadron. The group made rendezvous with the 4thFG at 1130 over Bradwell Bay and flew to Dunkirk, Roulers and Ostend. The fighters came out northeast of Ostend at 1159 after an uneventful trip. No hits, no fouls and all pilots were back down by 1250.

F.O. 131. The group went out again a fighter sweep to Roulers from 1805 to 1920. The weather was very bad and they turned back at Knocke after recall.

September 15

F.O. 132. The group was scheduled for a ramrod to cover the withdrawal of the bombers from Paris, but the mission was scrubbed at 1730. Tom Lea departed for Africa with a load of sketches.

September 22

F.O. 138. Major Tukey led a fighter sweep at the head of the 354FS. The 354th and 358FS made landfall at Sangatte at 1113 hours. The mission from Hazebroucke to Roulers to Zeebruge at 27,000 feet encountered moderate but accurate flak. No enemy fighters seen and both squadrons were down by 1206. Major Tukey then briefed both squadrons for a diversionary sweep for the second mission of the day.

F.O. 139. Major Tukey led the 358th and the 354FS on another sweep. They crossed Bradwell Bay at 1452, and made landfall over Furnes at 1515 hours and 26,000 feet. The formation swept from Lille to Ghent to Nieuwe Sluis. Two FW-190s were seen south of Ostend but spotted the 355th formation and immediately split-S for the deck before anybody got close. All aircraft were back on the ground at Steeple Morden by 1640 hours.

September 23

F.O. 141. Lieutenant Colonel "Speed" Hubbard, 355th Group Executive Officer, led the troops on a fighter sweep at the head of the 354FS. The group took off at 1459 hours, crossed Ostend at 1542 at 27,000 feet, and swept to Ghent and West Schouwen before coming back out at 1555 hours. A 20 vessel convoy was seen off Ostend heading Southwest. A couple of pilots returned late but everyone eventually made it back safely. No action yet.

September 24

The 354FS stood down for the next couple of days so that their Jugs could be modified for the new long range belly tanks.

F.O. 144. Colonel Bill Cummings, recently recovered from his ear infection, led the 357th and 358FS on a sweep from Furnes to Courtrai and back to Calais. No flak or fighters were seen and the group crossed out north of Calais at 1327 hours.

September 25

Lieutenant James Donovan, a new 354FS pilot, became the group's first casualty in England. On a flight to Goxhill for gunnery training, his flight encountered bad weather and Donovan's P-47 spun in near the Ossington-Wigsley area. Donovan died in the crash.

September 26

The 358FS stood down for belly tank modifications.

F.O. 145. Major Tukey led the group on a ramrod at the head of the 354FS. The 354th and 357FS furnished penetration support to the Forts and rendezvoused with the 4th Group over Dieppe. They escorted the Big Friends to Rouen but neither enemy aircraft nor flak was encountered and the group came out north of St. Valery at 1736 hours.

September 27

F.O. 147. Major Dix led a fighter sweep along the Blankenberg-Ghent line. Colonel Cummings had to return early because of an oxygen mask failure. The group came out over Haamstede at 1021 hours and 28,000 feet. Another boring deal and all pilots returned safely by 1114 hours.

September 28

More P-47D5-RE's were assigned to the 354th, 357th and 358FS to bring the group strength to 76 Thunderbolts.

October 2

F.O. 148. Colonel Cummings led the group on another boring ramrod covering the bombers' withdrawal from the Borkum Islands. No enemy fighters encountered yet. Even though the 355th had only been operational for two weeks, the pilots were getting restless. Lieutenant Dean landed at Bury St. Edmonds to refuel before coming home.

October 3

The group was alerted for Wing Field Order 73 but stood down at 0630.

October 4

F.O. 150. Major Dix, Group Operations Officer, led a ramrod to support the penetration to Frankfurt from 0950 to 1130 hours. The 355th rendezvoused with the Second Task Force over Knocke at 0953 and escorted the Forts as far as Eupen. Just as the group completed a 180 degree turn for home, about 20 FW-190s and Me-109s sailed over the rear of the Green flight of the 358FS. One Me-109 was immediately nailed by Cully Ekstrom for the 355th's first victory. An FW-190 slipped up on Ralph Dean and put several 20mm rounds in the wing root and tail causing Dean's gear to lower. Dean made it back to England and crash-landed near Monkton to try to save his P-47. He died later that night from resulting head injuries.

Claims: 1 Destroyed   Losses: 1

October 8

F.O. 151. Colonel Cummings led the 355th to the forward base of Hardwick where they refueled and took off again at 1504. They rendezvoused with their assigned wing of B-17s east of Meppel and provided withdrawal support. No fighters or flak were seen until flak was encountered in the target area. The trip was uneventful but the group heard that the 4thFG had scored on some FW-190s earlier in the day. All fighters returned safely by 1715 hours.

October 9

F.O. 152. Briefing was at 1430 and the group took off at 1528. Colonel Cummings led a ramrod to support the withdrawal of two wings of B-24's and two wings of B-17s. The 354FS failed to make rendezvous after flying through heavy overcast but the 358th and 357FS picked up the bombers over Holland and brought them home with no excitement along the way.

October 14

The 355th was scheduled for withdrawal support on the Schweinfurt deal. Unfortunately fog kept the 355th and most of the 8th Fighter Command on the ground in the area around London and the Eighth had its third worst day of the war as far as bomber losses were concerned. Sixty failed to return and many more were damaged. Only the March 6, 1944, and the April 29, 1944, raids on Berlin cost the Eighth more heavy bombers on a single day.

October 16

F.O. 159. Colonel Cummings led the 355th on a rodeo to support a Marauder strike in Holland. The group crossed at Noordval and swept toward Woerden until recalled at 1625. No flak or enemy aircraft were spotted and the boys came home by 1709.

October 18

F.O. 162. Colonel Cummings again led the 355th at the head of the 354FS. Major Joe Williams, the 354FS C.O., was still recovering from an ear infection.

The mission was a ramrod along the Gravelines-Brussels line but the bombers were recalled. The 355th then swept Brussels looking for enemy fighters but Jerry failed to materialize. Flak was encountered at Ghent, Cassel and Calais. Lieutenant Maben fell out of the formation near Cambrai and was last seen in a spin around 15,000 feet. No flak or fighters were in the area and the cause remains unknown. The group made landfall over Knocke at 1453 and came home.

Claims: None   Losses: 1

October 20

F.O. 163. Major Edward "Jonesy" Szaniawski led a ramrod at the head of the 357FS. Penetration support was provided to the Second Task Force on the way to Duren. Just before rendezvous west of Calais, the bombers fell under attack from a gaggle of about 25 Me-109s from their four o'clock position. The 109s immediately headed for the deck but the group stayed with the bombers.

Shortly after passing Cambrai, Major Raymond Myers bounced a pair of FW-190s. The 358FS C.O. sent one spinning into the overcast below and flamed the second one. Lieutenant Dissete damaged a lone Me-109 but the rest of the mission was uneventful.

Claims: 1 Destroyed   Losses: None

October 21

Colonel Cummings chewed the group out for too much chatter on the R/T and re-emphasized that the prime job of the 355th was to stay with, and protect, the bombers. "Engage the German fighters, drive them off, and come back quickly" was to become the standard 355th Fighter Group tactic for the duration.

No mission was scheduled because of heavy rain.

October 22

F.O. 165. Colonel Cummings led the group into the overcast for a ramrod for Ninth Air Force B-26s. Solid overcast continued through the rendezvous point. The 355th stayed on the briefed course for another 15 minutes and then turned back when they couldn't find the bombers. One pilot hit a bird but all pilots and planes returned safely to Steeple Morden.

October 24

Operations Order 44. The 357th and 358FS escorted the new crews of the 13th Wing on a practice mission over central England while the 354FS bounced them in repeated simulated attacks. The new group pilots flew on this mission and fun was had by all.

Fog shut group operations down through the first of November. During the week, pilots listened to intelligence reports, discussed tactics, participated in ditching drills, played cards and generally caught up on their sleep.

November 2

Decorations were presented in a morning awards ceremony to pilots in all three squadrons. The weather cleared sufficiently to finally allow the pilots a couple of hours in the air after nearly a week on the ground. The 355th bounced everything in sight and some of the mock dogfights ended up right on the deck because of the 1200 foot ceiling around the base. Colonel Cummings was infuriated over the low level antics and let everybody know it the next morning during the briefing.

November 5

F.O. 168. Colonel Cummings led the penetration support ramrod to Wilhelmshaven. The formation took off at 0930 from the advanced base at Bungay and made rendezvous with the First Bomb Division over the North Sea. Some intense jamming of C-channel by the Germans eliminated R/T contact with the bombers for most of the mission. Landfall was made over Tessel at 1245 and escort was broken off just short of the Initial Point at 1320 hours. Accurate flak was encountered over the Den Helder-Tessel area.

Speed Hubbard brought his Jug in with a blown tire but made a perfect landing, holding the bad wheel off until the last possible second.

November 5

F.O. 170.   Colonel Cummings led a ramrod to provide penetration support to B-17s attacking Gelsenkirchen. All P-47s carried the new 108 gallon belly tanks for maximum endurance and stayed with the bombers all the way. Landfall was made at 1258 near Westhoofel and shortly thereafter, Lieutenant Sluga latched onto a lone Me-210. He got behind it in a dive, scored after shooting most of his ammo and sent it smoking into the ground.

Shortly after coming away from the target, the group bounced a mixed gaggle of FW-190s, Me-109s and Me-210s. Lieutenant Charlie Sweat shot down an FW-190 for the 354FS's first victory and Pete Bauman and Fred Kelly also damaged a couple of 109s in separate engagements. Clark Collins of the 357th was shot down when a stafflen of Me-109s bounced his flight. A chute was seen to open near the ground but Collins did not turn up after the war. Collins thus became the first 355th pilot lost in air-to-air combat with the German Air Force.

Claims: 2 Destroyed   Losses: 1

November 7

F.O. 172.   Colonel Cummings led a ramrod to escort bombers attacking the Duren marshalling yards. During the briefing, Cummings repeatedly stressed that the prime duty of the 355th was to stay with the bombers.

The bomber formation was picked up over southeast Belgium and escort was continued until several pilots squawked about low fuel. The group had encountered a 90 knot headwind out of the Northeast and all the Jugs were running low.

On the way home Captain Norman Olson of the 357FS bounced an Me-210 scuttling along below his flight and flamed it. While diving through a cloud layer he lost Lieutenants Carlson and Westphall, who were believed to have collided during the dive. The 358FS Operations Officer, Captain Kossack, and Lieutenant Roach were last seen heading southeast toward a low lying cloud which closely resembled England. Both ran out of fuel over the Continent and landed. Carlson was later reported as KIA, while Westphall, Roach and Kossack were POW. Flight Officer Watson of the 358th also ran out of gas and bailed out six miles off the French Coast. Although reported to be POW in January, 1944, he was never seen again.

Only on the strafing missions of August 28, 1944, and April 16, 1945 would the 355th lose more pilots on a single day.

Claims: 1 Destroyed   Losses: 5

November 8

No mission today but Colonel Cummings called the pilots together to discuss yesterday's results. He first read a letter of commendation from General Kepner for the group's escort the day before. He then cautioned the pilots not to say anything over the R/T about low fuel. "Just call and say you're returning to base. If the Germans had been smart, they would have sent some fighters up to intercept us on the way out."

November 10

F.O. 175.   Colonel Cummings led a rodeo from 1349 to 1515. Landfall was over Ambeteuse at 1425 and the group descended to 12,000 feet to try to draw Jerry up. After 15 minutes of stooging around the group was recalled and came out over Le Touquet at 1446.

November 11

F.O. 177.   Colonel Cummings led a penetration support for bomber attacks by the First Division in western Germany. The group escorted the lead boxes of B-17s until the 78thFG joined the parade and assumed lead escort. The 355th then assumed escort positions above the trailing boxes for the rest of the mission. Four Me-109s were spotted slipping up on a crippled Fort, but the German fighters immediately turned into the clouds when they spotted the 355th. The mission was otherwise uneventful.

November 12

No operations today. The 354FS took the honors in the group skeet shoot. As a result, the 357th and 358FS waited tables for the 354th on Turkey Day—then pulled KP after the meal was over. Major Williams was still in the hospital with the flu and a high temperature.

November 13

F.O. 180.   Lieutenant Colonel Hubbard led the 355th on a ramrod after staging at Bungay and fueling up the 108 gallon drop tanks. The group furnished withdrawal support to the B-17s coming home from their attacks on Bremen and rendezvous was made over Cloppenburg at 1206 hours.

Near the Zuider Zee, a formation of FW-190s and Me-109s bounced the lead boxes of B-17s from above and behind. Just before the Germans pulled up in a zoom, Hubbard's P-47 started vibrating badly. Shortly thereafter, Hubbard's engine broke loose from its mounts and he bailed out. The group turned into the German fighters and, in the ensuing fight, Lieutenants Neal and Vincent and Captain Olson each destroyed an Me-109. Lanphier was last seen near the Ems River being chased by a pair of 109s into a nearby cloud and was presumed shot down. Hubbard evaded capture to return after D-Day but Lanphier was later reported KIA.

Claims: 3 Destroyed   Losses: 2 (1 pilot evaded)

Major Dix presided over the debriefing after the mission to critique the tactics plus qualify procedures for bounces and dropping belly tanks. The squadron commanders were instructed to act as traffic cops and execute, at their discretion, the bounce after reported sightings of enemy aircraft. Although Fighter Command had directed the groups to conserve belly tanks, Dix directed the pilots to use their own discretion. Under no circumstance was saving a belly tank to assume priority over risking a fighter pilot's aircraft or life.

November 15

Lieutenants McGraw and McNally of the 357FS took off for a weather reconnaissance flight at 1100 hours. They were later heard over the radio to say that they were about to go down though a small hole in the overcast and were never seen or heard from again. As they were never found and German records make no mention of claims on two P-47s from either air combat or flak, it is presumed that they were not shot down and probable that their loss was weather related.

Claims: None   Losses: 2

November 19

F.O. 184.   Major Dix led the group in a penetration support ramrod to Gelsenkirchen. The escort route was Egmond to Gelsenkirchen and back to Ijmuiden at 29,000 feet. Escort was broken at 1225 over Ijmuiden and the fighters came home without incident. No fighters were seen and no losses were experienced by either the escort or the bombers.

November 26

F.O. 191.   Colonel Cummings led a ramrod to Bremen with 108 gallon belly tanks. The group staged out of Bungay and made rendezvous with the bombers near Papenburg at 29,000 feet and 1229 hours. Escort was provided along the withdrawal route until 1302 when the group crossed Den Helder. No enemy aircraft were seen and flak was moderate but inaccurate. The only excitement occured when two 356thGP Jugs flew through the 354FS at right angles and clipped Starr's vertical stabilizer.

The 56th Group had a field day when they bounced a large gaggle of Me-110s, 109s and FW-190s. They collected a record 22 scalps for the loss of one pilot. The 355th saw the scrap below them but stayed with their lumbering Big Friends.

November 27

The 354FS of the 355th swapped commanders with the 361FS of the 356th Group. Major Williams was given a farewell party and Major Claiborne Kinnard, Jr. made Steeple Morden his new home.

November 29

F.O. 192.   Colonel Cummings led a ramrod to Bremen after staging from Hardwick. Shortly after rendezvous with the bombers, Lieutenant Woertz led Green flight of the 358th Squadron on a bounce and clobbered an Me-109 near Bremen.

After noses were counted following the mission, quite a few pilots were found located at various bases along the English coast where most had landed on gas fumes. Lieutenants Peery and Hecht from the 358FS and Del Negro of the 354FS failed to return. Peery and Hecht were forced down in Holland after running out of fuel and Del Negro just disappeared. No fighters or flak were reported in the area, he simply disappeared during an "S" turn over the B-17s while following Kurtz. Del Negro was the first 354th Squadron pilot lost during a combat mission. Major Kinnard arrived at Steeple Morden during the mission to formally assume command of the 354FS.

Claims: 1 Destroyed   Losses: 3

November 30

F.O. 193.   Major Dix led the group on a ramrod to furnish withdrawal support to the First Bomb Division. Rendezvous was made north of Aachen at 1135 hours. The group chased away two separate gaggles of six to eight Me-109's at 1145, but did not pursue when the Jerry fighters split-S for the deck. No engagements, no wins, no losses.

During the debriefing, Cummings and Dix stressed tighter flight formations, less talking on the R/T and more shooting at enemy aircraft. Major Kinnard, grounded for awhile because of an ear infection, made a presentation on the new water injection boost to be installed on all P-47s for emergency power.

December 1

F.O. 194. Colonel Cummings led a ramrod penetration support to bombers attacking Solingen. The group made rendezvous at 1115 hours 30,000 feet over Julich and were bounced a couple of minutes later by a gaggle of 25 to 30 Me-109s from out of the sun.

The Jerries were described as "skilled and aggressive" and eager to take on the fighters. In the resulting scrap, Johnston and Bernoske of the 357FS each claimed an Me-109 for their first victories. Macurdy and Ekstrom also claimed single Me-109s for the 358FS. The 354FS was otherwise occupied evading bounces from P-38s and P-47s from other groups in a couple of cases of mistaken identity.

The rest of the mission was uneventful until Jim Hull of the 358FS took his flight through a cloud bank near Lierre during a flak barrage. When the flight emerged from the clouds, Hull was missing and presumed lost due to flak. Hull was later reported KIA. Jesse Williamson of the 357FS was hit by flak near Koblenz and bailed out shortly afterwards to become a POW.

Claims: 4 Destroyed   Losses: 2

December 4

Lieutenant Vincent, a well liked West Pointer, was killed during a fighter tactics training flight when the tail of his Jug came off during a dive. Vincent was the second 354FS pilot to die in a non-combat related accident.

December 5

F.O. 196. The group staged at Thorny, fueled up their drop tanks, and took off on a ramrod at 0915. Major Dix led the group on the penetration support to Bordeaux. The escort was uneventful and no enemy fighters were seen.

Visibility was terrible on their return and the group pilots landed all over England. The visibility around Steeple Morden remained essentially zero for several days and none of the pilots returned until the 9th and 10th of December.

December 11

F.O. 198. Colonel Cummings led a ramrod to support B-17s attacking Emden. Following rendezvous with the Third Bomb Division at 1235 hours over Groningen, the 354th and 357FS escorted the bombers over the target and back over the North Sea.

The mission was uneventful until Jack Woertz stalled out just before final approach to Steeple Morden and was killed in the crash.

Claims: None   Losses: 1

December 13

F.O. 199. Major Dix led a ramrod at the head of the 358FS. After staging from Hethel at 0840, the group provided withdrawal support to heavy bombers attacking Bremen. The mission was uneventful except for take off when Lieutenant Laing of the 357FS clipped a tree. Colonel Cummings took off to inspect the damage as Laing climbed to get more altitude. After a visual check, Cummings advised Laing to go over the side. Laing bailed out but broke his leg on the tail and spent many weeks in the hospital getting patched up.

December 16

F.O. 203. Major Dix led the ramrod after Major Myers turned back due to fuel feed problems. The mission was another escort to Bremen and the weather was appalling. The rendezvous with the bombers was not made until the B-17s were well over the North Sea. The Continent was completely covered with clouds so Bremen was eventually bombed through the overcast. Considerable flak was encountered but no enemy fighters penetrated the cloud cover to challenge the mission. Because the weather was also bad over England, most of the pilots landed on other fields and did not completely return to Steeple Morden until December 19th. Lieutenant Macurdy made a dead stick landing at Rock Heath after running out of fuel. His Jug was completely and thoroughly wrecked but Macurdy walked away without a scratch.

December 20

F.O. 204. More of the same. Colonel Cummings led the group on the second leg of penetration support to the bombers attacking Bremen. The mission was another milk run and all pilots returned safely by 1320. A number of the pilots made remarks about the unusually large numbers of B-17s, B-24s, P-47s and P-38s which participated in the raid.

The group flew to Hardwick that night to stage for a raid the next day. The mission was scrubbed and all fighters returned to Steeple Morden on the afternoon of the 21st.

December 22

F.O. 207. Major Dix, acting Group Exec since Hubbard went down, led a ramrod to Osnabruck. Rendezvous was made according to plan and the penetration escort was continued until 1350 hours.

Just after the group was relieved by the 56thFG, Me-109s bounced the 56th. It was later learned that Captain Walker Mahurin raised his score in this scrap to 15 to lead all ETO Aces. The 355thFG continued to be where the Germans weren't, and all the pilots were feeling a little testy.

December 24

In the briefing before the mission, Colonel Cummings read a field order to the group pilots which reflected somewhat new thinking on the part of the Eighth Air Force. In effect, the memo stressed the importance of aggressively driving off enemy fighters whenever they were seen in the area of the bombers. The pilots were not yet given the complete freedom to range further away from the bombers but more aggressive pursuit following contact was being encouraged.

F.O.209. Colonel Cummings led the ramrod after the group patrolled from Le Treport to Amiens to Harcourt and the Tocqueville area before turning for home. The bombers proceeded to bomb long range gun emplacements around the Pas de Calais area. Very little flak and no enemy fighters were observed.

On the way back, Captain Curtis Johnston bounced a pair of fighters closely resembling Me-109s. After raking one from wingtip to wingtip, he quickly broke off after recognizing it as the new P-51 Mustang. Fortunately, the P-51 was able to fly on and nobody was hurt.

December 29

The group received a briefing from Major Blakeman of Military Intelligence. He briefed them on German interrogation tactics, successful evasion and escape histories and compared the German interrogation tactics to those of the Allies.

December 30

Just before briefing, a fully loaded B-17 from neighboring Bassingborn crashlanded on the western edge of Steeple Morden. The 91st Bomb Group Fortress narrowly missed the big engineering hangar and all the crew got out safely.

During the briefing, Major Dix placed particular emphasis on watching out for the new Mustangs. Major Kinnard then made a presentation regarding a new assembly tactic for grouping up after takeoff. Essentially, the new tactic was a spin off of the assembly and formation procedure used by the bombers and offered excellent opportunities to conserve time and fuel.

F.O.210. Major Dix led the group on a ramrod to provide withdrawal support for an attack on Ludwigshafen. Landfall was made over Gravelines at 1224 and rendezvous occurred at 1315.

Following rendezvous with the bombers, the group provided escort until 1340 when they turned for home. Following their 180 degree turn, a gaggle of Me-109s bounced another nearby formation of bombers. The 355th turned back immediately and traded head on passes with the 109s near Rheims. In the scrap that followed, Ray Murdoch broke away from his flight to shoot down a 109 and was quickly shot down after following several more down to the deck. Flight Officer Wambier was last seen just before the head on pass with the 109s while flying Markin's wing.

Ekstrom was last seen strafing flak installations near St. Inglevert on the French coast and later reported to have been shot down and killed by flak. Flak also heavily damaged Lieutenant Hovde's horizontal stabilizer, but he made it home O.K. Ekstrom was one of the best of the group pilots and the first of a long line to fall to German flak while strafing.

Claims: 1 Destroyed   Losses: 3

December 31

F.O. 211. Colonel Cummings led the group on a ramrod to Bordeaux. The 355th was up at 0908 hours, made rendezvous near Lannion at 1014 hours and returned from the uneventful mission at 1213 hours. All pilots returned safely.

SUMMARY OF COMBAT OPERATIONS, 1943

The 355th Fighter Group had started its combat career against the Luftwaffe with about the same overall results as most other new P-47 Groups in the ETO.

The initial missions were fighter sweeps under the command of experienced pilots from the 56th and 4th Groups, plus rodeos and ramrods providing withdrawal support, to provide valuable combat experience without risking particularly high losses.

During the last 100 days of 1943, the 355th Fighter Group developed a style and purpose relative to their role as an escort group which changed very little over the next 16 months. Specifically, the 355th Fighter Group adhered to the general tactic of "hit 'em and come back" during bomber escorts when enemy fighters were seen. This particular tactic probably cost the group more air victories but saved a lot more bomber crews from death or capture. The Luftwaffe started using the tactic of sending two gaggles of fighters in on the bombers. The first made a quick pass and broke for the deck. If the escort followed, the second force attacked the bombers. If the escort stayed, the first German force reformed and climbed back to support the second force again to repeat the tactic. The 355th countered the tactic by turning into the fighters, breaking up the attack and then returning to the bombers instead of pursuing the Germans in force. Gradually, the Eighth Fighter Command built up enough strength to allow the fighter escort to send one or two squadrons in pursuit and keep a reserve with the bombers to counter the next German attack.

The overall record of the 355th during combat operations in 1943 included claims for the destruction of thirteen German fighters for the loss of six pilots in aerial combat. The group lost an additional seventeen pilots to flak, running out of gas, weather and accidents. Most of the pilots were far more concerned about weather than the Luftwaffe.
The ground crews put tremendous effort and long hours to keep 'em running and the effort paid off with one of the best maintenance records in the ETO. In all, the combined efforts of leadership, pilots and ground support would pay handsome dividends for the rest of the war.

1. The 355th's headquarters personnel, before shipping overseas in 1943. (Williams, Minchew)
2. 357th FS CO Szaniawski and ground exec Williams during P-40 training in Florida. (Williams)
3. Many a 355th soldier relaxed away from Steeple Morden by visiting nearby Cambridge. (Minchew)

4. Kossack, Hovde, Ekstrom, MacCurdy, Dissette, Bauman and Flanders relax in an English pub during the fall of 1943. (Hovde)

5. Cummings "communicating" in typical fighter pilot language to 355th pilots, 1943. (Minchew, Hart)

6. Jugs of the 354th FS rolling out for element takeoffs, early 1944. (Barnhouse)

7. Crew Chief Barnhouse in front of WR-U. "Miss Behave" nose art is one of the top examples of ETO artistry, typical of DeCosta's style. (Barnhouse)

8. Two R-2800s pulling a pair of 357th FS Thunderbolts off the runway at Station F-122. (Bille, Butcher)

9. Szaniawski and OS-A, "Available Jones," ready to lead the 357th on another penetration. (Butcher)

10. Burroughs and the rest of the 357th weaving down the line in preparation for another ramrod. (Hart, Bille, Butcher)
11. Sergeants McCarville and McFall with Laing's OS-X of the 357th FS. (Brennan, Kidwell, Hart)
12. Mendenhall, Neal and Barnhouse loading .50 cal. for WR-J. (Barnhouse)
13. The 355th Group's first, longest and oldest boss, Colonel Bill Cummings in OS-V, "Wild Bill." (Hovde, Lenfest)
14. Speed Hubbard's WR-P before flak nailed "Lil Jo" on November 13, 1943. The air exec evaded and returned in June 1944. (Kucheman)

15. Kucheman and the captured Me-109G at Steeple Morden in January 1944. (Kucheman)
16. A British "traveling circus" brought this Me-110 through Steeple Morden for 355th cockpit familiarization. (Lenfest, Hovde, Kidwell)
17. DeCosta and Butler admire DeCosta's latest work. Combined with the 355th's Fighter Comets band, the art was a heavy draw for visiting pilots and brass. (Haviland)
18. Closeup of "Miss Behave," the author's favorite example of ETO nose art—a masterpiece. (Barnhouse, Haviland)
19. 355th pilots looking over the competition. (Lenfest, Kucheman)

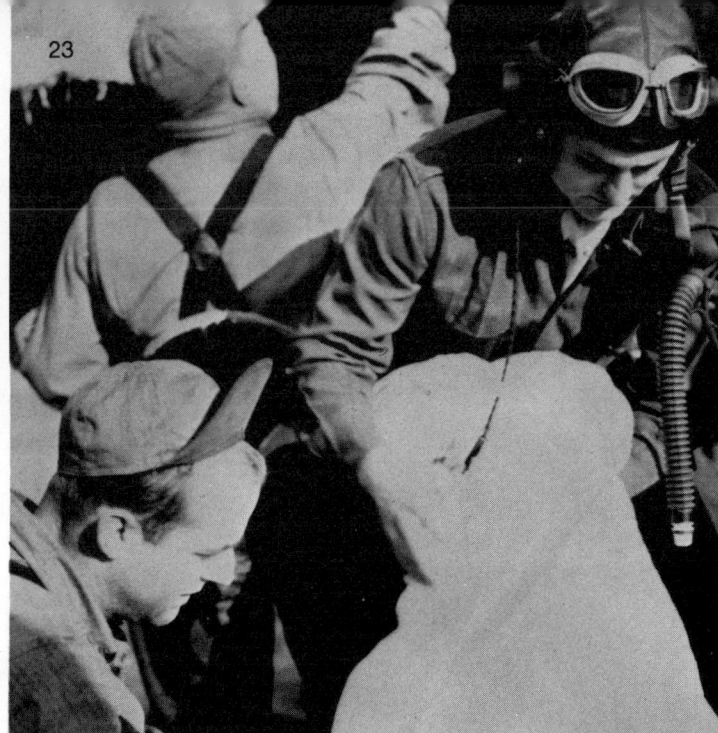

20. Ground exec Glynn Williams and group operations officer Gerald Dix in early 1944. (Williams, Haviland)
21. Chester Butcher's OS-F, "The Butcher," after a belly landing in January 1944. After skin repairs and a new engine, OS-F flew again. (Butcher, Hart)
22. Jonesy Szaniawski and Norm Olson in front of Olson's OS-P, "Ma Fran 3rd." Picture taken in February 1944 after Olson became the group's first ace. Both pilots became victims of accurate German flak, with Olson KIA and Szaniawski POW. (McNeff, Butcher)
23. Lieutenant Sluga pulling the silk after his first successful jump after spinning out in extremely bad weather. His third, and last, combat jump 15 months later would leave him safe but a POW. (Sluga, Hovde)
24. James Westphall and OS-L "Alabama Bound." He had to bail out after colliding with Carlson during a diving bounce. (Hart, Ramsdell)

25. & 26. Jim Duffy's WR-Y, nearly shot down by flak over Antwerp on February 11, 1944. The P-47 was a rugged ship. (Vose, Baldwin)

27. Korky Koraleski's WR-L, "Miss Thunder," of the 354th FS in early 1944. (Bennett)

28. Captain Reed Butler's OS-H sporting non-regulation hubcaps in February 1944. (Barnhouse, Torrey, Wing)

29. Sergeants Carter and Tabacchi on WR-M in early 1944. (Barnhouse)

30. DeCosta's trail is everywhere in the officers' club at F-122. (Mendenhall, Bennett, Hart, Barnhouse)
31. Jack Woertz of the 358th, known as a good pilot, stalled on final in early 1944 and was killed in the ensuing crash. (Hovde)
32. Top-notch group intelligence officer Danny Lewis. He was said to have a nose for Luftwaffe reaction. (Williams)
33. Crew chief Jones and pilot Butcher in front of OS-F. Butcher survived a spectacular high-speed crash on March 27, 1944 to become a POW. (Butcher)
34. Steeple Morden's perimeter as seen from the air. (Hovde)

COMBAT OPERATIONS DIARY
1944

January 2

The 355th stood down on this day. Instead, the pilots and crews drilled in the loading of 500 pound bombs on the fuselage racks of the P-47s.

January 4

F.O. 212. The Eighth flew two significant missions on the fourth. One 120 bomber effort went to Munster and an 840 bomber force was sent to Kiel. Major Dix led the group on a ramrod to provide withdrawal support for the Munster effort.

Rendezvous was made at 1056 hours and 27,000 feet over Brielle and continued until 1142 hours. Captain Koraleski broke into a pair of Me109s chasing a 356th Group P-47 but the 109s quickly broke down and away and no claim was made. The mission was otherwise uneventful.

January 5

F.O. 213. Colonel Cummings led a penetration support to Tours. The 352ndFG was scheduled for the penetration effort but had trouble getting off on time so the 352nd and 355th swapped assignments. Because the 352nd now had the target support responsibility, the 355th pilots bitched long and eloquently as the target support usually was where the action was.

Major Everett Stewart of the 352nd Group, and future C.O. of the 355th, got credit for one third of a kill on a He-177 near the channel while the 355th watched from above.

January 7

F.O. 215. Major Dix led a ramrod to cover the withdrawal of the Ludwigshafen mission. Heavy undercast along the route prevented identification of landmarks and except for heavy flak, the mission was uneventful.

January 11

F.O. 216. Major Dix led a ramrod to provide withdrawal support from Brunswick. Shortly after takeoff, Lieutenant Sluga of the 358FS bailed out when his instruments failed during the IFR climb out. His P-47 nosed into a nearby field seconds after bailing out. The unbelievable weather completely disrupted organized assembly and only a few flights ultimately made rendezvous with returning B-24s. Most never saw anything but thick clouds, but all ultimately returned tired but safe.

January 12

Captain Abbey, Liaison Officer with British Air Ministry Intelligence, briefed the group on several new German fighters expected over the next several months. Particular emphasis was placed on the new Me-163 and Me-262 jets and their projected performance.

January 14.

F.O. 217. Major Dix led the group on a circus. The 355th patrolled the Abbeville - Amiens area while the bombers pounded V-1 sites in the Pas de Calais region. The most excitement the group had all day was dodging 91st Bomb Group B-17s landing at nearby Bassingbourn.

January 19

Major Kinnard called the 354th Squadron pilots together and apologized for his lack of visibility to the pilots since arriving in late 1943. He reported that his ear infection had nearly healed, commended the ground crews for one of the best maintenance records in Eighth Fighter Command and promised that action and victories would soon come at an accelerated rate. Kinnard's hearing worsened during the war, to the point his R/T volume had to be set at maximum.

January 21

F.O. 221. Colonel Cummings led a circus to patrol the Evreux-Abbeville line. The 355th's instruction were to engage and pursue any enemy fighters seen in the area. The mission was entirely uneventful until the group turned for home.

At 1405 hours FW-190s bounced both the 354th and 357FS. Lieutenant Jim Duffy shot down one FW-190 for the 354th and Captain John Wilson of the 357th got another. Several pilots chased FW-190s all the way to the deck, some above the streets of Paris, but no other claims for destruction were made.

Following the debriefing, the group was commended by Colonels Auton and Zemke for their aggressive behavior. A lot of pilots privately wondered about the special commendations for aggressiveness as they thought that was their purpose in life in the first place.

Claims: 2 Destroyed   Losses: None

January 24

F.O. 224. Major Dix led the group on a ramrod to furnish withdrawal support from the Frankfurt strike. Initially Colonel Cummings led at the head of the 358FS and the 355th made rendezvous with the bombers about 40 miles east of Ostend. Cummings had to abort shortly after R/V and Major Dix took over. No enemy air action was experienced but several fighters were damaged by accurate and persistent flak.

Lieutenant Sweat had a two square foot hole in the side of WR-R but returned safely. Lieutenant Pipher was lost after flak tore off part of his wing as the 357FS reached the French cost on the way home. He spun into the Channel from 1000 feet and no chute was seen.

Claims: None   Losses: 1

January 25

No mission on this day, but in the late afternoon, a British "traveling circus" comprised of an Me-110, Ju-88 and an Me-109G came to Steeple Morden. For the next couple of days, RAF pilots lectured the group on starting procedures for both the FW-190 and the Me-109 as well as comparative merits of both fighters vs the Thunderbolt in combat. Lieutenants Duffy and Williams of the 354FS escorted the captured German fighters to their next stop on the 27th of January.

January 29

F.O. 226. Colonel Cummings led the group on a ramrod to Frankfurt. The penetration support for the First Division was uneventful until reaching the Koblenz - Limburg area. Everybody was low on gas and the 355th had just started for home when 20 to 25 FW-190s and Me109s bounced the 357th and 358FS from out of the sun.

In the running fight that followed, Lieutenants Macurdy and Rankin chased a 109 down on the deck where they ran into a trap of six to eight Me-109s. Macurdy shot down two before taking 20mm hits in the wing and breaking away from the fight. Bart Rankin was last seen in a chandelle with two 109s on his tail. He called in later to say that he had been hit in the side and on his way home but was never seen again. Macurdy limped toward home but another 109 got on his tail and forced him to crash land. Macurdy evaded capture and fought with the French Maquis for six months before he returned to England.

The 357FS lost Captain Ben Martin to unknown causes and Major Fisher, on temporary duty from the newly operational 362nd Group, also went down in the scrap. Martin evaded and returned in August while Fisher turned up POW.

Claims: 2 Destroyed   Losses: 4 (2 pilots evaded)

January 30

F.O. 227. Lieutenant Colonel Stewart, the new Executive Officer led a penetration support to Brunswick. The 355th relieved the 361stFG just east of the Zuider Zee at 1139. The bombers were strung out all the way to the target, making it difficult to cover them well, but fortunately no enemy fighters showed up. The mission was uneventful and all fighters were back by 1345.

January 31

Wing Field Order 85. Lieutenant Colonel Stewart led two flights each from the 354th and 357FS on a circus dive bombing effort while the rest of the group provided top cover. They dive bombed the German airdrome at Gilz-Rijen, starting their dives from 17,000 feet and releasing at 10,000 feet. Several 500 pound bombs apparently struck a fuel and ammo dump which caused an amazing blast and quickly raised a column of black smoke to 8,000 feet. The 4th Group followed the 355th into the target area and got into a fight with German fighters, claiming six. In the following morning's debriefing, hoots of laughter greeted a report that the 4th Group also claimed hits on the fuel and ammo dump.

The group was informed by the Germans that Kossack, Roach, Watson and Peery were alive and prisoners of war in Germany. Watson later failed to turn up after the war and presumed dead.

February 2

F.O. 231. Lieutenant Colonel Stewart led a ramrod for general area support to mediums and heavies hitting Crossbow targets in the Pas de Calais area. The only excitement of the day occurred when Stewart took Red flight of the 354FS down to bounce suspicious looking twin engine fighters near a formation of B-25s. The flight pulled away after the fighters were identified as British Mosquitos. Everybody returned by 1527 hours. Major Laughlin of the new 362nd Group was assigned to temporary duty with the 355th for combat training to replace Fisher.

February 3

F.O. 232. Stewart led a ramrod to Wilhemshaven. The group provided an uneventful penetration support and all fighters returned by 1320. After returning from the mission, Kucheman and Jeeter Neal scooted back up in the London area to shoot down a couple of errant barrage balloons.

February 4

F.O. 234. Lieutenant Colonel Stewart led a ramrod to cover the bombers withdrawing from Frankfurt. The 65th Wing Commander, Colonel Auton, flew Stewart's wing on the mission. Three FW 190s were spotted several miles away from the group but departed when the 354FS turned into them. The mission was otherwise boring and all pilots returned by 1524 hours.

February 5

F.O. 235. Stewart led a ramrod to cover Liberators bombing German airfields around Tours. The mission was uneventful for the 354FS but the 357th and 358FS shot down two plus damaged several other fighters.

Captain Olson's flight chased ten Me109s through the low box of B-24s and Olson shot down a pair to raise his score to four, the group high.

The route was Fecamp to Mortagne to Tours to West Mamers and back over the Channel near Trouville at 1320.

Claims: 2 Destroyed   Losses: None

February 6

F.O. 236. Stewart led another ramrod to cover the withdrawal of bombers striking German airfields near Romilly. Shortly after takeoff, Stewart had to turn back due to failing prop pitch controls and Major Szaniawski moved the 357FS up to lead the group. The 355th made the rendezvous point between Le Touquetant Coulommiers at the appointed time but couldn't find the First Task Force. After sweeping from Amien to Arras and Hesdin, the controller vectored the 355th over to Dieppe to pick up their "missing" charges. No enemy aircraft were seen although light concentrations of flak pursued them along the route.

The group's fifth mission in five days was starting to show as all the pilots were a little tired.

February 8

F.O. 237. Major Kinnard led the 354FS for the first time to cover bombers withdrawing from Frankfurt. Lieutenant Colonel Stewart led the group at the head of the 358FS and they made rendezvous with the bombers east of Charleville at 1247 hours.

Two FW190s and six Me109s bounced Kinnard's squadron but broke for the deck when the 354FS turned into them. No shots were fired by the Germans and they flew into some thick clouds at 9,000 feet, not to be seen again. The rest of the ramrod was uneventful and following landfall over Dieppe, the group left the bombers and returned home.

Two other notable events occurred on February 8. Lieutenant James Morris of the 77th Squadron, 20th Group, shot down two FW-190s and two Me-109s in a P-38 to become the first 8th Air Force pilot to shoot down four in one mission.

The second, and more far-reaching event, was the directive from Eighth Fighter Command which accompanied F.O. 237. "If bombers are not being attacked, groups will detach one or two squadrons to range out searching for enemy aircraft. Upon withdrawal, if endurance permits, groups will search for and destroy enemy aircraft in the air and on the ground." The 355th had gotten the Field Order which was to set the style for the group for the rest of the war.

Additionally, the Eighth Air Force decided to award ground scores on the same basis as air to air victories towards the status of Ace. The result was a virtual "free for all" by several groups in their pursuit of the Luftwaffe in the air and on the ground. Many more Eighth Air Force fighters were lost to flak than German fighters and few survivors of strafing attacks against heavily defended airdromes would ever dispute the courage required to do it more than once.

February 10

F.O. 239. Colonel Cummings led a ramrod to support the Second Task Force on attacks against the Gilze-Rijen airfields. The mission was uneventful, much to the disgust of both the fighter pilots and their crews. The group picked up the bombers west of The Hague and proceeded to Eindhoven and back over Flushing without incident.

February 11

F.O. 240. Colonel Cummings led a ramrod along the final penetration route to an area just short of the Initial Point to Frankfurt. Rendezvous was made with the rear boxes of bombers over Eupen at 1113 hours.

The 56th FG had the lead escort position and got into a brawl below and to one side of the lead elements of B-17s. Shortly after the 56th engaged, a few more FW-190s and Me-109s were attacked by Major Szaniawski and Lieutenant Burroughs. Jonesy quickly hit an FW-190 but overran it and Burroughs slipped in to blow it apart. Szaniawski then shot down another FW-190 plus destroyed an attacking Me-109 with a large angle deflection shot into the cockpit.

Lieutenant Roland Dufresne went down with a sick engine for unknown reasons after this engagement. He bailed out near Cologne, evaded capture and returned in the late summer.

Lieutenant Duffy of the 354FS had an oxygen malfunction, blacked out, and fell away from the formation in a steep dive. Duffy recovered consciousness and pulled out about 4,000 off the deck, then proceeded home at low altitude. After skirting Antwerp and shooting up some barges, he was clobbered by flak and struggled home with extensive damage to his nose and tail.

Claims: 3 Destroyed   Losses: 1 (pilot evaded)

February 12

Two separate missions were scrubbed but British Intelligence presented the pilots with another excellent briefing on the latest German intelligence methods. The briefing may have been prophetic as many pilots of the 355th would have an opportunity to view German interrogation procedures first hand after the strafing activity picked up.

February 14

An escort mission to support a dive bombing attack by the 356th Fighter Group was scrubbed due to impossible weather conditions of 10/10 cloud cover and ice over the target. Rain and fog grounded operations from Steeple Morden until February 20.

February 20

F.O. 245. Approximately 600 heavy bombers opened up Big Week with attacks on the German aircraft industry at Leipzig, Aschersleben, Bernburg, Gotha, Brunswick and Halberstadt. Additionally, the new 15th Air Force bombed Regensburg, Augsburg and Stuttgart.

Despite heavy overcast, Lieutenant Colonel Stewart led a maximum effort ramrod to provide withdrawal support to five wings of bombers. The 355th made rendezvous with the Big Friends about 28,000 feet over Marienberg at 1417 hours. German fighters were attacking the five wings of bombers withdrawing from Brunswick and Halberstadt.

The 355th sailed into the attacking Me-109s at the rendezvous point and quickly drove them away. In the ensuing scrap, Captain Olson bagged an Me-109 to become the group's first ace and Lieutenant Dickson of the 358FS got another one.

Several 109s were damaged by all three squadrons but only the 357th and 358FS claimed credit for confirmed victories. After an otherwise uneventful escort, the group broke escort and made landfall over Blankenberg at 1506 hours. All pilots returned safely.

Claims: 2 Destroyed   Losses: None

February 21

F.O. 246. Colonel Cummings led another ramrod on the second day of Big Week to support B-17s over the target on Diepholz Airdrome. All the pilots expected and anticipated a scrap because they were escorting the bombers over the target.

The bombers were 10 minutes late however, and the group had to turn back before reaching the target because of dwindling fuel reserves. The 357FS managed to score just as they turned for home when Olson took his flight down to bounce 15 FW-190s at 15,000 feet. The rest of the 357FS followed quickly and shot down three FW-190s in short order. Captain Olson got victory number six, future ace John "Moon" Elder got his first victory and Ben Johnston also scored. No more enemy fighters were seen for the remainder of the mission and all pilots returned to Steeple Morden by 1510 hours.

Claims: 3 Destroyed   Losses: None

February 22

F.O. 247. Lieutenant Colonel Stewart led a penetration and area support to bombers attacking Gotha and Schweinfurt. As the group met the bombers near Munster, Stewart led Red flight of the leading 358th Squadron on a bounce to break up an attack by 10 to 12 FW-190s and Me-109s.

Paul Kenney and future 355th ace Billy Hovde each destroyed an FW-190 while Dickson damaged another. The German fighters broke off the attack and dove for the cloud cover below. The bombers flew an excellent formation and no more enemy fighters were seen. All pilots returned safely.

Claims: 2 Destroyed   Losses: None

February 24

F.O. 250. Colonel Cummings led the group on a ramrod at the head of the 354FS. Despite excellent prospects for enemy fighter resistence along the bomber withdrawal route from Schweinfurt and Gotha, no enemy fighters made an appearance in their area and the mission was uneventful. Just before briefing, Flight Officer Sheehan of the 56th Group related his experiences of bailing out and evading capture through Holland, Belgium, France and Spain.

February 25

F.O. 251. Major Szaniawski led the group on a ramrod to provide withdrawal support to the trailing boxes of the Third Bomb Division on their way back from Augsburg. While the target support groups (comprised of the 4th, 56th and 354th Groups) encountered significant resistance, the 355th had another "milk run". All the pilots cursed the Luffwaffe, the luck of the draw, and continued low activity of German fighters in their vicinity. The mission on this day included more than 1200 heavy bombers and 1000 escorting fighters.

Despite the directives from Eighth Fighter Command, the fighters had not yet started raising hell on the deck to a large degree.

February 26

The 355th was assigned two of the brand new Mustangs for familiarization and training. As the new 354th Group had quickly established an impressive string of victories with the new P-51B, the group was eagerly awaiting conversion. Rumors of several nagging mechanical bugs dampened their enthusiasm somewhat but most pilots remained convinced that the P-51 with its performance and range potential was "IT".

February 28

F.O. 254. Colonel Cummings led the 355th on a circus to patrol the Le Treport - Arras - Hazebrouck - Boulogne area. The patrol turned out to be another milk run and all pilots returned safely by 1642 hours.

More 355th pilots continued to check out in the new P-51B. The month of February had resulted in 11 confirmed victories for the loss of one aircraft but no pilots. The pilots weren't entirely happy with the relatively calm nature of the missions but the activity was definitely picking up.

February 29

F.O. 255. Lieutenant Colonel Stewart led the group on a circus. The 355th provided area support over the Zuider Zee for the bombers retiring from Brunswick. The 355th hoped to find Jerry but the mission was boring as usual, and review of mission summary reports from Eighth Fighter Command revealed that the total claims for the day was one Me-110 shot down by Major Gerald Johnson of the 56th Group. Where was the Luftwaffe?

March 2

F.O. 257. Colonel Cummings led the group on a mission to provide withdrawal support to bombers retiring from the Frankfurt area. The 355th's 56 P-47s operated under Type 16 control and were directed to escort specific stragglers along the withdrawal route.

At approximately 1410 hours, the 358th Squadron bounced two FW-190s southeast of Charleroi and three Me-109s near Liege. All were shot down in two short engagements for no loss. Neither the 354th nor the 357th Squadrons were in position to attack, so the mission remained uneventful for them. Myers, Blair and Hoffman each got a 109 while Gresham shot down an FW-190 and Fussell and Dudley shared the other one. It is probable that one of the two FW-190 German pilots shot down in this action was the great German ace Egon Mayer, who was killed in this area.

Egon Mayer was the Luftwaffe's top fortress killer at this time and his passing probably meant salvation for many more B-17 crews. Based on analysis of combat film and recollection (long range, high deflection) from Mayer's wingman, it is probable that Walter Gresham was the pilot who shot Mayer down.

Claims: 5 Destroyed   Losses: None

March 3

F.O. 259. Lieutenant Colonel Stewart briefed the group for the Eighth Air Force's first Big B (Berlin) strike at 1100 hours. The 355th's assignment was to cover the withdrawal of the First Task Force from the vicinity of Koblenz westward. As Stewart led 52 P-47s off at 1253, he received word that the mission to Berlin had been scrubbed. Some of the Task Force Bombers were directed to secondary targets in Hamburg so the 355th patrolled northern Holland hoping to pick up bombers on the way back. No bombers were seen and no enemy fighters were encountered. The group learned that the 55th Fighter Group, a Lightning group assigned to target escort over Berlin, did not hear the recall and became the first Eighth Air Force fighter group over Berlin.

Landfall out was made over Egmond and everybody was home by 1455.

March 4

F.O. 260. Colonel Cummings, with 65th Wing Commander Auton on his wing, led the group back to the Berlin. Thirty two P-47s and 14 P-51s made the trip to cover the First Task Force withdrawing from attacks on the Erkner plant in Berlin.

Rendezvous was not made even though they orbited the rendezvous area of Cologne and Bonn for about 20 minutes. Although no enemy fighters were encountered, the flak was intense and accurate. Several fighters, including some of the 357FS's brand new Mustangs, received flak damage but all returned safely. Norman Olson had an entire exhaust stack blown away from his new Mustang.

Prior to the start of the mission, Colonel Auton described a new Thunderbolt group being formed to develop tactics for low level strafing attacks and asked for volunteers. Several pilots from the 355th volunteered for consideration.

March 6, 1944

F.O. 262. The 355th loaned 16 of their brand new Mustangs to the 4th Group for the maximum effort escort to Berlin. As a result, the 355th flew mostly Thunderbolts on this important day.

Lieutenant Colonel Stewart led the 355th to support the B-17s and B-24s on the withdrawal route. The group reached the rendezvous point just past Nienburg at 1430 hours. By leaning fuel mixtures to the maximum, they were able to stay with the bombers longer than usual and the 355th had its best day to date.

Captain Walter Koraleski of the 354FS led all scorers with two victories over Me-109s and shared a third with Bud Fortier and Clarence Barger after a lengthy chase on the deck. Stewart, McCasland (his first mission), Easterly and Hill from the 357FS plus Dickson from the 358FS each scored single victories over FW-190s or Me-109s.

In all, the Eighth Fighter Command claimed 82 German fighters destroyed for the loss of eleven fighters. The 355th and 357th Groups alone accounted for 28 with no losses. The group made landfall over Ijmuiden at 1545 hours and all returned safely by 1612.

Claims: 8 Destroyed   Losses: None

March 8

F.O. 263. Colonel Cummings led the group back to Berlin for another withdrawal support to the First Task Force. The 355th picked up 60 B-17s over Dummer Lake at 1435 hours and 27,000 feet.

As in the previous Berlin mission, the bombers were under heavy attack when the 355th arrived. Major Dix quickly shot down an FW-190 which had shot down a P-38 only seconds before and Lieutenant Norman of the 357FS blasted a long nose FW-190 moments after it shot down Lieutenant Rothenberg. While flying Norman's wing, Rothenberg over ran the FW-190 and paid the ultimate price.

After the fight, the 354FS released escort duty and slipped down to the deck to see what they could find. One flight led by Johnston, claimed six JU-88s plus an Me-110 on the ground. Henry Brown started his long rise to the top of 355th Group's victory list by claiming the Me-110 and a shared JU-88 with Curtis Johnston. Sweat was shot down and killed after destroying the first JU-88, and Barger was wounded and nearly shot down after claiming three. Had Barger been flying the newer Mustang instead of his ragged Jug he probably wouldn't have made it back.

After a review of the films, Brown was awarded 3.5 Ju-88s and one Me-110 for a total of four and one half for the day.

Claims: 8 Destroyed   Losses: 2

March 9

F.O. 264.   Major Dix led the 355th "A" Group on a penetration support to Berlin. The A Group was flying Mustangs and stayed with the bombers all the way to the target where they were relieved by P-38s. The mission was completely uneventful except for heavy flak on the way in.
   The 355th "B" Group, flying 29 Thunderbolts, picked up the withdrawing bombers near Hannover and escorted them to the coast. Neither force encountered enemy resistance but lost Lieutenant William Momberger, who crashed shortly after take off near Bassingbourne for unknown reasons.

Claims: None   Losses: 1

March 11

F.O. 265.   Lieutenant Colonel Stewart led a ramrod to Munster with a full complement of 50 Mustangs.

The 355th experienced the same mechanical problems and failures which had plagued other groups equipped with the high performance, but temperamental, Mustangs earlier in the year. Flight Officer John Chalot was last seen on the penetration leg in a 45 degree dive and did not respond to repeated R/T appeals. Shortly thereafter, Pop Allard called in with news that he had to bail out and went over the side. The cause for Chalot's and Allard's losses were believed to be oxygen failure and oil pressure loss, respectively. Both turned up as POW's later. Chalot was sent to Buchenwald and barely survived the war.

No enemy fighters were encountered in the otherwise uneventful target escort over Munster and all other Mustangs returned by 1150.

Claims: None   Losses: 2

March 14

No mission today after an engine dropped out of another group's Mustang, killing the pilot. Eighth Fighter Command immediately issued orders to ground the P-51s until all engine bolts were thoroughly inspected. As the engines had to be pulled to remove the bolts, all Mustangs were grounded for a couple of days.

March 15

Starr, Fortier, Williams and Wright left the 354th Squadron for detached service with a new low level attack outfit flying Thunderbolts under the command of Colonel Glenn Duncan, 353rd Group C.O.

March 16

F.O. 270.   Lieutenant Colonel Stewart led the troops on a target support to Augsburg. Landfall was made with 44 Mustangs over Ostend, and rendezvous with the bombers occurred over the Nordlingen area. The 355th joined the 4th FG and the bombers were escorted over the target. First contact with Jerry was made after the bomb run when 40 plus Me-109s were spotted queuing up for a pass on the low box of B-17s. One B-17 was seen going down with no chutes seen. The 354FS entered the scrap with seven Mustangs and emerged with 7 destroyed for no loss after a chase that ranged all the way to the deck.

Captain Neal was high scorer with two confirmed 109s and a shared victory with Lieutenant Lenfest. Lenfest also shot down another 109 while Koraleski, Duffy and Morris each scored singles.

Stewart led the 358FS into the brawl and Stewart, Rosenblatt, Kenney, DeGeorge and Gresham each chalked up an Me-109 destroyed. Dickson scored a pair to raise his total claims to four.

The 357FS, at the trailing edge of the fight, scored when Burroughs and Colson each shot down an Me-109. Lieutenants Bille,

Kirby and MacFarlane also claimed a shared Me-109 south of Reutlingen.

Lieutenant Carver of the 358FS was shot down in the fight and Don Wright was last seen chasing two Me-109s and also failed to return. Both later turned up POW.

During debriefing, the group pilots expressed opinions that the quality of the German pilots encountered ranged from very good to inexperienced.

Claims: 17 Destroyed   Losses: 2

March 17

General Auton visited the base to extend a personal commendation to the 355th pilots. Stewart took the opportunity to press Auton to expedite delivery of the Malcom Hood canopy to improve visibility and the 100-mil gun sights to replace the old 70-mil sights. The hundred mil gun sight was far better than the 70 mil sight for lead calculation on large deflection shots.

March 18

F.O. 273A. Lieutenant Colonel Stewart led 47 Mustangs on a ramrod to support bombers attacking targets near Munich and Augsburg. When the bombers swung away from Munich at 1420, several large gaggles of mixed Me-109s and FW-190s made aggressive attacks on both the bombers and escorts.

Lieutenant Hovde of the 358FS scored a double, knocking down two FW-190s and damaging another, to raise his score to three. Lieutenants Lenfest and Mendenhall shared a 109 while Neal and Henry Brown each scored singles. Neal raised his score to four and one half in the air to become the 354FS' leading scorer. Stewart also shot down an Me-109 to raise his total to four.

During the mission, a straggling 357th Group P-51 marked G4*H tacked on to the 358FS but could not make R/T connection. During the initial bounce by FW-190s the 357th Group pilot (believed to be Constantin Vogel of the 362nd Squadron) failed to break and was shot down. All 355th pilots returned safely.

Claims: 6 Destroyed   Losses: None

March 20

F.O. 275. Lieutenant Colonel Stewart led a ramrod to the Frankfurt area for withdrawal support of Third Task Force B-24s. Major Kinnard reminded the pilots one more time "to stick together, particularly in a fight". Bad weather prevented rendezvous at the designated location and the three squadrons operated a "shuttle service" for returning boxes and aborting bombers.

Henry Brown spotted a lone FW-190 making attacks on a struggling Fort from the six o'clock position at 7,000 feet. Brown called the bounce and swooped down from 15,000 feet to hammer the FW-190. After two good bursts with strikes all over, the FW flicked into a snap roll and headed straight down. Brown followed him into the clouds below but only claimed a probable.

Koraleski and Duffy destroyed two locomotives on the way home and all fighters returned safely.

March 22

F.O. 277. Lieutenant Colonel Stewart led the 355th for another run on Berlin. The group dispatched 45 Mustangs to support Second Task Force B-17s attacking the Basdorf aircraft engine plant and rendezvous was made northwest of Muritz Lake at 1302 hours. No enemy fighters were spotted but the 354FS was bounced by "friendly" P-38s. No harm, no foul and escort was broken over the Channel at 1520 hours. Prior to coming home, Woody and Duffy destroyed a couple of trains.

March 23

F.O. 278. Colonel Cummings led a routine ramrod to Brunswick with 45 Mustangs. Rendezvous was made early east of Munster and the 354th and 357FS escorted five boxes of B-17s over the target and back to the Channel. The 358FS missed the rendezvous when their bombers were 25 minutes late and swept the area to Hanover before returning.

A burning Air Sea Rescue launch was spotted on the way home in the Channel.

March 24

F.O. 279. Colonel Cummings led the 355th on a ramrod to Schweinfurt. Complete cloud cover obscured the target area and the mission was uneventful except for flak. On the way home, the 354FS dropped down to the deck and shot up several trains near Ulzen and Cologne.

Twenty fighter groups were up on this day and the old hands remembered that just five months past, four groups was a maximum effort.

March 26

No mission today, but Kucheman, Koraleski, Neal, Mendenhall, Brown, Perry, Duffy and Boulet of the 354th Squadron took off for some formation publicity shots for Eighth Fighter Command.

Kenneth Williams, on recent special assignment to "Bill's Buzz Boys" was shot down while attacking Chateaudun airdrome on the new group's first combat mission. He evaded successfully and returned to Steeple Morden in mid April.

March 27

F.O. 282.   Colonel Cummings led a maximum effort penetration, target and withdrawal support ramrod. The bombers from the First Task Force bombed German airfields near Biarritz, just a few miles north of Spain. Following the bombing, the 357th was released from escort duty and dropped down to strafe.

The 357FS made one pass on the Bicarrosse Airdrome before pulling away. Major Crossen shot down an Me-109 in the traffic pattern and blew up a JU-88 on the field. Captain Wilson and Lieutenant Reedy shared in the destruction of another 109 near the airdrome after a short chase on the deck.

Lieutenant Butcher led his flight down for a second pass and was clobbered by light flak after heavily damaging two JU-88s. Butcher was too low to bail out and his P-51 made one snap roll before he managed to skid off to one side and crash into a hill. Everybody throught he had "bought it" but Butcher miraculously turned up POW in a German hospital several months later.

Claims: 3 Destroyed   Losses: 1

March 28

F.O. 283.   Lieutenant Colonel Dix led the group to support attacks on German airfields near Dijon. The 355th picked up their B-17s over Chateau Thierry and shortly after R/V the 354FS was jumped by two flights of Lightnings for the second time in a week. No damage was inflicted but tempers were running pretty high.

Major Szaniawski took the 357FS down to Dijon airdrome after escort was broken and the "Jones Boys" established a new ETO record by destroying a record 19, probably destroying one and damaging 31 German aircraft on the ground. Top scorers were Szaniawski with four and Johnston with three. The 354FS added four and the 358FS added one more when Hovde shot up an HE-111 on another airdrome near Compeigne.

Captain Neal became the first combined air and ground ace for the 354FS when he added one (shared with Minchew) on the ground to his 4.5 in the air. Szani awski's and Johnston's ground scores raised both their combined scores to six and five, respectively. Even better, the group suffered no casualties in the deal.

Bud Mahurin and Gerald Johnson, two top scoring aces of the 56th FG, were shot down this day. Mahurin evaded, but Johnson became POW.

Claims: 24 Destroyed   Losses: None

March 29

F.O. 284.   Lieutenant Colonel Stewart led a ramrod from 1124 to 1609 hours. The 355th group provided target support for the Big Friends over Brunswick.

At approximately 1320, Kinnard led the 354FS into a gaggle of approximately 50 plus FW-190s which were approaching the B-17s from the Southwest. In the engagement, the group shot down 14 with Stewart, Burroughs and Ben Johnston getting two each. Following the escort, the 354th and 357FS went down on the deck to destroy two more enemy aircraft on the ground plus two trains. Stewart became the 355th's second air ace on this day while Koraleski raised his total to four and one third. Johnston's engine blew during the scrap and he crash landed on a German field about 5 minutes after the fight.

Lieutenant McConnell of the 358FS was shot down by flak near the Dutch coast and Bud Lambert bailed out over the Channel after running out of gas. Lambert drowned despite all efforts by the group and Air Sea Rescue.

Claims: 16 Destroyed   Losses: 3

The 355th closed out March operations by destroying 40 out of its total 110 victories in the last two missions of the month and received two Special Commendations from Eighth Fighter Command for their outstanding performance.

During March, the 355th leap-frogged its way to number seven (7) on the top scoring list of the 8th Fighter Command groups; behind the 56th, the 4th, the 354th (on loan from the 9th Air Force), the 78th, the 357th and the 352nd, in that order. Going into April, the 355th Fighter Group was about 250 victories behind the 56th and about 185 behind the second place 4th Group.

Two more weeks would again dramatically change the order and the 355th would jump to number three in the scoring race and remain there for the rest of the war. Interestingly enough, the 355th would outscore all other groups in the ETO, including the 4th, from April 1, 1944 to the end of the war by destroying approximately 755 more German aircraft in the air and on the ground.

Leadership, opportunity and luck dictated the fortunes of various fighter groups during WWII.

April 5

F.O. 288. Colonel Cummings led a fighter sweep to the Munich area from 1247 to 1820 hours. The results of this mission set a record which stood for five more months before finally being broken by the new 479thFG. The targets for the 355th were the Oberpfaffenhofen, Landsberg, Lechfeld, Penzig, Ottingen and Denigen airdromes southwest of Munich.

The group made landfall over Ostend and Cummings led the 355th down through the overcast to navigate one and one half hours in miserable weather before reaching the target area. The group entered the target area and split up into three separate forces to attack the airdromes.

After boring through a swirling snowstorm and withering flak for 40 minutes, the group departed the target area with claims of 51-2-81 for the loss of three of their own. The 358FS took top honors with claims of 24-1-41 and established a new single squadron record in the ETO.

Major Kinnard of the 354FS took top honors with one air victory plus four on the ground. Koraleski shared three in the air to raise his air total to five and one half and become the group's third air ace. Brady Williamson nailed one by himself and shared two more in the air. Houston and Myers each claimed three on the ground while Cummings and Beckman scored doubles. In all, 42 pilots claimed either damaged or destroyed aircraft during the mission.

Lieutenants Hill, Culp and Ondris were all killed. Hill and Culp were shot down by flak and Ondris was last seen being chased by 109's over Landsberg airdrome. The 355th started the month of April with a bang and eventually received a Distinguished Unit Citation for the mission. The group's last three missions resulted in destruction of over 90 German aircraft plus 120 more damaged or probably destroyed.

Claims: 51 Destroyed   Losses: 3

April 8

F.O. 291. Lieutenant Colonel Stewart led the next mission on a ramrod to the Brunswick area from 1145 to 1640 hours. As rendezvous was being made near Gardlingen, approximately 50 to 75 Me-109s and FW-190s from JG 3 were ripping up the B-24s with "company front" attacks. The 357FS stayed with the Liberators as the 354th and 358FS waded into the German fighters.

In a short and violent clash, the 355th claimed seven for one loss (Dickson) but eight B-24s were seen going down before Jerry broke for the deck. Those pilots making claims included Henry Brown, Kurtz, Minchew, Hovde, Sluga and Harrington.

The 354th and 358FS rejoined the bombers while the 357FS went down to strafe Gifhorn A/D. The 357th destroyed five on the ground and Szaniawski shot down an Me-109 for the loss of two. Reedy was shot down by 109s and Olson was hit by flak after destroying an Me-109 on the ground. After climbing away, McNeff saw Olson slump forward in his harness, make a slow 200 degree turn and dive into the ground near Hoefer, northeast of Celle. Dickson of the 358FS was last seen chasing several Me-109s and FW-190s near Emden and also turned up KIA. With the passing of Norm Olson, the 355th lost their first ace and their only air ace KIA for the entire war.

Interestingly enough the 355th did not lose an ace in air to air combat during WWII, which may be a unique accomplishment for a top scoring fighter group in the ETO.

Claims: 13 Destroyed   Losses: 3

April 9

F.O. 292. Colonel Cummings led a ramrod to the Warnemunde area from 1002 to 1500 hours. The 355th furnished an uneventful target and withdrawal support and broke escort near the Zuider Zee. No enemy fighters were seen but two B-24s were seen going down near the target due to flak. The 56thFG and 354thFG got some action but not much else was going on.

April 10

F.O. 293. Lieutenant Colonel Stewart led a ramrod to Tours and Bourges from 0845 to 1234. They picked up the bombers north of Vendome and escorted them to the target. Bombing was reported to be excellent and after the bombers turned for home, the 354FS dropped down to strafe. Kinnard, Austin, Duffy, Woody and Kurtz each destroyed one aircraft with one pass and came on home. All pilots returned home by 1234 hours.

The 4th had a big day on the ground with a score of 28 on a deep penetration to Germany.

Claims: 5 Destroyed   Losses: None

April 11

F.O. 295.   Lieutenant Colonel Stewart led a ramrod to attack aircraft engine plants near Sorau. A gaggle of 20 to 30 twin and single engine Jerry fighters was spotted queing up near Stargard for attacks on the bombers as the 355th made R/V with the bombers.

The 354th and 358FS bounced while the 357FS stayed with the Big Friends. The Me-210s, 410s and JU-88s were the first "easy meat" the group had encountered since November and they flamed seven quickly before the Me-109s and FW-190s arrived to break up the party. Two more German fighters were shot down out of the top cover for no loss and the rest of the enemy fighters broke for cloud cover to survive to fight another day. The 358FS rejoined the bombers while the 354th and 357FS dropped down to strafe the Strasbourg airdrome. Fourteen more aircraft were destroyed on and near the ground before the group turned for home.

Curtis Johnston destroyed three on the ground to take honors for the day but both Johnston and Easterly were shot down by flak to become POWs.

Brown bounced four Me-109s stalking two other 355th Mustangs. After a ten minute rat race with empty guns, he finally bluffed the 109s into breaking for the deck. As Brown was out of .50 caliber, he declined to pursue the chase. In this fashion Henry Brown survived to become the group's top ace and received the Distinguished Service Cross.

The 357thFG also had a very big day, destroying 25 German fighters further along the penetration route. The new 357th Fighter Group was quickly establishing an excellent reputation for air victories in the ETO.

Claims: 23 Destroyed   Losses: 2

April 12

F.O. 296.   Colonel Cummings led the 355th on a ramrod from 1222 to 1620 hours. Landfall and rendezvous with the bombers was made over the Walcheren Islands at 1315. The group provided penetration and target support to heavies striking Hanover and Bremen. Flak was moderate to heavy but no bombers were seen to go down.

April 13

F.O. 298.   Major Kinnard led a ramrod from 1210 to 1738. The 355th provided penetration and target support to bombers attacking airdromes at Lechfeld and Oberpfaffenhofen near Munich.

En route to the target, the 357FS bounced 14 Me-109s and shot down five plus claimed two probables without loss. Szaniawski, Bille, Hillman, Sturm and Wilson got one each. Near Nordlingen, Major Myers took Red flight from the 358FS and jumped four FW-190s, getting one before the others broke into the cloud cover.

The 354th and 357FS dropped down to the deck after the bombers turned for home and swept Oberpfaffenhofen and Grailsheim airdromes. The 354th got 19 on Oberpfaffenhofen. Kinnard got four to briefly take the lead in the group scoring race, while the Browns (Rich and Henry), Duffy, Barger, Morris and Williamson each got two. Browning and Woody each destroyed singles. The 358FS had no luck at Lechfeld but the 357FS picked up three shared aircraft on the ground at Grailsheim.

The group returned home to receive their fourth Special Commendation in the last six missions from General Auton. Following the results of the day's mission, Henry Brown had regained the scoring lead over Kinnard and now had a total of 11.7 to 10, respectively.

Claims: 28 Destroyed   Losses: None

April 15

F.O. 299.   Major Myers led a rodeo to the Glienicke and Wagonoff area from 1150 to 1630. Landfall was made at 1255 over Ijmuiden. When the group was near the target area, two squadrons split up to strafe separate airdromes. The 358FS dropped down to strafe Glienicke A/D, the 357FS attacked Wagonoff and the 354FS orbited to provide top cover for both attacking squadrons.

The 358th bagged ten for the loss of Kenney, who was hit by flak and crashed nearby. McElroy destroyed five DO-217s on the ground while Myers, Kenney, Dissette, MacConkey and Beckman each destroyed one DO-217. Moon Elder, leading the 357th, got a stray Me-109 over Wagonoff and MacFarlane got one on the ground for the loss of Joe Kerch to flak. Walter Koraleski, the leading air ace of the 354th, reported mechanical problems near Utrecht and bailed out. All three pilots became POW.

The 355th made landfall over the Hague and all other pilots returned safely.

Claims: 13 Destroyed   Losses: 3

April 18

F.O. 304.   Major Kinnard led a ramrod for penetration and target escort to Orienburg and rendezvous was made at 1422 hours near Wittenberg. The bombers flew a good formation and no Jerry fighters were encountered by the 355th.

Twenty to thirty German fighters did jump the 4th Group near Rhin Canal and were clobbered. Light but inaccurate flak was encountered over the target and landfall was made over the Hague where the 355th broke off the escort.

April 19

F.O. 305.   Lieutenant Colonel Stewart led a penetration and target support to Kassel and Eshwege from 0816 to 1237. The 355th made rendezvous with the bombers south of Brunswick at 1000 hours and 15,000 feet.

Near Magdeburg the 354th and 358FS climbed to investigate contrails at 37,000 feet and were bounced from above by 30 plus Me-109s and FW-190s. As the German fighters passed through, Woody, Fussell and Meteyer shot down one each for the loss of MacConkey. Several FW-190s cornered MacConkey on the deck and blew him up before Hoffman could help. The German fighters continued on the deck and the two squadrons returned to escort the bombers. The 355th policy continued to be "Break up the attack and return to the escort."

Landfall was made south of Ostend when escort was broken off.

Claims: 3 Destroyed   Losses: 1

April 20

F.O. 307.   Major Kinnard led a ramrod to the coast of France from 1610 to 2045 hours. The 355th provided area support to bombers attacking targets in the Cherbourg area. Landfall was made near Fecamp at 1755 hours and the bombers were picked up near Bernay at 1805. No fighters were encountered and the flak was meager.

The 354FS dropped down to strafe Blois Airdrome and Kurtz got two while Houston and Browning each destroyed one. Heavy flak was encountered around the drome and only two passes were made. All returned by 2045.

Claims: 4 Destroyed   Losses: None

April 21

Under Secretary of State Edward Stettinius accompanied Generals Spaatz, Doolittle, Kepner and Auton on a visit to Steeple Morden. The mission scheduled for that day was scrubbed due to bad weather.

April 22

F.O. 309.   Major Myers led the 355th on a fighter sweep and area patrol from 1626 to 2055. The group swept to Hanover at 1756 but no enemy fighters were seen. The 358FS let down from 8,000 feet and shot up barges on Steinhuder Lake plus several trains in the same area. Flak was intense and accurate, damaging several Mustangs, but all returned safely.

Shortly after the 355th returned to Steeple Morden, German intruders in the form of Me-210s and Me-410s slipped into some Second Division landing patterns and shot down nine B-24s.

April 24

F.O.312.   Lieutenant Colonel Dix led a ramrod to the Munich area from 1106 to 1632. The 355th provided target and withdrawal support to First Division B-17s bombing Oberpfaffenhofen. Rendezvous was made at 1315 north west of Munich.

At 1330, the B-17s came under heavy attack by 70 plus FW-190s and Me-109s. Kucheman led the 354FS into the gaggle and the 354th engaged for about 20 minutes in a wild scrap ranging from 35,000 feet to the deck.

Woody led his flight into one bunch of Me-109s and quickly flamed four. Boulet got strikes on number five but pulled off as Woody slid in and put a solid burst into the engine and cockpit. Number five fell off pouring smoke, coolant and oil and finished in a tight inverted spin before blowing up. Woody then put another concentration of strikes into a sixth Me-109, from about 60 degrees deflection, before finally running out of ammo. The 109 fell off in a spin but Woody only claimed a "damaged". In all, Woody, Fortier and Boulet destroyed nine in this encounter and Woody received a DSC for his role in the mission. Kucheman and Henry Brown destroyed three and two 109s respectively to wrap up the squadron's score for the day. Woody and Brown became the group's fourth and fifth air aces.

Meanwhile, the 357FS was also turning in a solid day's work by nailing six. Dix, Bille and Wilson got singles while Demers got a double and shot up a third before McNeff and Butler finished it off.

Raymond Demers was killed when the wings came off his Mustang as he strafed two barges and was hit by light flak in a steep dive. Jack Sturm was shot down by an Me-109 and Lieutenants Norman and Hillman of the 357th were lost later in the mission due to unknown circumstances. Both were seen chasing a 109 through a box of B-17s and may have been shot down by the Forts. Sturm turned up later as POW. The rest of the mission was uneventful and all other pilots returned by 1632.

Bob Woody became the first fighter pilot in the Eighth Air Force to shoot down more than four German fighters in one day.

Claims: 20 Destroyed   Losses: 4

April 25

F.O.313.   Lieutenant Colonel Stewart led a ramrod to Dijon from 0752 to 1250. The group provided penetration and target support to First and Third Division B-17s attacking airfields in the Dijon area. The 357FS left the bombers on the way home and strafed targets of opportunity. They damaged a couple of unidentified twin engine fighters and shot up some hangars and flak towers but didn't find much. No enemy aircraft were seen in the air and flak was light.

April 26

F.O.315.   Lieutenant Colonel Dix led a ramrod from 0722 to 1255 hours. The group provided penetration, target and withdrawal support to Third Division B-17s attacking Brunswick and Fallersleben. Rendezvous was made near Steinhuder Lake.

Mustangs of the 354FS were fired upon several times by gunners of bombers they were escorting. After one of these incidents, Boulet reported rising engine temperatures and bailed out to become POW. The escort was otherwise uneventful and the bombers flew an excellent formation. No enemy aircraft was seen.

Boulet remained in solitary confinement for several weeks because the Germans thought he was a plant. Vernon Burroughs, shot down in May after transferring to the 4th Group, confirmed Boulet's story and Boulet was released to POW camp.

Claims: None   Losses: 1

April 27

F.O.317.   Major Szaniawski led the 355th on a ramrod from 1655 to 2120 hours. From landfall near Knocke, escort to the target at Luneville and return, the flight was boring and uneventful. The bombers flew an excellent formation once again, making them easy to cover. All Mustangs returned by 2120 hours.

April 29

F.O.320.   Lieutenant Colonel Dix led a ramrod to Berlin from 0846 to 1425 hours. Landfall was made over Egmond and the 355th orbited for an hour near Steinhuder Lake before the bombers finally made rendezvous.

On the way into the target Captain Neal and his wingman Lieutenant Fritts, bounced four FW-190s west of Berlin. The FW190s broke away and Neal's two ship element pursued them into an undercast at 7,000 feet. Fritts started to pull out at 4,000 feet while still in the cloud cover and broke out just above the treetops. When Fritts couldn't raise Neal over the R/T, he made the long climb back to rejoin the formation. Fritts believed that Neal and maybe some of the Germans might have gone in together, but Neal was never seen again.

The Luftwaffe failed to attack the 355th or their escorted bombers, but 200 plus heavily armed FW-190s and escorting 109s made a shambles of other boxes of bombers. Over 20 Second Division B-24s were shot down quickly near Hanover and 64 bombers failed to return for the second worst day in Eighth Air Force history.

Henry Brown evened the score for Neal when he slipped up on a large gaggle of 109s near Brunswick, blew one up and slipped away. The 355th broke off escort at 1235 and everybody but Neal was on the ground by 1425.

Neal was a very popular guy in the 354FS and the group mourned the loss of a damned good and aggressive fighter pilot.

Claims: 1 Destroyed   Losses: 1

April 30

F.O.321.   Lieutenant Colonel Dix started a patrol at 0733 but Major Rosenblatt took over when Dix aborted shortly after take off. The 355th made landfall over St. Valery at 0817 and swept the area between Clermont and Lyon.

35. Olson and OS-P "Ma Fran 3rd." Olson, the only 355th air ace KIA, was shot down by flak on April 8, 1944. No 355th FG ace was shot down by a German fighter. (Wilkerson, Seidl, Hart)

36. Les Minchew and WR-M before transferring from the 354th FS to group operations. (Minchew)

37. Barger and WR-C nearly paid the ultimate price during the 355th's first strafing attack on an airfield, March 8, 1944. (Baldwin, Barnhouse, Vose)

38. Captain James McConnell and YF-C, "Dual Purpose." McConnell was shot down March 29, 1944 by flak while riding his new Mustang. (Hovde)

39. This lucky 91st BG Fortress bellied in with leaking fuel and a full load of bombs. The date was March 6, 1944, the day the Eighth Air Force first hit Berlin. (Lenfest)

40. Bennett and Gertzen working on Bob Woody's WR-W. (Haviland)

41. Crew chief Coraggio painting Gresham's first kill on YF-T, "Trigger II." Gresham may have been the pilot who shot down the great Luftwaffe ace Egon Mayer on March 24, 1944. (Hovde, Gresham)

42. Crew chief Launer and assistant Gerry Thompson check out Ev Stewart for Big B on March 6, 1944. (Stewart, Launer)

43. Billy Hovde of the 358th FS, who scored his first kill in a P-47 and went on to become a Mustang double ace. (Hovde)

44. 354th FS armament officer Scott and two of his armorers trying to figure ways to reduce stoppages. (Kucheman)

45. Ev Stewart in April 1944, after making ace. (Thompson, Stewart)
46. "Ole II" in the 358th FS area during mid-April, 1944. (Hovde)
47. Henry Brown, top 355th Texas ace, sporting a new set of flying boots, April 1944. (Mendenhall, Dumas)
48. Many airmen in the ETO traveled from far and wide to see DeCosta's mural in the 355th officers' club. (Lenfest, Mendenhall, Sims)

49. The 355th switched from P-47s to P-51s in late February and early March. Lenfest's old and new mounts are seen here. (Lenfest, Caldwell)

50. Szaniawski and crew chief Schultz bringing "Available Jones" victory total up to date on March 27, 1944. (Hart, Ramsdell)

51. An element of 354th FS Mustangs in the spring of 1944. (Brown, Sims, Duffy, Kucheman)

52. Jack Beckman, American transferee from the RCAF, joined the 358th in 1943. He went MIA on March 1, 1945 upon being hit by flak while chasing an Me-262. (Hovde)

53. John Wilson and Floyd Kelly of the 357th FS. Wilson was lost in a crash in early 1945. (Williams, Hart)

54. Jim McElroy destroyed five Do-217s on the ground during his first strafing mission in April 1944. (Hovde)
55. Captain Les Minchew and crew after a long ride to Germany and back (Haviland)
56. This highly-polished bird, WR-B, was possibly flown by Williams. (Bennett)
57. Norman "Bud" Fortier, a 354th ace, in an early Mustang, April 1944. Two of his seven victories were shared, for a total of 5.83. (Fortier)
58. Captain Walter Koraleski and WR-L just before becoming a POW on April 15, 1944 due to engine failure. Koraleski was the "Bulldogs" first ace. (Kinnard, Sims, Bennett)
59. Elder and Feldman in front of Elder's first Mustang, 05-R, "Moon," April 1944. (Ramsdell, McNeff)

60. Clay Kinnard and his first "Man O' War" Mustang after the April 13 raid on Oberpfaffenhofen. (Kinnard, Lenfest)

61. Kurtz's WR-A "Hat Jane" in April 1944. (Kurtz)

62. Duffy and crew on WR-Y in April 1944. (Baldwin)

63. Mort Braun paying off a one-pound bet to Henry Brown after the latter picked off another one. (Braun)

64. Several 354th FS Mustangs as viewed from the right waist position of a B-17. Kucheman, Brown and Neal are closest to the camera. (Bennett, Sims, Braun)

65. Stewart buzzing Steeple Morden after shooting down number five on March 29, 1944. (Haviland)
66. Photo formation for the 355th with brand-new Mustangs on March 26. (Kucheman, Caldwell)
67. Boresighting a 358th Mustang in May 1944. Note the unusual, short-lived color scheme of black nose. (Hovde)
68. Clarence "Fid" Barger and WR-C both went missing on May 28, 1944. (Kurtz)
69. Under Secretary of State Edward Stettinius with air exec, Ev Stewart, viewing a dingy demonstration by Sargeant Estabrook. (Hart)

70. Bert Marshall's first victory was September 11, 1944. This Me-109 blew up as "Jane III" zoomed over him in a high-speed pass. (Marshall)

71. Marshall became an ace in 61 days, on August 6. It was the fastest record from first mission to fifth kill of any 355th pilot. (Marshall)

72. Elder, Stewart, Stettinius, Kurtz, Kinnard, Walsh and Williams on the Steeple Morden tower, April 21, 1944.

73. Bob Woody was the first Eighth Air Force pilot to nail more than four airborne Germans in one mission, April 24, 1944. He's joined by crew chief Gertzen and Bennett on WR-W, "Woody's Maytag," after scoring 4½ Me-109s. (Woody, Gertzen)

74. Raymond Myers, CO of the 358th FS, was also the "Angels'" first ace. He bagged number five on May 24, 1944. (Myers)

The group escorted a couple of boxes near Bourges and then were vectored under Type 16 control to pick up a different bunch of B-17s when Jerry fighter action was reported. No enemy aircraft were seen and the bombers were left at 1045. All fighters returned to Steeple Morden by 1250.

Following review of April results, the 355th had charged past several other groups to assume third position behind the 56th and 4th Groups. After a review of claims for destroyed and probables, the 355th was awarded 157 confirmed victories for the month to raise their total to 267.

May 1

F.O.323. Lieutenant Colonel Dix led a ramrod from 1631 to 2055 hours. The group provided penetration, target and withdrawal support to bombers attacking Metz.

On the way in, 75 to 80 Me-109s traveling on a northeasterly heading started to attack the bombers but broke off when the 355th positioned to bounce. One flight of the 357th was hit from out of the sun near Hannover by five or six Me-109s. They shot down Lieutenant Kaminski and continued to dive into a cloud layer below. On the way out, Captain Dissette took Red flight of the 358FS down on four Me-109s near Traben-Trabach and shot down one.

Landfall out was made at 1955 over Ostend and everybody but Kaminski was home by 2055.

Claims: 1 Destroyed   Losses: 1

May 4

F.O.326. Lieutenant Colonel Dix led a ramrod from 0838 to 1300. The 355th furnished target and withdrawal support to bombers attacking Brunswick and Halberstadt. Landfall was made north of the Hague at 0931 and bad weather conditions were encountered. At 1015 the group was recalled near Halberstadt just before rendezvous.

Near Hannover, the 358FS was bounced by 35 plus Me-109s. Yellow and Blue flights scored two destroyed, two probables and three damaged. Martyn got two probable Me-109s and damaged another before two more 109s slipped in at six o'clock and shot him down. Robinson got one plus a probable, Captain Gresham got another probable plus a damaged and Blair damaged an Me-109 before disengagement.

The group came out north of The Hague at 1203 and 10,000 feet.

Claims: 2 Destroyed   Losses: 1

May 7

F.O.329. Lieutenant Colonel Szaniawski led a ramrod from 0807 to 1341. The group provided penetration, target and withdrawal support for First Task Force bombers attacking targets in Berlin. Landfall was north of Ijmuiden at 0915 and rendezvous was made at 1040. The continent was covered with 9/10 and 10/10 overcast but heavy, intense flak was encountered over Bremen, Hannover and Berlin. No enemy fighters were seen and the 355th was relieved by the 56th FG near Brunswick at 1144. Landfall out was again north of Ijmuiden at 1245 hours and 20,000 feet.

May 8

F.O.331. Lieutenant Colonel Stewart led another boring ramrod to Berlin. Following an 0615 briefing, the 355th departed Steeple Morden at 0805 and made landfall north of The Hague at 0913. Rendezvous with the Second Task Force was made at 1038 just short of Berlin and the group furnished penetration and withdrawal support until 1210.

Twenty-five plus Me-109s were spotted near Brunswick by the 358FS but Stewart denied permission to bounce as the group was the only fighter escort for two large formations. The 352nd FG did bounce them and shot down 29 in the ensuing scrap. Heavy and accurate flak was experienced near Hannover, Brunswick and Berlin and a couple of B-17s were seen to go down along the way. Landfall out was made north of Egmond and all Mustangs were home by 1340.

May 9

F.O.333. Lieutenant Colonel Dix led the 355th from 0756 to 1120 on a penetration, target and withdrawal ramrod for bombers attacking the Luftwaffe night fighter base at St. Trond. The mission started out as a fighter sweep but Second Division B-24s called for help on C-channel near Dinant and the group pulled up to provide support. Rendezvous was made in the Namur area at 0918.

Following the bombing, the 358FS dropped down to strafe the airdrome but the smoke was too thick to pick up ground targets and the 358th made only one pass on St. Trond with no verifiable results. No enemy fighters were seen and the B-24s were reported to fly an excellent formation. Landfall out was near Flushing and all fighters returned safely.

May 10

F.O.334. Lieutenant Colonel Dix led a ramrod from 0714 to 1005 to support First Task Force bombers attacking targets in Rotenberg. Landfall was made at 0808 north of Egmond but the weather was so bad that the bombers were recalled before R/V. The 355th then swept south to pick up some of the recalled boxes of bombers coming home. Landfall out was north of Egmond at 0907 and all fighters were down by 1005.

May 11

F.O.336. Lieutenant Colonel Szaniawski led a ramrod from 1651 to 1955. The 355th furnished an uneventful penetration and target support for bombers attacking targets near the Saarbruecken area. Landall and rendezvous was made over Dunkirk at 1731. The bombers were escorted to the target and back until escort was broken off at 1803 near Liege. No enemy aircraft were seen and landfall out was made over Cayeux at 1904.

May 12

F.O.337. Lieutenant Colonel Dix led a ramrod to support First Task Force B-17s attacking targets in Zwickau. This day marked the start of the Eighth Air Force campaign against the German oil industry. The 355th's mission was to escort the bombers attacking the Focke-Wulf repair depot in Zwickau. The other Task Forces and the majority of the fighter escort went after German oil.

Briefing was at 0900, take off at 1026 and landfall was made at 1122 over Ostend. The 355th escorted the Forts from Bonne to Falkenstein where the 358th Squadron departed to escort some Third Division bombers. On the way in, some 109s started to attack Woody's flight, but broke away after he turned into them. The 355th was relieved on the way back and broke escort at 1450. Everyone came back over Ostend and all pilots were on the ground at 1550.

May 13

F.O.338. Lieutenant Colonel Dix led a ramrod to Poznan, Poland from 1157 to 1757 hours. This particular mission was the longest escort by the Eighth Air Force Fighter Command until very late in the war, covering 1480 miles. The 355th was assigned to protect First Task Force B-17s attacking the Focke Wulf assembly plant at Poznan while others covered the force attacking the synthetic oil plant at Politz, near Stettin. (The 355th would take the same approximate route on September 18, 1944 for the last Shuttle Mission.) The 354th and 357FS were assigned to the two wings attacking the first Poznan target and the 358FS covered the second Poznan effort. Fifty three Mustangs took off at 1157 and 48 made landfall south of Egmond at 1257. Rendezvous with the Forts was made east of Berlin at 1440 and the group split up to cover the seperate efforts.

Shortly before reaching the target, Lieutenant Fortier took Falcon Blue flight of the 354FS down to bounce a JU-88 and quickly shot it down. The rest of the 354th then wheeled into some 15 to 20 Me-410s attacking the B-17s from the 12 o'clock position and shot down six.

Dix and Morris each bagged a pair and Brown shot down one to raise his total of air kills to eight and his combined air/ground tally to sixteen. Only Kinnard was close with ten. Lieutenant Martin shot down an He-129 near the deck for his first air victory and ended up coming home alone. Fortier took his flight into four FW-190s flying line abreast near Hannover and shot down one while Perry flamed two and damaged a third, to bring the day's total to ten for no losses.

The rest of the trip home was uneventful and the pilots all landed safely by 1757.

Claims: 10 Destroyed   Losses: None

May 19

F.O.342. Lieutenant Colonel Szaniawski led a ramrod from 1044 to 1555. The 355th escorted one Task Force to Brunswick and another bomber force to Berlin. The Berlin effort was cancelled and rendezvous with the Brunswick effort was missed because of bad weather.

After relief from escort duties by the Controller, the 354th and 357FS dropped down to strafe Solingen and Diepholz airdromes. Jonesy was hit by flak and lost all engine coolant shortly thereafter. After Szaniawski successfully bellied in "Available Jones V" and ran into the woods, Bud Fortier destroyed the grounded Mustang. Hudson Packard of the 357FS spotted a DO-217 on the deck near one of the airfields, broke formation to give chase, and was never heard from again. No other enemy aircraft were seen and the group returned home by 1555 hours.

Claims: None   Losses: 2

May 20

F.O.343. Colonel Cummings led a ramrod to the Bierset/Liege area from 0915 to 1216. The 355th made rendezvous with four combat wings near Namur. As two of the bomber wings remained uncovered, Cummings dispatched five flights to cover them also and the 355th provided the sole escort for all four wings.

Near Maastricht, the 354FS climbed to intercept some FW-190s forming in front of the lead wing of B-17s and were quickly bounced from above and behind by six FW-190s and Me-109s painted similarly to Mustangs. Donaldson and Jacobson were quickly shot down and the Germans continued their dive before they could be engaged. The large gaggle in front of the bombers turned away when the 354FS did not pursue the diving German fighters. No bombers were lost and the fighters returned around 1216.

Claims: None   Losses: 2

May 21

F.O.344.   The Eighth Air Force sent the first large force comprised strictly of several fighter groups out for strafing and low level attacks. Colonel Cummings led the 355th on the CHATTANOOGA to the Bergen area from 1033 to 1545 hours. The 358th and 354FS shot up several trains, a small factory, several radio stations and one flak tower. MacFarlane and Englebreit potted an Me-108 near Schwerin and the 357FS destroyed four more aircraft on the ground.

In addition to the five destroyed aircraft, the group also clobbered eight trains, four trucks and raised merry hell all over the area.

Claims 5 Destroyed   Losses: None

May 22

F.O.346.   Lieutenant Colonel Dix led a ramrod to Kiel from 1053 to 1521. The 355th provided penetration, target and withdrawal support to the bombers along the Bremen-Hamburg-Kiel route.

Dix took the 358FS in to break up one attack by 20 FW-190s and chased them to 10,000 feet before coming back to the bombers. The 354FS chased 40 to 50 S/E fighters southwest of Redsburg but couldn't catch them. After the squadron returned to the bombers they spotted another 15 to 20 Me-109s at 32,000 to 38,000 and climbed to engage. They too turned away but not before Dix managed to shot one down. The 358FS chased some high flying Me-109s flying an American style formation, but they outpaced the Mustangs. Landfall was made over Friedrichskoog at 1336.

Claims: 1 Destroyed   Losses: None

May 23

F.O.348.   Lieutenant Colonel Dix led a ramrod to Chaumont from 0724 to 1212 hours. The bombers were met according to plan at 0857 but neither the rendezvous point nor the area short of the target could be seen because of the solid cloud cover. The escort was broken off around 1118 close to Dieppe.

May 24

F.O.349.   Lieutenant Colonel Myers led a ramrod to Berlin. Six wings of Second Task Force Forts were picked up over St. Peter. In an 8th AF experiment, Colonel Blakeslee of the 4th Group was to control and direct all fighters of four separate groups.

Just after reaching the target, 75 plus Me-109s and FW-190s of JG 3 were spotted at 12 o'clock to the bombers. The 355th split into three sections with the 358FS directed to the enemy fighters while the 354th and 357FS stayed with the bombers. One half of the gaggle dove for the deck, hoping to draw the 358th away but Myers led his squadron into the remaining Germans in a head on attack. The fighters were driven off before reaching the bombers and Myers got one to become the group's sixth ace. Lieutenant Foster of the 357th picked off another Me-109 for no loss to either the fighters or bombers.

Bombers escorted by other fighter groups suffered heavy losses to JG 1 and JG 3 when they pursued the decoys to the deck and left the bombers open to attack. The disciplined 355th passed up an opportunity for a big day by sticking to the primary job —PROTECT THE BOMBERS.

On the way home Fortier and Fritts were bounced by 109s, turned into them, and escaped before dropping to the deck to strafe a train. Fritts crashed and blew up on the pass for unknown causes, either flak or loss of control.

Claims: 2 Destroyed   Losses: 1

W.F.O.99.   Lieutenant Colonel Dix led a dive bombing effort to Beaumont-sur-Oise from 1720 to 1940 hours. The 358FS provided top cover while the 354th and 357FS tried to take out a railroad bridge. The target was dive bombed from 12,000 feet and bombs were released at 5,000 feet with generally poor results.

Perry and Duffy strafed an FW-190 taxiing on Cormeilles en Vexin airfield and destroyed it before being chased off by heavy flak. They also caught a train before turning for home.

Landfall out was made over Cayeux at 1905 and 15,000 feet. This mission was a milestone for the 355th as it was the first time the group flew two in one day.

Claims: 1 Destroyed   Losses: None

May 25

F.O.350.   Lieutenant Colonel Dix led a ramrod from 0710 to 1128. The group provided target and withdrawal support to bombers attacking Metz. Rendezvous was made with five wings of B-24s at 0823 hours near Meaux and escorted over the target and back. Two Me-109s were spotted with blue nose 352ndFG P-51s in pursuit near Charleroi. No flak or fighters were encountered, landfall was made over Coxyde at 1100 and everybody was back by 1128.

May 27

F.O.351.   Lieutenant Colonel Kinnard led a ramrod to provide target support to bombers attacking the Strasbourg marshalling yards from 1021 to 1509.

Rendezvous was made with the Third Division near Neufchateau at 1219 and the escort was uneventful except that one box of bombers shot at the 358th, mistaking them for enemy aircraft.

May 28

F.O.352.   Lieutenant Colonel Kinnard led a ramrod to Ruhland, northeast of Leipzig, from 1148 to 1652. Kinnard returned shortly after crossing the channel with radio problems and Captain Colson took over the lead. The 355th picked up the Forts near Celle at 1331 hours and escorted them over the target and back to Bad Nauhein at 1535 hours.

The 354FS's last flight was bounced from above near Wittenberg at 1335, and Lieutenants Barger and Christensen were shot down. The 354th had been climbing to engage more than 50 Me-109s and had been hit from behind by the unseen top cover. Barger was heard to acknowledge a break by his wingman and neither were seen to go down, but both failed to return. The large gaggle left to look for easier pickings. On the way home, MacFarlane and Eshelman of the 357th bounced a flight of Me-109s and shot down one each.

Claims: 2 Destroyed   Losses: 2

May 29

F.O.353.   Colonel Cummings led a ramrod to Poznan, Poland from 1019 to 1637. Rendezvous with the First Division was made near Poznan at 1310. The bombers were escorted over the target and back along the withdrawal until 1415. No enemy aircraft were seen and the mission was just another 1400 mile milk run. All fighters returned by 1637.

May 30

F.O.354.   Lieutenant Colonel Kinnard led a ramrod to Halberstadt from 0854 to 1335 hours. The 355th furnished target and withdrawal support to First Division B-17s after rendezvous was made west of Dummer Lake at 1030.

At 1100 hours, Blue flight of the 358FS sailed into a gaggle of 40 FW-190s and Me-109s southwest of Brunswick. Lieutenant Santos exploded two FW-190s while Donovan shot down an Me-109 and shared another Focke Wulf with an unidentified Mustang pilot from the 353rd group. This half credit stuck with the group until July when Minchew shared a kill with a P-38. Robinson also nailed an FW-190 to raise the squadron total to four and one half.

Following completion of escort duties the 357FS dropped down to strafe targets of opportunity near Aurich, including two clobbered trains and two barges. Following the mission, a Big Discussion was held about R/T chatter fouling up a chance at a big score because the 354th and 357FS were not able to get a clear picture of the location of the enemy fighters.

Claims: 4-1/2 Destroyed   Losses: None

May 31

F.O.355.   Lieutenant Colonel Dix led an area support to bombers attacking Hamm, from 0833 to 1323. Landfall was made over Ijmuiden at 0935 and the group covered the northern flank of the bomber route in a freelance patrol.

At 1115 the bombers were picked up south of Hamm for withdrawal support and escorted to the coast. Nothing of interest was seen along the route and landfall was made over Coxyde at 1302.

June 2

F.O.358.   Lieutenant Colonel Kinnard, then Captain Blair, led a fighter sweep under Type 16 (Beachy Head) control to the

Compiegne-Paris-St. Quentin area. Kinnard aborted after take off due to faulty tanks and Captain Blair assumed command. The 355th swept the Paris-St. Quentin-Lille area from 1145 to 1330 with no contact or encounters and all P-51s came home. A boring introduction to the busiest month yet.

June 3

F.O.364. Lieutenant Colonel Kinnard led an area patrol to the Montdidier area under Type 16 control. Colgate vectored the group to Montdidier for about 90 minutes and then brought them home at 1455. Lieutenant Browning of the 354FS went down west of Paris with engine coolant trouble at 1425 hours to become POW. Nothing else exciting happened and landfall was made south of Calais.

Claims: None   Losses: 1

June 4

F.O.367. Lieutenant Colonel Dix led an area patrol from 1330 to 1616 hours under Type 16 control. The 355th swept an area from Abbeville to Amiens to Cambrai before turning for home at St. Valery at 1540. Flight Officer Davis of the 354th had coolant problems short of St. Quentin and dropped down to 4,000 feet when 20mm flak hit him hard. Davis crashed and exploded on the beach. The 354FS continued a run of losses for the squadron which started on May 20 and now reached seven straight for the group. All other P-51s returned by 1616.

Claims: None   Losses: 1

F.O.368. Lieutenant Colonel Dix led a ramrod from 1840 to 2221 hours to provide penetration, target and withdrawal support near Versailles. Heavy flak was encountered over Le Havre but no enemy aircraft were seen. Escort was broken over the Channel at 2130.

June 5

F.O.369. Lieutenant Colonel Kinnard led a Type 16 control area patrol along the Graville-Vire-Falaise axis from 0812 to 1103. No enemy aircraft were seen and the group came out north of Bayeaux at 17,000 feet.

The last couple of days were remarkable for the number of new pilots which went through Goxhill (and Stud Starr's tutelage) and became replacements for the group. Included in this batch of pilots were several future 355th aces including Lieutenants Cullerton, Hauver and Priest and Captains Haviland and Marshall. Of all the new pilots assigned to the group after June, 1944, only Gordon Graham would score five or more aerial victories before the end of the war.

At 1900 hours Colonel Cummings tracked down the group intelligence and operations officers, the three squadron C.O.'s and the weather officer. After locking the group operations room, Cummings, Major Lewis, Captain Mason, Captain Schmucker, Captain Nicholson, Lieutenant Colonel Dix, Major Rosenblatt, Lieutenant Colonel Kinnard, Lieutenant Colonel Myers and Captain Ramsdell worked to plan the routes, the squadron assignments, timing and armament for the following day's invasion. At the same time, the line crews were busy painting the black and white invasion stripes around all the Mustangs' fuselages and wings.

According to the field orders, the 354th and 357th Squadrons' P-51s were topped off with fuel, the 108 gallon long range tanks were loaded and all the guns were loaded with tracer and API.

Cummings called the briefing for 2400 hours and broke the news of D-Day to an excited bunch of pilots. All routes for the following day for penetration and withdrawal were planned to avoid the shipping lanes.

Additionally, Cummings instructed the pilots to be very cautious about shooting up possible civilian rail or road traffic. All pilots were also advised to saddle up in their Mustangs a little early to familiarize themselves with cockpit procedures and give their eyes time to adjust to flying.

June 6

F.O.371-"FULLHOUSE". Lieutenant Colonel Dix led the 354th and 357FS to the Alencon area southwest of Paris from 0251 to 0821 for an area patrol. The weather was lousy but, except for a fair amount of flak, the mission was uneventful. The entire mission was flown under Type 16 control.

F.O.371-Part B. Lieutenant McGinty led the 355th B Group (358FS) on a Type 16 control area patrol after Meyers aborted with engine trouble. The 358th had a good day strafing trucks, trains and barges around Alencon and near Dreaux.

Donovan, Covault, McNally and Humphrey shared in the destruction of two locomotives, four barges and two tugs while McNally and Pardee shot up two locomotives and two trains at the Bleury railroad station. All returned safely although several had flak damage. Everybody was up by 0601 and back by 1030.

F.O.371-"STUD". Colonel Cummings led the 357FS on its second mission of the day on a fighter bombing Mission. Each Mustang was loaded with 250 pound H.E. bombs to attack some targets near Dreaux that the 358th squadron had spotted earlier. Off at 1106, and directed to an area southwest of Paris, the 357th Squadron pounded bridges, armored vehicles, trucks and horse drawn goods wagons heading toward the beaches. Lieutenant Phillips of the 357FS was hit hard by flak near La Mailleraye and was killed when he struck the stabilizer after bailing out. All other P-51s were back by 1405.

Claims: None   Losses: 1

F.O.371-Part B. Lieutenant Colonel Kinnard led the 354FS on another fighter bomber sweep to the Le Mans area from 1315 to 1420. In the briefing, Kinnard remarked that they may want to look some targets over before bombing to "Make sure we do some good." The 354th caught a load of rail cars and ammo trucks near Le Mans and bombed, then strafed with spectacular results. Several ships came back with pieces of exploded trucks, rail cars and armored cars stuck in various locations on the bottoms of their birds.

F.O.371-Part C. Lieutenant Colonel Myers led the 358FS on a combined fighter bomber/escort mission near Mamers from 1320 to 1650 hours. The squadron patrolled the Mamers area from 1430 to 1543 at altitudes ranging from 15,000 feet to the deck. The 250 pound bombs were dropped on targets of opportunity and the Mustangs strafed their way back to the beach perimeter.

F.O.372-"ROYAL FLUSH". Lieutenant Colonel Dix led the 354th Squadron on an area patrol in the Chateaudun area. The squadron was vectored by Colgate over toward the Channel after shooting up three trains near Chartres, and then joined the 357FS to jump 20 Stukas near the deck at 2105.

Dix got one in the air and shared one on the ground after the JU-87s tried to save themselves by landing in nearby fields. Fortier and Perry each got one while Silky Morris shared one with Floyd Taylor, one of the new pilots. Captain Bert Marshall got his first air victory in this short scrap, on his second day of combat. Several probables and damaged were also claimed.

All pilots returned by 2020.

Claims: 7 Destroyed   Losses: None

F.O.372-Part B. Captain Wilson led the 357FS on an area patrol in the same general area as the 354FS from 1810 to 2230. The squadron shot up several columns of German road traffic around 2030 and spotted the 15 JU-87s near Janville heading toward the beaches at 2058. Captain Kelley shot down two, while James, Bernoske, Fuller and Cotter got one apiece. Minchew Fuller, James and Wilson each damaged one before they broke into the low clouds and escaped. James also claimed two more probables. On the way home, Lieutenant Douglas was hit by flak near Calais and bailed out to become POW.

Claims: 8 Destroyed   Losses: 1

After the two squadrons had come home with claims of 15 of the total day's bag of 26 for the Eighth AF, they were reminded that things didn't always go their way when they received news of the 4th's bad luck. The 4th FG had been jumped from above while strafing and lost seven pilots including two aces. Six were killed and one evaded.

June 7

F.O. 373 and 375. Myers led the 358FS, Kinnard the 354FS and Colson the 357FS on three separate efforts during the morning and early afternoon. Myers took the 358th to Evreaux from 0505 to 0800 and strafed German road traffic and positions in the area. Intense and accurate flak was encountered at the marshalling yards at Evreaux but all Mustangs returned safely.

Lieutenant Colonel Kinnard took the 354FS up for an area patrtol near Evreaux. The squadron strafed trains near Evreaux and La Chappelle Vendemotse and slipped over to Nogent le Routrou to beat up tanks and trucks northwest of the city. Flak was moderate to heavy. Bob Couture was hit and bailed out but evaded capture to return later.

Captain Colson took the 357FS on a fighter bomber sweep to the Chateaudun-Mantes Gasscort-Bonniere area from 0653 to 0940. The 357th bombed and strafed a convoy near Chateaudun and Foster was killed by the concussion of his own bombs exploding an ammo train. Harrell was shot down by flak but bellied in near Chateaudun and escaped the Germans. West of Aquigny, 15 FW-190s bounced Yellow flight on the deck and shot down MacFarlane, Guerrant and Hollman. Only MacFarlane survived to become POW. The 357th had its worst day of the war with five down in one day.

Claims: None   Losses: 6 (2 pilots evaded)

F.O.376-Part 1. Lieutenant McGinty led the 358FS on its second mission, an area support in the Paris area, from 1030 to 1600 hours. After patrolling at 15,000 feet from 1145 to 1345, the 358th dropped down to strafe the Vendome marshalling yards. One train, several locomotives and three tanks were destroyed or heavily damaged before the squadron returned home.

Earlier in the day, Lieutenants Blaylock and Winn escorted two photo reconnaisance Mosquitos over Normandy from 0706 to 1215.

F.O.376-Part 2. Captain Kelley led the 357FS on an area patrol from 1721 to 2140. The patrol east of the Fe Camp area was uneventful, although one B-17 was seen to go down near Rennes at 1930.

F.O.376-Part 3. Colonel Cummings took the 354FS up to 20,000 feet to protect B-17s and B-24s attacking Angers and Tours. The Patrol was up at 1722 and back down at 2135.

June 8

F.O.377. Lieutenant Colonel Dix led the group on an area support effort in the Bordeaux - Poitierre area from 1432 to 1920 hours. Shortly after strafing a train south of Niort, Dix lost coolant and bellied his Mustang in to become POW.

Lieutenant Donovan was hit by flak near Libourne and bailed out. He evaded capture and returned later in the month. McGinty and Brien dropped down on a small airfield and destroyed an He177 in the pattern. Flight Officer Williams was hit hard by flak in the same area and struggled back to Eyeworth only to die in the crash landing.

Claims: 1 Destroyed   Losses: 3 (1 pilot evaded)

With the loss of Gerald Dix, combined with Everett Stewart being home on leave, several command vacancies opened up and a variety of changes in the 355th occurred over the next several days. Kinnard moved to acting Group Executive Officer, Kucheman took over command of the 354th Squadron and the newly arrived Marshall became Squadron Ops Officer for the 354th.

Speed Hubbard returned to England after evading through the occupied countries to Spain. Because Hubbard evaded via the underground pipeline, he was permanently removed from combat duty and sent back to the States in July.

June 10

F.O.379-Part 1. Captain Kelley led the 357FS on an area patrol near Nantes and Chartres from 0445 to 1015. The patrol was completely uneventful except for a couple of early returns.

F.O.379-Part 2. Lieutenant Colonel Kinnard led the 354th and the 358FS on a fighter sweep and area patrol. The group had no particular bomber escort assignment and swept along the Fe Camp to Nantes area from 0640 to 0835 hours.

Neither fighters nor flak was encountered and all group fighters returned by 1035. The uneventful missions were serving the valuable purpose of indoctrinating the new replacement pilots of the last 30 days in the local geography and formation flying that the old hands took for granted.

F.O.380. Major Kucheman led the group on an area patrol in the Chartres area from 1202 to 1604 hours. The 355th swept along the Fe Camp-Chartres-Cayeux line and the 357FS strafed 15 to 20 rail cars near Bolbec. The patrol was otherwise uneventful and all returned safely.

F.O.381. Lieutenant Colonel Myers led an area support to the Loudec area from 1804 to 2135. The 354FS encountered 10/10 coverage near Mortain so they dropped their 250 pound eggs on a rail line and went home. The 357FS obtained excellent results in their glide bombing effort and the 358FS also had good results. Many vehicles, rail cars and armored vehicles were strafed from Loudec to Lande. No losses.

June 11

F.O.382-Part 1. Lieutenant Colonel Kinnard led the 354FS on a fighter bombing sweep to the Chateaureaux area from 0620 to 1040. The squadron let down through an overcast and shot up gas tank batteries, trucks, transformer stations and trains before returning home with no losses.

F.O.382-Part 2. Captain Colson led the 357th and 358FS on a bombing mission to the Nogent le Roton marshalling yards from 0716 to 1040. Several rail cars, trucks and warehouses were hit by 250 pound bombs and all pilots returned by 1040.

F.O.382-Part 3. Colonel Cummings led a dive bombing mission to the Redon area from 1159 to 1600 hours. Road, rail and water targets were bombed and strafed by the group from Redon to Nantes and Plelan. Several trains, bridges, tunnels and many trucks were hit and Kucheman also skip bombed a small tanker with 100 pound bombs with no visible effect. No losses or major damage to the group.

June 12

F.O.383. The three squadrons flew an area support in the Cambrai area from 0636 to 1118 under Type 16 control. Major Kucheman led the 354FS on a patrol near Lille and Cambrai while Minchew and the 357FS patrolled near St. Omer. Lieutenant Colonel Myers took the 358FS along the Cambrai - Brussels - St. Quentin line before returning home. No enemy aircraft were spotted.

F.O.383-Part 2. Lieutenant Colonel Kinnard led the 354FS on a ramrod to Mantes Gassicourt. Kinnard flew his brand new P-51D "Man O'War" on an escort for B-26s from 1845 to 2115 hours. Before the mission, Kinnard briefed the 355th on the prudence of watching out for a "Red Hot" Me-109 Gruppe which had nailed the 353rd Group in the same area the day before for eight 353rd ships, losing only three of their own. No German fighters were encountered however, and all ships returned safely.

F.O.384. Major Rosenblatt led a ramrod to the same Mantes Gassicourt target from 1837 to 2130. The 357th and 358FS escorted the B-26s from St. Valery to the target and back. Only light flak was encountered and all fighters returned safely.

June 13.

F.O.386. The 355th provided escort to three separate heavy bomber boxes attacking targets at Beauvais - Nivilliers, Illiers and Amiens airdromes from 0651 to 1010. Eight unidentified S/E ships were seen climbing in the Rouen -Beauvais area by the 357FS, but they managed to climb into cloud cover and slip away. Due to bad weather, the entire group landed at Manston and other coastal bases before returning by 1340.

Generals Marshall, Arnold, Doolittle and Auton visited the 355th in the early afternoon, inspected the base, watched some combat film and attended a mission briefing before leaving in the early evening.

F.O.387. Major Kucheman led a ramrod to the Beauvais-Tille area from 1839 to 2220 hours. The 355th was vectored by Colgate several times to suspected enemy fighters but none were encountered. After sweeping Brussels to Ghent to Flushing, the group came out over Walcheren Island at 2125.

June 14

F.O.388. Lieutenant Colonel Myers led an area patrol to the Paris area from 0637 to 1034. The group broke escort at 0920 and the 357FS dropped to the deck to shoot up trains and trucks near Paris and Laon. Fifteen unidentified aircraft were spotted over Paris but broke away when the 354FS turned into them. Flak was heavy around Paris but all returned safely.

June 15

F.O.390. Lieutenant Colonel Kinnard led a ramrod to Bordeaux from 0540 to 1105. Because of the length of the mission, all the 108 gallon drop tanks were topped off. Kinnard emphasized the need for all the pilots to maintain strict R/T discipline, pointing out the problems encountred in May when several excellent opportunities to really punish Jerry had been lost because of too much chatter, too little information. He also announced that the new 150 octane fuel would soon be available with claims for significant boosts to climb and speed performance.

Landfall was made near Fe Camp and the bombers were picked up at 0708 hours over Loudon. Bombing results were reported as excellent but no enemy aircraft were seen. Landfall out was over Brest and everybody came home safely. Brown and Duffy followed such old hands as Bille, Woody, Elder, Lenfest, Hovde, Gresham, Williamson and Stewart home for a well deserved 30 days leave.

In the last 30 days the 355th lost nearly all their top pilots and aces to leave or transfers. Only Minchew, Kinnard, Fortier and McElroy and a few others remained to help provide leadership to the new group pilots.

June 16

F.O.393. Major Rosenblatt led a ramrod under Type 16 control to Beauvais-Tille area from 1444 to 1733. Rendezvous was made at 1550 hours near Evreaux and broken off at 1653 near mid-Channel. One flight of the 357FS dropped down to strafe a couple of trains near Rosieres. No German aircraft were spotted and flak was light.

June 17

F.O.394. Colonel Cummings led a ramrod to the Beauvais-Tille area from 1015 to 1440. The 355th escorted the B-26s from 1109 near Evreaux till 1412 near Thorny Island. Heavy cloud cover obscured the target and the bombing results were not seen. Boring trip.

F.O.395. Lieutenant Colonel Myers led a ramrod from 1931 to 2320. The three squadrons escorted different bomber boxes to and from three separate targets.

The 354FS covered withdrawal from Alencon and several different boxes were picked up and shepherded along the Alencon -Dieppe line before breaking escort at 2245 and returning home.

The 357FS made rendezvous near Le Mans at 2040, brought their bombers back to the Channel and returned to pick up one more box.

The 358FS escorted the bombers to Tours and back to Trouville when escort was broken off at 2215.

June 18

F.O.396. Lieutenant Colonel Kinnard led a ramrod to Hanover from 0641 to 1110. This marked a trend "back to normal" for the 355th which had conducted area supports, patrols and fighter bombing sweeps over France since the beginning of June.

Landfall was made over Cuxhaven where the 354FS split to cover some unescorted bombers while the 357th and 358FS made rendezvous with their assigned heavies near Wessermunde and Bremen. Flak was heavy and accurate over the target and nine FW-190s were spotted near the Channel but too far away to attack. Another relative milk run.

June 19

F.O.399. Major Kucheman led another ramrod to Bordeaux from 0649 to 1149. The 354th and 358FS made rendevous with the bombers near Villers and escorted them to the target. The 357FS picked up their boxes at 0725 over southern England and escorted them to the Merignac airdrome. Flak was heavy and accurate over Bordeaux. Lieutenants Coleman and Reeves were last seen in a spin over the target but the exact cause, flak or weather, was unknown. The weather was miserable all the way back to Brest but everybody except Coleman and Reeves made it back safely.

Claims: None   Losses: 2

June 20

F.O.402. Major Kucheman led a ramrod to support bombers striking at oil refineries in Ostermoor and Politz. Up at 0621, the 355th flew across Hamburg toward the rendevous point over the Rugen Islands. The bombers were five minutes early so Kucheman cut across to Darsser and made rendevous at 0900.

After making one orbit around the B-24s, Perry spotted 30 - 40 Me-410s queing up on the bombers from four o'clock. Three B-24s blew up and two stragglers dropped out of formation by the time the 354th Squadron waded in. Ten or more Me-109s and a couple of FW-190s also joined the scrap.

The 354th engaged and Kucheman, Graham and Taylor each shot down an Me-410 while Huish and Williams shared another one. Several more 410s were heavily damaged before the Me-109s and FW-190s arrived to spoil the fun. In a short time, Martin got two 109s, Hoffman got another and Wright got a pair. Marshall shot one off Graham's tail, destroyed another Me-109 which was shooting at Wright and then added the finishing touch to Wright's second 109. All the rest of the Jerries dove away to cloud cover near the deck to fight another day.

At the same approximate time, another 75 plus 410s and 109s made a single pass from the North near Pommersche Bucht and the 357FS intercepted. The German fighters didn't stay but Lieutenants Fuller and Buckles each got an Me 410 while Captain Minchew hammered an escorting Me-109. Several Mustangs, low on gas and ammo, turned for home while the rest of the 355th continued the mission. Escort was broken off at 0950 by the 354th and 357th while the 358th stayed until 1100 when they broke escort over the Terschelling Islands.

All returned safely by 1145 and the 355th held a big party to celebrate being the third group in the 8th to pass the 300 destroyed mark. The tally from D-Day had pushed them over the top.

Claims: 13 Destroyed   Losses: None

F.O.405. The three squadrons went their separate ways on a rodeo from 1648 to 2000. The 354FS provided top cover while Lieutenants McNeff and Beckman led the 357th and 358FS on a strafing mission to the Paris-St. Quentin-Noyan area. The bag on the ground included a couple of trains, 32 barges and two trucks.

June 21

F.O.407. Kinnard led a ramrod to Ruhland from 0734 to 1420. The 355th covered one Task Force on a round trip while the 4thFG and one squadron of the 352FG took their B-17s all the way to Russia for the historic first Shuttle Mission.

Rendevous was made near Wittenberg and Belziz and the target was bombed at 1035. The 357FS bounced some 109s near Brunswick and Bernoske, Salinsky and Chapman each got one. Captain Fred Haviland started his string with another Me-109 in the same scrap. The 354FS dropped down to strafe near Wittenberg to destroy or heavily damage five trains, four barges and two launches. The 358FS spotted some JU-88s but Kinnard told them to stick with the bombers and no bounce was made. Everyone came out over the Zuider Zee around 1345 hours at 24,000 feet.

Claims: 4 Destroyed   Losses: None

June 22

F.O.411. Lieutenant Colonel Kinnard led a glide bombing mission to the Rennes -Chauny - Fisme area from 1414 to 1732. The bridge at Fisme was obscured by weather so the 354FS first bombed an airfield under construction then strafed a parked troop train near Suippes. The 354th left after shooting up German troops, rail cars, locomotives and trucks. The 357FS bombed more rail traffic near Chauny and 30 to 40 rail cars were seen to blow up. Myles King lost his coolant shortly afterwards and bellied in near the target to become POW. The 358FS strafed and bombed trains near Rennes then shot up a camouflaged airfield near Plancoet. No enemy aircraft were seen.

Claims: None   Losses: 1

June 23

F.O.414.   Lieutenant Colonel Myers led an area support to the Paris-Reims area for his last mission. The group patrolled the area from 1928 to 2110 hours at 24,000 feet. Control reported German fighters but none were seen. Flak was light over the target and everybody was home by 2200.

June 24

F.O.415.   Lieutenant Colonel Kinnard led a patrol under Type 16 control from 0638 to 1200 hours. The 355th was vectored from Dreaux to Paris to Beauvais and Etampes but no German aircraft were spotted. The group strafed several trains and hit several trucks and armored cars on their way to Caen before Lieutenant Salinsky of the 357FS uncovered a well camouflaged fighter strip near Angers. Salinsky destroyed three, damaged two and Forker got two more. After carefully noting the location, they pulled away to report their find.

Claims: 5 Destroyed   Losses: None

W.F.O.105.   Lieutenant Colonel Kinnard took the 354th and 357FS back to Angers to finish up what Salinsky and Forker started. Up at 1708, the group arrived at the grass landing field, grid co-ordinate 2V09789, at 1830 hours.

After shooting up the flak guns on the first pass, the 355th set up a classic gunnery pattern and shot hell out of the parked 109s. Kinnard, Morris and Haviland each destroyed three while Ellison, Martin, Perry, Crandell and Spencer got two. Trembarth, Hulderman, Cross, Forker, McHugh and McNeff each destroyed one. Several more 109s were shot up by the group but no more fires were seen. The 355th departed the area at 1850 and returned by 2015. Big Party after the mission.

Claims: 25 Destroyed   Losses: None

June 25

F.O.417.   Major Kucheman led bleary-eyed pilots on a ramrod to support First Division Forts attacking targets near Toulouse from 0613 to 1210. Rendezvous was made near Tours at 0754 and escort was broken off over Cape Breton at 1013. Bombing appeared excellent and the mission was uneventful.

F.O. 418.   Captain Kelley led the 355th on an area support to the Auxerre area from 1734 to 2125. Landfall was made near Dieppe at 20,000 feet and the assigned area was patrolled from 1907 to 1930. The 355th swept along the bomber withdrawal route until crossing out over Dieppe at 2035. The 357th Group bounced the 354th squadron and closed in a head on pass before recognizing "friendlies" and breaking away. No harm, no foul.

June 27.

F.O. 420.   Major Rosenblatt led a fighter bomber sweep for targets of opportunity near Paris. After landfall near Dieppe at 1819, the 355th patrolled their assigned area under Type 16 control until 1915.

The group then dropped down to bomb and strafe some marshalling yards near Laon and Hirson. At the same approximate time, ground control vectored Austin's flight from the 354FS to escort some stragglers near Pas de Calais. The flight split up near a large cloud formation along the way and ran smack into what looked like 15 plus Spitfires with no invasion stripes. Austin's split flight was immediately bounced by the strangers near Chateau-Thiery and Ruark was heard requesting help over the R/T. A silver Mustang was seen spinning down below the clouds, but Ruark bailed out and evaded capture. The rest of the flight slipped into the clouds and got away. Landfall out was over Calais at 2030 hours.

Claims: None   Losses: 1 (pilot evaded)

June 28

F.O.421.   Major Kucheman led an area support under Type 16 control from 0531 to 0940 over the Chartres area. On the way to Chartres, 12 unidentified, single engines bogies were spotted flying unmolested by flak over Paris. The 354FS gave chase but could not close and returned to the group. Following the fruitless chase, the 355th patrolled the Chartres - Paris area from 0735 to 0835 and crossed out north of Boulogne at 0845 and 18,000 feet.

June 29

F.O.422. Lieutenant Colonel Kinnard led a ramrod to Leipzig from 0645 to 1230 hours. Rendezvous was made as the First Task Force bombers came off the target at 0910 and 26,000 feet. The bombers were escorted along the withdrawal route past Dummer Lake and escort was broken off at 1045 near Lingen. Except for intense and accurate flak over the Leipzig targets the mission was boring.

Hubbard visited Steeple Morden for the first time since he went down on the 13th of November, 1943. While two other pilots reported seeing German fighters near the area, Speed indicated that flak damage was the cause of his engine breaking loose from it's mounts.

June 30

F.O.424. Major Kucheman led a combined ramrod/fighter bomber sweep from 1303 to 1616. Rendezvous was made at 1402 and the group escorted, with 100 pound bombs instead of drop tanks, until 1420 after the B-17s dropped on Montdidier.

The 355th then dropped down to attack water traffic near Lurches and St. Quentin plus marshalling yards near Valencennes. The results were generally fair to poor because of the minimal capabilities of the 100 pound bombs and delayed fuses. The group left the target area by 1530 and came out near Calais at 15,000 feet.

July 1

F.O.425. Lieutenant Colonel Kinnard led the group off at 1800 for a sweep to St. Quentin, Soissons and Senlis area but the mission was scrubbed shortly after take off due to extremely bad weather.

July 2

F.O.426. Major Kucheman led an area support to the St. Quentin-Cambrai-Peroune area. Three boxes of Second Division Liberators were picked up at 1337 near Poix and escorted to the coast. Landfall was made over Cayeaux. Milk Run.

July 4

F.O.430. Colonel Cummings led a ramrod to escort some B-17s attacking railroad bridges near Gien.

Rendezvous was scheduled for Trouville but a group of P-47s came roaring through the 355th west of Paris just before R/V. The group was scattered all over the area trying to avoid mid-airs. Various flights picked up separate boxes of bombers, escorted them to Gien and back out to a point north of Caen before breaking escort. Strictly routine except for the excitement with the Jugs.

July 5

F.O.431. Lieutenant Colonel Kinnard led a ramrod to support bombers attacking Beziers. The 355th was to relieve the 4thFG on the way home from the first Shuttle Mission.

Following take off at 1207, rendezvous with the bombers was made over the target at 1325 and escort was maintained until 1515 near Chattlelleraut. The 355th dropped down to strafe on the way back.

Victor Denti of the 354FS pulled out of formation just prior to the strafing attack on Chateauroux airdrome and crashed on the southern edge of the field. Nobody knew just what the problem was as no flak had been yet encountered. Schwab shot down a JU-88 off Schutt's tail while Kinnard and Hulderman shared one on the ground.

Claims: 2 Destroyed   Losses: 1

July 6

F.O.432. Colonel Cummings led a ramrod to Kiel to support Second Division B-24s. Rendezvous was made at 0905 over Heligoland at 24,000 feet. The 357FS provided close escort while the 358th and 354FS swept to Muritz Lake at 33,000 feet. Nothing of interest was spotted so the two squadrons picked up stragglers and escorted them back to the coast. Landfall out was over Egmont at 15,000 feet.

Lieutenant Norm Dixon of the 357FS was hit by flak at approximately 1020 hours over Schwerin. He went over the side to become POW.

Claims: None   Losses: 1

F.O.435. Major Kucheman led an uneventful ramrod to Gien from 1733 to 2150 hours. Rendezvous was made at 1907 near Argentan and escort was broken near Fe Camp at 2048.

An unidentified fighter group was observed strafing a dummy airfield near St. Andre.

A new flight (E flight) was formed with brand new P-51D-5's in the 354FS to support Bud Peaslee's First Scouting Force.

July 7

F.O.436. Lieutenant Colonel Kinnard led a ramrod to Leipzig and Halle to support B-24s attacking oil and aircraft assembly targets. Rendezvous was made at 0808 near Lingen and The force penetrated to the target. As the formation swung to the northeast, they encountered 100 plus single and twin engine fighters between Halle and Merseburg.

Kinnard bent his throttle to intercept and his lead flight of the 354FS surged way ahead of the rest of the group. The 358FS maintained close escort while the rest of the 354th and the 357FS broke into the Me-410s and Me-109s.

Kinnard quickly shot down two Me-410s and then shot down an Me-109 to become the 355th's seventh air ace. Lieutenant Huish collided with large debris from an exploding Me-410 to become the group's first loss of the day.

Captain Minchew led the 357th into the scrap and quickly shot down two 410s and shared a third with a 20thFG P-38 which cut in front of him. Minchew damaged two more while Haviland and Cross each shot down a pair. Fuller, Cotter and Perry each shot down an Me-410 while McNeff got an Me-109. Betounes and Bob Taylor shared a 109 before the rest escaped below.

Lieutenant Fuller chased another Me-109 on the deck near Naumburg and was hit by flak. He bailed out and his chute was seen to open but he did not turn up after the war.

Claiborne Kinnard received the group's third DSC for his leadership and courage in this day's action.

Claims: 14 Destroyed   Losses: 2

July 8

F.O.437. Major Kucheman led an area patrol to the Montmiral-Provins area from 0646 to 1010. Following a forty minute patrol of their assigned area, McHugh of the 357FS spotted a well camouflaged airdrome near Gaye and dropped down to strafe.

The 355th rotated squadrons for top cover and left the field at 0915 with claims of 20 destroyed and 19 damaged. Morris, Kucheman, Williams and McHugh led all scorers with two each. Most of the destroyed aircraft were Me-109s and Me-410s.

Lieutant Jim Lowder of the 358FS crashed into some trees at the edge of the field after a pass on the field and his Mustang was seen to blow up.

Claims: 20 Destroyed   Losses: 1

July 9

F.O.439. Captain Minchew led an area patrol to the Arras-Hazebrook-St. Omer - Amiens area. Flak over Lens and Calais was heavy but nobody was hurt and the group broke escort at 1355 hours. Everybody was down by 1447.

The 355th ground crews spent a busy afternoon and night removing Invasion stripes from the top sufaces of the wings and fuselage above the star insignia.

July 11

F.O.441. Major Kucheman, then Captain Fortier, led a ramrod to Munich from 0936 to 1515. At 1150 the 355thFG made rendezvous with the lead boxes of B-17s just south of Ludwigshafen. Overcast made observation of ground targets impossible and heavy flak was encountered over Munich from the Initial Point all the way in. At 1323 escort was broken and landfall out was made over Calais at 1439.

Floyd Trembarth encountered severe weather near London while returning from a radio relay and spun out. He bailed out OK and his bird went into an empty field north of London.

July 12

F.O.442B. Lieutenant Colonel Kinnard led another ramrod to the Munich area from 1023 to 1620. Rendezvous was made near Mannheim at 1230 with First Division B-17s. The 355th furnished penetration, target and withdrawal support before escort was broken at 1510 near Valenciennes. The target was obscured, so the bombing results were not observed. No action other than heavy flak.

July 13

F.O. 444. Colonel Cummings led a ramrod to the Bordeaux area from 0606 to 1222 and rendezvous with First Division B-17s was made near Strasbourg at 0832.

Just after the bombers were left at 1055, they called the 355th on C-channel to report 15 to 20 Me-109s making head on attacks. Kinnard took the 354th and 357FS back to the Augsburg area to help out. Hendrickson and McHugh jumped four 109s around 1108 hours for claims of 1-1-1 before the rest dove away. One B-17 was seen leaving the formation with two engines feathered before the 355th could break up the attack.

Claims: 1 Destroyed   Losses: None

July 14

F.O. 446. Major Kucheman led a boring ramrod to Vendome from 1648 to 1235 hours. Escort was continued to Evreux and broken at 1055.

July 16

F.O. 450. Captain Fortier led the 355th back to Munich for the third time in less than a week. Following takeoff at 0735 the group made contact with the Third Division Forts over Louviers at 0909. The target was bombed at 0949 and escort was broken off near Ghent near 1100. No fighters were spotted although heavy flak was encountered near Munich and Brussels.

Although the mission was uneventful, the radio relay team of Priest and Wright was bounced by Me-109s disguised with invasion stripes. The relay Mustangs evaded the bounce and returned home. Additionally, Sumner Williams' P-51 was hit by a B-24 gunner and limped home on one bank of cylinders.

July 17

F.O. 451. Captain Hovde led an area support to B-17s and B-24s attacking targets near Etempes. The group was up at 0902, rendezvous was made near Chartres and escort was completed at 1215 over Dieppe. No enemy fighters were seen and everybody came home by 1310.

F.O. 453. Captain Hovde led the second mission of the day on an area support along the Boulogne - Rouen line. The 355th patrolled their assigned sector from 1950 to 2120 and made landfall over Dieppe at 2130. All Mustangs were down at Steeple Morden by 2210.

July 18

F.O. 454. Major Kucheman led a ramrod from 0636 to 1400 to support a bomber task force attacking Peenemunde. The bombers were picked up short of the target at 0947 at 25,000 feet, escorted to the target and back to the Channel at 1045. Bombing results appeared excellent and no enemy fighters were encountered although the group watched from above as the 352nd ripped up a large German force near the target. The 352ndFG scored 21-0-11 for the loss of two.

Fred Johnson's engine quit over the Ditch and he bailed out to become the group's first Air/Sea Rescue customer.

Claims: None   Losses: 1 (pilot rescued)

July 19

F.O. 456. Lieutenant Colonel Kinnard led a ramrod to the Munich area again. Up at 0644, the 355th met the bombers at 0825 east of Namur.

Just short of the target, the 355th was bounced by 15 plus Me-109s and FW-190s out of the sun when the group went after some decoy Ju-88s. The 357th and 354FS pursued the first gaggle, but only John Folger closed to shoot down an FW-190.

While the two squadrons were pursuing the first gaggle, another batch of German fighters sailed into the unprotected area and two B-17s were shot down before Captain Hovde could get the 358 FS in position to intercept. The Germans had pulled a successful "bait and switch" tactic and it payed off.

Hovde, Covault and Thompson each claimed an Me-109, while McElroy shot down an FW-190. Hovde's victory made him the group's eighth ace.

Flight Officer Duppstadt, joined a flight of red and white checkered nose 339th Mustangs on the way home and strafed an unidentified airfield with his new friends to get two more.

Lieutenant Schwab of the 354FS had a runaway prop on the way into the target just before the bounce, and bailed out to become a

POW. Everyone else came home by 1245 after breaking escort near Antwerp.

Claims: 7 Destroyed   Losses: 1

July 20

F.O.457.   Lieutenant Colonel Kinnard led the fighters back to the Munich area for another pass on the cloud covered targets. Up at 0805, the group made rendezvous at 0950 near Cologne and escorted the B-17s over the target at 1130.

A gaggle of 50 plus Me-109s and FW-190s was bounced by the 354th and 358FS. Captain Fortier of the 354FS shot down an Me-109 near Chemnitz to become the group's ninth ace. Lieutant Peters shot down two FW-190s, shot down a DO-217 near an airfield close to Leipzig, and then strafed the airfield to destroy a JU-88 and an He-111. Peters later received a DSC for this day's work and Peterson also shot down an Me-109 plus damaged another one over Chemnitz.

While the 355th blunted the attack and destroyed five for no losses, the large gaggle closed with the bombers and shot down eight B-17s for the heaviest confirmed loss to 355th escorted bombers during the war.

Lieutenant Costello of the 357FS got separated after a long chase on the deck, and was hit by flak on the way back. He bailed out, evaded, and returned to Steeple Morden later. Strachan's engine quit over the Channel and he bailed out to be the second Air/Sea customer in three days.

Claims: 7 Destroyed   Losses: 2 (pilots rescued, evaded)

July 21

F.O.458.   Captain Fortier led a ramrod back to Munich from 0722 to 1317. Overcast covered the Continent all the way to the target but the rendezvous point was believed to be near Saarbruecken at 0915.

Lieutenants Thompson and Humphrey spotted several Me-109s near the target and bounced them. Thompson shot down one but broke off the engagement when he realized that the rest of the 358FS failed to hear his R/T call or follow his bounce. The group broke escort shortly before landfall over Schouwen.

Claims: 1 Destroyed   Losses: None

July 24

F.O.461.   Captain Hovde led the 355th to strafe Lechfeld and Landsberg airdromes near Augsburg. The group was to join the 4th and go after the new German jets but the 4th didn't make R/V.

After landfall near Ostend at 1012, the Mustangs penetrated to the target area and started shooting at 1200. The fighters made one pass, flew about 10 miles, reformed and turned back to make another pass. Hovde's wingman, Walburn, was hit by flak on the second pass but crash landed and managed to evade.

Sawchuck of the 354th was killed when he was hit while climbing out away from Lechfeld. Fortier, Hoffman, Patterson, Cotter and Guilleland returned with claims of five jets. In all the group returned with claims of 12-0-11

Claims: 12 Destroyed   Losses: 2 (1 pilot evaded)

July 25

F.O.464.   Major Kucheman started a patrol to the Brussels area but the mission was scrubbed while climbing through heavy weather.

July 27

Lieutenant Garth Spitler rejoined the the 354FS as a replacement pilot. Spitler was unique because he served with the squadron before as a crew chief while the group was in Florida. He was accepted into flight training before the 355th moved to England.

July 28

F.O.469.   Captain Marshall led a ramrod to the Merseburg area. Rendezvous was made at 0922 near Kassel and the B24s were escorted to the target.

A gaggle of Me-109s and FW-190s, flying an American style formation, engaged the 355th at 1000 hours. The German force split into two groups with one group attacking and diving away to try to sucker the escorts into following, while the second force pressed the attack on the bombers.

75. Kucheman and crew discussing "their" triple in the big battle of April 24. Hank brought his total to four aerial victories with a single in June. (Kucheman, Barnhouse)

76. For a brief period the group used a black nose and cowl band in addition to ETO stripes on wing and tail. This ship is Lenfest's WR-F in May 1944. (Lenfest)

77. Hank Kucheman lounging on WR-U, "Lil Jo" in April 1944. (Kucheman, Barnhouse)

78. Steeple Morden tower—not constructed to Debden standards. (Bennett)

79. Olson's first P-51 was coded OS-X, "Ma Fran 4th." This photo was taken shortly after Olson went down in another Mustang. Szaniawski's OS-A is seen in the background. (Kidwell)

80. Henry Brown's WR-Z, serial 42-106448, in mid-May just before he went home for a short rest. (Brown, Williams)

81. Boulet's WR-E after a belly landing in April, 1944. Boulet was accidentally shot down by B-17s on April 26, becoming a POW. (Hart)
82. Chuck Lenfest with the new WR-F, "Lorie III," soon after Boulet was shot down in "Lorie II" by B-17s. (Lenfest, Caldwell)
83. Lieutenant Colonel Myers "explaining" number five to his crew in May 1944. (Myers)
84. Major Fred Ramsdell during his assignment as 357th CO in 1944. The Mustang is OS-T, "Eager Eve." (Ramsdell and Bille)
85. The 358th FS ready room can be seen behind the YF Mustangs in mid-1944. (Hovde)
86. Henry Brown and Jimmy Doolittle chatting about Brown's DSC mission of April 11. (Brown)

87. Henry Brown's "Hun Hunter from Texas" in pre-D-Day history. Invasion stripes came later, as per no. 91. C on rudder indicates C Flight. (Marshall)
88. Captain Bert Marshall and "Jane" shortly after D-Day. This P-51B was the first of six by that name lost or damaged by German flak. (Marshall)
89. Haviland and Torrey working over OS-H, "Barbara." Haviland joined the group around D-Day. (Gertzen)
90. New 354th FS ops officer, Bert Marshall, after shooting down one on D-Day. (Haviland)
91. Marshall flew Brown's WR-Z during his first week of combat. (Braun)
92. Lieutenant Royce "Deacon" Priest was the first pilot to rescue a fellow flier from behind enemy lines in the ETO. The author remains grateful for the rescue of his father. (Silva)

93. Lee Mendenhall in WR-P. (Marshall)

94. Generals Auton, Marshall and Colonel Bill Cummings during the June 13, 1944 visit to Steeple Morden. "Man O' War" in background. (Stewart, Kinnard)

95. Kucheman's last P-51B, just after taking over the 354th FS from Kinnard in early June. (Barnhouse)

355th FIGHTER GROUP ASSN.

1942 - ORLANDO, PHILADELPHIA, STEEPLE MORDEN, GABLINGEN - 1945

WR 354 ★ OS 357 ★ YF 358

August 26, 1985

FOUNDING
SECRETARY-TREASURER
HISTORIAN-EDITOR:
Gordon H. Hunsberger (Dec'd)

PRESIDENT:
*Brady C. Williamson
13 MacAfee Road
Somerset, NJ 08873
201-846-2607*

1st VICE-PRESIDENT:
*Elmer L. McElwain
Box 214
Big Run, PA 15715
814-427-2310*

2nd VICE-PRESIDENT:
*James E. Brown
227 W. 406 North
Valparaiso, IN 46383
219-462-3633*

SECRETARY-TREASURER:
*Robert E. Kuhnert
4230 Shroyer Road
Dayton, OH 45429
513-294-2986*

BOARD OF DIRECTORS:
*James E. Brown
John A. Chalot
Ward H. Douglass
Robert E. Kuhnert
Elmer L. McElwain
James P. Murphy
Joseph G. Myers, Jr.
Ralph W. Purvis
Fred L. Roberts
C. Kenneth Robinson
Charles J. Rosenblatt
Philip O. Tilghman
Mark Waldo
Douglas B. Warden
Brady C. Williamson*

LEGAL:
*Robert C. Grasberger
Philip O. Tilghman*

SWEETHEART:
June Allyson

STEEPLE MORDEN
MEMORIAL:
*Henry D. Wertz
Harrison T. Price
A.W. Channing
David C. Crow
Ken Jarman
Malcolm D. Freestone*

STEEPLE MORDEN
ENGLAND:
*David C. Crow
Rutland House
21 Hay Street
Steeple Morden
Royston, Herts
SG8 CPO*

Dear Tony:

Good to get your letter today, so I'll spring into action before I permit your letter to slide into the basket and have other letters land on top of it.

I'll send a copy of the book and if the cost is more than you bargained for I'll cover it. I realize I'm acting without telling you the cost, but I think you will enjoy having it. You'll recognize many faces, I'm sure. Bill did a nice job on it, but there are a few mistakes.

The big boo boo is listing the Memorial Dedication as 1980, when it was 1981. Then, too, Marzo's name is misspelled Marza a couple times in the book. (He's the guy who was badly injured when the B-17 blew up, you will recall).

We were advised by Champlin Press that the retail is $14.95, which is what we will get over the counter at the reunion, but by mail we're asking a donation of $16.00 to cover prep and postage. (This puts us a few cents under the retail, but since we got the dealers' discount, we will still make a couple bucks for the outfit).

What is still needed is a text listing every soul who was assigned to the 355th, more complete lists of airplanes, pilots, ground crews. Maybe that can come to pass one day. I would like to work on something like that but haven't had the time to touch it. I have a tiger by the tail in the Sec/Treas job and it keeps me hopping every day. I hope to catch up with all back correspondence this year and then get more involved with our Communications gang again. I feel bad that I've let slip my correspondence with all of you, but believe me I think of you all so often and wish so much we could all get together before more of us pass away.

Glad you're enjoying your <u>great</u> grandchildren. You've got us beat. We have two grand, a girl nearly 6 and a boy 3½. They just returned to the USA after 3 years in Dusseldorf, Germany. They will be in South Bend, IN, which is just about 5 hours away. Bettye and I want to make a run through the Canadian northwest and go through your state, maybe next spring. If so we'll give you a holler.

Don't mention getting old, we're just getting better, right? All the best to you both. We'll miss you in Memphis.

Cheers,

Bob Kuhnert

96. Tabacchi, Berg and Durham surveying Morris' flakked-up Mustang just after D-Day. (Barnhouse)
97. Bad news for the Wehrmacht is carried by this 355th Mustang, loaded with parafrags. (Hart)
98. Duffy's WR-Y at Steeple Morden after a disagreement with German flak gunners. (Mendenhall)
99. Clarence Graham, Gil Wright and Bert Marshall discussing a good day, June 20, when the trio shot down four Me-109s. Marshall's double was scored when he shot a pair off Graham and Wright's tail. (Marshall)
100. Robert O. Peters destroyed three in the air plus two on the ground, July 20, 1944. Shortly after receiving the DSC, Peters fell to another Mustang over Warsaw. (Hovde)

101. Kinnard's birds usually had "different" camouflage schemes from May to November 1944. This P-51D-5 was Kinnard's until he took over the Fourth Group in the fall of 1944. (Marshall)
102. Group air exec Clay Kinnard in July, 1944. An acknowledged innovator of tactics and superb combat leader, he briefly commanded the 4th FG before taking over the 355th. (Kinnard)
103. High-schoring 357th FS ace, Captain Fred Haviland, approximately August 1944. (Haviland, Bille)
104. Mendenhall's last WR-X, "Texas Terror IV," in the summer of 1944. (Marshall)
105. Dick Cross' WR-L, "Dottie," after a July engine failure on takeoff. (Mendenhall)
106. Crew chief Seidl, pilot Cullerton and armorer Woodnail with "their" OX-X. (Seidel, Cullerton)
107. Lieutenant Dillon's YF-N, "Rugged Rebel II," shortly after tearing up an Me-109 while flying relay on August 1, 1944. (Hart)

108. Gilleland's OS-Q, "Georgia Peach," being prepared for a morning run in July or August, 1944. (Badavas)
109. WR-M after a change in management from Morris to Clarence Graham. (Graham)
110. Marshall's WR-B "Jane II" in August 1944. (Marshall)
111. Pilots of the 354th Squadron in late August 1944.

112. Bill Martin, Moss and Bunt on WR-J, "Martin's Gloria." Martin was killed in a thunderstorm after rotating back to the States in September 1944. (Graham)

113. John Gilmore looks over a close call by flak on August 15. His luck ran out for good while strafing in the Metz area two weeks later on the 355th's worst day of the war. Eight Mustangs and three pilots were lost on August 28. (Hovde)

114-119. Me-109s in various stages of distress as viewed from 355th gun cameras. (Marshall, Kinnard, Hart, Galer, Dumas)

120-123. Several shots of 355th Mustangs performing what they did better than any group in the ETO. (Galer, Marshall, Kinnard, Hart, Dumas)

124. Silky Morris and crew just before he finished his ops in July 1944. The Mustang is WR-M. (Haviland)

125. Priest rescues Marshall on August 18, 1944 after the latter was shot down by flak. (Hess, Pritchard)

126. Royce Priest helping Bert Marshall out of the rescue ship, WR-E, named "Eaglebeak." Priest inherited WR-E from Taylor and later renamed it "Weepin' Deacon." (Hess)

127. Woolard and Woods describing top cover during Priest's rescue. Woolard was later captured and was killed during an escape attempt with Lenfest. (Marshall)

128. Crew chief Mort Braun standing on the last "Hunter from Texas." (Braun)

129. Henry Brown's WR-Z soon after his return from Stateside leave in late August. He destroyed at least 13 more German aircraft before being captured in October. (Brown, Lenfest, Shiller)

130. Lieutenant Colonel Stewart's WR-S in September 1944. In early to mid-October, all 354th FS ships had red cowl bands and rudders. (Mendenhall via Bennett)

131. Hovde's YF-I, "Ole III," just before its near-fatal crackup. (Hovde)

Marshall ignored the diving fighters and jumped the second force. Marshall shot down an Me-109 after a wild chase on the deck and Lieutenant McElroy shot down a pair to raise his total to 3 air, 6 ground. Marshall and Hauver destroyed an unlucky pair of trains before making the long climb back to escort duties.

The escort was discontinued at 1130 near Liege and the group returned to Steeple Morden by 1230.

Claims: 3 Destroyed   Losses: None

July 29

F.O.470.   Captain Minchew led a ramrod to Merseburg from 0728 to 1250 hours. The 355th made rendezvous at 0850 and escorted five boxes of B-17s to Dummer Lake. At 0930, Minchew led the 52 Mustangs away from the Forts and swept Dummer Lake to Merseburg. No enemy fighters were encountered and the 355th returned to escort duties west of Merseburg. Escort was broken at 1200 near Den Helder. Steeple Morden was socked in so everybody landed at Martlesham Heath, home of the 356thFG.

July 31

F.O.472.   Captain Hovde led a ramrod to Munich from 0944 to 1620. The 355th swept the Ostend-Munich-LeTouquet line and escorted stragglers on the way out. No enemy aircraft were seen and everyone returned by 1620.

Major Kucheman completed his tour of 82 missions and six victories and turned over the reins of the 354FS to Captain Marshall. Kucheman took over group ops while awaiting orders to go home. At this time, all three squadrons were led by Captains (Marshall, Minchew and Hovde) which was fairly unusual for the Eighth Air Force at this stage of the war. Majors Elder and Sluga were just returning from leave and would soon change the situation.

August 1

F.O.473.   Major Kucheman led an area patrol near Paris from 1328 to 1755. Although many bandits were reported southwest of Paris, no enemy fighters were encountered after sweeping the area. The group orbited the enemy airdrome that they had pounded on July 8, but the field was abandoned and they left the area at 1645 to start for home. On the way out, Lieutenant Debacker of the 357FS suffered an engine failure and bailed out over the Channel where he was picked up by Air-Sea Rescue.

Lieutenants McNally and Dillon were flying a bomber relay near Chateaudun when Dillon spotted three Me-109s, slipped in to 50 yards and clobbered one. The Jerry managed to bail out before his ship blew.

Claims: 1 Destroyed   Losses: 1 (pilot rescued)

August 2

F.O.475.   Major Elder led an area support for heavy bombers attacking tactical targets in northeastern France. The 355th patrolled the assigned area from 1845 to 2015, then joined two other groups to strafe rail and transportation targets near Paris and Amiens.

Lieutenant Orr of the 358FS was shot down and killed by flak between Forges and Londimierres at 2035. Lieutenant Gower of the 357FS was hit hard by flak while strafing barges near St. Poi but bailed out and evaded capture. Elder was also clobbered by flak near Albert but managed to struggle back to the Channel for a successful ditching. After floating around for 45 minutes, a French fishing boat picked Moon up and took him to Allied held France.

Claims: None   Losses: 3 (one pilot)

August 3

F.O.476.   Captain Hovde led a ramrod to Strasbourg on the German-French border from 1242 to 1745. Rendezvous was made south of Eindhoven and the bombers were escorted to the target.

Several Me-109s were seen climbing through an undercast and Captain Kurtz of the 354FS took his flight down to engage. As Kurtz made his bounce, several more 109s were seen climbing through the same area. Kurtz opened fire on the leader of one gaggle but was hit in the throttle linkage, lost all power control to his Mustang and coasted all the way down to Germany for a crash landing and severe head injury.

Marshall led the rest of the 354FS down on the bounce and lost Hoffman and Patterson to a mid-air collision. Patterson was killed but Hoffman bailed out, broke his leg on landing and evaded capture for several weeks before getting picked up by the Germans near the Alps. Marshall latched onto the tail of a real pro but couldn't pull enough deflection on the Me-109 so Lenfest swooped down from a different angle and blew him up. Flight Lieutenant Peglar, on loan from the RCAF, shot down an Me-109 and then an FW-190 to score a double kill.

About ten miles southeast of Mannheim, the 357FS was bounced by ten Me-109s and FW-190s. Captains Minchew and Haviland shot down one apiece. Minchew's victory over the Me-109 made him the tenth 355th air ace. Lieutenant Cotter shot down one Me-109 and chased another down to the deck before getting hit by flak and crashing into some trees. Cotter survived the high speed crash to become POW.

Lieutentant Floyd Taylor of the 354FS had an engine failure but made it to Switzerland and returned in September. All in all, the 355th did not have one of its better days with six victories for the loss of five and everyone remarked that the enemy pilots encountered were several cuts above the average.

Claims: 6 Destroyed   Losses: 5 (one pilot evaded)

August 4

F.O.478.   Lieutenant Colonel Kinnard led a ramrod to escort B-24s bombing targets in the Rostock, Schwerin and Wismer area. The group made rendezvous at 1320 near the Danish coast, escorted the B-24s over the target and back and broke escort over Borkum Island at 1520. The target was completely obscured by clouds and bombing results could not be observed.

August 5

F.O.483.   Captain Hovde led a ramrod to Fallersleben's aircraft factories from 1046 to 1540. The B-24s were picked up south of Heligoland at 1226 and escorted to the target. Bombing results appeared to be excellent and escort was broken off near Ijmuiden at 1450. Some Me-262s were seen south of the Zuider Zee but no contact was made.

August 6

F.O.487.   Captain Marshall led a ramrod to Berlin to escort B-17s attacking aircraft and tank engine factories. The bombers were picked up over Cuxhaven at 1055 and escorted to the target and back along the withdrawal route.

Between Hamburg and Bremen Green flight of the 354FS was bounced from six o'clock high by six to eight Me-109s. Flight Officer Folger evaded the bounce with a climbing right turn and called in OK shortly thereafter but was never seen again. Marshall picked up the leader and shot him down after a hard chase on the deck to become the group's eleventh ace.
The German pilot was probably Leutnant Auguste Mors from JG 5, a 60 victory ace of considerable skill. Captain Lenfest shot down the leader of the second element to become the group's twelfth ace and Lieutenant Martin shot down another Me-109 to raise his combined air and ground score to 7.

In a separate encounter, Captain Bill Preddy of the 352FG shot down six to tie the current ETO record.

Claims: 3 Destroyed   Losses: 1

August 7

F.O.490.   Captain Hovde led an area support to B-24s attacking oil dumps north of Paris from 1014 to 1405. Heavy thunderstorms in the vicinity of Charleroi prevented progress along the planned route so the controller vectored the group to the Charleroi - Amiens area.

West of Amiens the 357th and 358FS dropped down to shoot up several trains and flak towers. Several more locomotives were strafed near Foullens before the guys broke off and came home.

August 8

F.O.494.   Lieutenant Colonel Kinnard led a fighter bomber sweep in the Paris area from 1205 to 1535. All three squadrons had a field day destroying trains, armored vehicles, trucks, flak towers, oil tank batteries, barges and destroyed or heavily damaged 10 locomotives. No enemy aircraft were seen, but the 357FS lost two Mustangs to flak. Bernoske was shot down near Vitry but bailed out and evaded capture while Lee was killed northwest of St. Dizier when his ship crashed and burned.

Claims: None   Losses: 2 (one pilot evaded)

August 9

F.O.496.   Captain Hovde led a ramrod to support bombers attacking Nurnberg. The bombers to be escorted by the 355th aborted so the group tacked on to the first box of unescorted bombers they spotted. Their new friends went to Karlsruhe and after providing penetration, target and withdrawal support, the 355th broke escort over Schouwen Island at 1152.

August 10

F.O.498.   Lieutenant Colonel Kinnard led a ramrod to support Second Division B-24s attacking bridges and marshalling yards near Joigny. Rendezvous was made over the Channel near Selsey Hill at 0900 after orbiting for 18 minutes. The target was bombed at 1111 but the results were sad, probably due to the sorry formation the Libs were flying. The mission was otherwise totally uneventful and everybody was home in time for a late lunch.

August 11

F.O.503. Major Elder led the group on a penetration, target and withdrawal support to bombers attacking Strasbourg and Saarbrucken. The 355th joined the 357thFG and 55thFG near Ghent at 1400 and the B-24s were escorted over the target and back to the Metz area at 1530, when the escort was terminated.

The 354FS swept the deck and Peglar destroyed a JU-52 on the Dole Tavaux airdrome. The 358th and 357FS destroyed five locomotives in the Goudrecourt, Besancon, Mirecourt and St. Dizier areas. Lieutenant Michela of the 358FS was hit by flak and heard to say he was bailing out. Although he had plenty of altitude, no one actually saw him bail out and his ship went in at Pont-A-Mousson.

Claims: 1 Destroyed   Losses: 1

August 12

F.O.506. For the first mission, Lieutenant Colonel Kinnard led a ramrod to support bombers attacking airfields at Laon, Athies, Juvincourt, Laon Couvron and Mormelon. Up at 0731, the 355th joined the 4th FG and Second Division B-24s near Rennes at 0920. The target was bombed with good results and escort was continued until 1120 over the Channel.

F.O.508. Captain Hovde led the next mission to bomb and strafe transportation targets of opportunity in northern France. Results were mixed but several locomotives, bridges, trucks, flak towers, oil storage tanks and freight cars were destroyed or damaged. Lieutenant Eshelman of the 357FS lost his coolant and bailed out near Meaux but managed to evade and returned to Steeple Morden a couple of weeks later.

Claims: None   Losses: 1 (pilot evaded)

August 13

F.O.511. Captain Lenfest led the group to France to strafe rail and road traffic, from 0814 to 1130. Targets of opportunity north of the Seine, near Rouen and Gournay, were shot up and bombed and results were generally excellent. Several bridges, 22 trucks and five half trucks were destroyed. No enemy aircraft were encountered and no losses were experienced.

F.O.512. Captain Marshall led a ramrod to St. Malo for the 355th's second mission and the group made rendezvous with Second Division B-24s over the Channel near Isigny at 1325. The escort to and from the target was completely uneventful and the group left the bombers over the Channel at 1500 hours to return home.

F.O.511-Part 2. Captain Hovde took the 358FS back to the Rouen area for a fighter bomber sweep from 1718 to 2015. The squadron bombed and strafed rail and road targets from Sommery to La Hallotierre with good results.

August 14

F.O.513. Major Elder led a ramrod to Stuttgart. Following landfall near Ostend at 0952, the group picked up the First Division B-17s near Freiburg. Escort was sustained through the target area and broken at 1345 near Charleroi.

The 354FS strafed a marshalling yard near Saverne, destroying a locomotive and a warehouse while damaging 25 locomotives, 80 trucks and 40 flatcars. The 357FS destroyed three trains near Bischwiller and shot up an airfield near Saarebourg. Elder, Forker and Shade destroyed one JU-88 apiece. Shade was hit by flak and bellied in several miles away but he evaded the Germans and returned in September.

Claims: 3 Destroyed   Losses: 1 (pilot evaded)

August 15

F.O.516. Captain Marshall led a ramrod to Vechta from 0950 to 1430. The group made rendezvous with the wrong bomb groups near Terschelling Island at 1130 but hooked up with the right bunch north of Groningen shortly thereafter.

Following the bombing, the squadrons broke escort and dropped to the deck to strafe targets of opportunity. Captain Gresham of the 358FS picked off an Me-109 circling the airfield near Zwolle for the only score of the day and Mike Graczyk became a POW after getting hit by flak near Lingen.

Marshall received severe flak damage in the cockpit area and brought his ship back to Steeple Morden with over 50 holes in her.

Two trains were destroyed and several were severely damaged before the group returned home.

Claims: 1 Destroyed   Losses: 1

August 16

F.O.518. Lieutenant Colonel Kinnard led the 355th A Group on a ramrod to support bombers attacking Magdeburg, Dessan, and Kotchen. The group, composed of the 354th and 357FS, made rendezvous with the bombers near Gramsbergen at 1000.

The 357th was bounced by 20 plus Me-109s near Hildesheim at 1030 but scored heavily before the Jerry fighters could break away. Elder scored a double to become the 355th's thirteenth ace. Bille, Cullerton and Spencer also scored doubles while Lamer, Crandell and Michels each got one Me-109 to raise the total claims to 13. John Dix Riggs was last seen trying to evade three Me-109s and was later reported KIA. Escort was continued until 1250 near Egmont.

Captain Sluga led the 358FS (B Group) on a ramrod to provide target and withdrawal support to heavies bombing Magdeburg. The bombers, observed flying a sloppy formation, were picked up at 0945 near Zwolle. Two B-24s were seen to blow up over the target and a straggling B-17 was escorted back to the Channel. Landfall was made over Ijmuiden at 1240 and all pilots returned by 1420. No enemy fighters were seen on this deal but the flak was intense.

Claims: 13 Destroyed   Losses: 1

August 17

F.O.519. Captain Lenfest led a ramrod to support ten B-24s attacking the Les Foulens railroad bridge east of Paris. The 355th joined the 4thFG over Selsey Bill at 0918 and landfall was made at 0940. Escort was provided to the target area but, because of heavy cloud cover, the bombers did not bomb the assigned target. The 355th escorted the Second Bomb Division bombers back to Selsey Bill where the escort was broken off at 1340.

August 18

F.O.522. The group split into three separate forces to execute fighter bomber sweeps north and east of Paris. The 358th and the 354FS encountered most of the opportunities and delivered some heavy blows to several marshalling yards. The results were not entirely one way, however, because of the skill of German flak gunners.

Lieutenant Brien of the 358FS was hit near Soissons, bellied in, and walked away to become a successful evader. Captain Sluga was also hit hard but managed to struggle back to the Channel where he made his second successful jump. Sluga was picked up by a mine sweeper after 15 minutes in his dingy and made it back to Steeple Morden shortly thereafter.

Marshall, leading the 354FS, was shot down near the German border but made it back to Steeple Morden before Sluga. Shortly after crash-landing, Marshall's number three man, Lieutenant Royce Priest, landed a quarter mile away in the same wheat field. After throwing out his parachute and dingy to make room for his squadron C.O., Priest sat on Marshall's lap and took off in "Eaglebeak" for the first successful rescue of an American pilot in Europe. "Deacon" Priest was awarded the Distinguished Service Cross to join Brown, Woody, Kinnard and Peters in a very select 355th Club.

The only problem Marshall and Priest faced on landing was Lenfest's "wrath" over Marshall losing Charlie's brand new Mustang after borrowing it for the mission.

Claims: None   Losses: 3 (all evaded or rescued)

August 19 - 23

Sorry weather provided the group with a much needed five day rest to catch up on their sleep and bring their fighter strength back to par.

August 24

F.O. 527. Lieutenant Colonel Kinnard led a ramrod to Hanover from 0818 to 1425. The group made rendezvous near Heligoland with Second Division B-24s and took them over the target at 1141. Following the bombing, the 355th swept southeast to pick up First Division B-17s prior to bombing Weimer. Escort was broken near Zwolle at 1330. No enemy fighters were seen and the mission was uneventful.

August 25

F.O.529. Major Elder led a ramrod to Lubeck to support Second Division bombers. Following rendezvous northwest of Kiel at 1050, the 355th escorted the B-24s to the target and back to Heligoland where escort was broken off at 1330. Boring, but a good deal for the B-24s.

F.O.531. Captain Hovde led a ramrod to the Brussels - Liege area for the 355th's second mission of the day. The B-24s were escorted from the Walcheren Island to the target near Brussels and back to the Walcheren Islands at 1935.

August 26

F.O. 532. Captain Lenfest led a ramrod to Ludwigshafen from 0811 to 1235. The group made rendezvous with the Third Task Force south of Antwerp at 0925. The target was bombed at 1028 and escort was broken over Schouwen Island.

Lieutenant Bill Cullerton spotted an FW-200 on final approach over the Speyer airdrome and poured the coals to "Miss Steve" but didn't get close enough to clobber him until the FW-200 was on the ground. Four locomotives were damaged near Liege to round out the day's activities.

Claims: 1 Destroyed   Losses: None

F.O. 534. Captain Hovde led the second mission of the day and crossed the Channel at 1808 near St. Quentin to look for targets of opportunity. The weather grew progressively worse as the group penetrated the Continent and Hovde finally wrote the mission off near Rethel. All pilots returned home by 1950.

Lieutenant Daves, assigned to Air Sea Rescue patrol from the 358FS, dove into the Channel for no apparent reason. The visibility was poor due to an intense haze so disorientation was possible.

Claims: None   Losses: 1

August 27

F.O. 535. Captain Lenfest led a ramrod to support bombers of the Third Task Force. Up at 1220, the 355th orbited the rendezvous area until notified that their assigned bombers had aborted. Lenfest then distributed the squadrons to cover other unescorted bombers attacking targets of opportunity and then provided a "ferry escort service" to escort various bomber boxes from Zuider Zee to England. No fighters, no flak and all were home for dinner by 1720.

August 28

F.O. 538. Major Elder led a strafing mission to support Patton near Metz and the 355th suffered its highest loss of aircraft of the war to German flak gunners.

Up at 0654, the group split into separate forces to attack rail and road targets. Marshall's 354FS provided top cover for the other two squadrons until they pulled away from the target area. He then led the Red flight of the 354th down to strafe a crowded marshalling yard. Marshall took a series of direct hits in the wing and canopy of his Mustang while strafing and told the rest of the group to stay away. In the same pass he lost his wingman, Bert Smith, who bailed out of his flaming ship but managed to evade back to Third Army lines. Marshall brought "Jane II" in for a belly landing at Manston with his vision obscured by blood from cuts on his face and a four square foot hole in his left wing.

In Elder's 357th squadron, Lieutenants Hurley and Phillips were also shot down by flak. Both evaded capture and returned to Allied lines.

Hovde's 358FS suffered the heaviest losses and came away from the target with renewed respect for Jerry flak but without Hughes, Duppstadt, Tolby, Weber and Gilmore. Gilmore's ship was seen to blow up and Weber bailed out but his chute didn't open.

On the plus side of the ledger, eleven locomotives were destroyed or heavily damaged as well as 169 other vehicles, trucks, box cars and flatcars with troops tanks and trucks on them. Two marshalling yards were also thoroughly shot up. While the cost was high, the group put in one of its more effective strafing days under extremely adverse circumstances.

Claims: None   Losses: 8 (6 pilots evaded)

During the month of August, 1944, the group lost 28 Mustangs plus several more so heavily damaged that they were "Class 26's" (Scrapped). More importantly, 13 pilots were killed or captured. Only two of the 355thFG pilots were shot down in air to air combat. Only April had proved more costly to the group in planes and pilots.

Several significant command changes also occurred during the July and August. Stewart returned from leave to resume his leadership as Group Executive Officer. Kinnard left the group to assume the number two position, and ultimately, Group Commander of the 4th FG. Kucheman finished his ops and turned over command of the 354FS to Marshall while Lenfest became Squadron Operations Officer. Sluga and Hovde emerged as 358FS C.O. and Ops Officer, respectively. Elder returned from leave to take over the reins of the 357FS from Minchew, who moved on to Group.

September 1

F.O. 543. Lieutenant Colonel Stewart led his first mission since returning from the states in August. The mission was a ramrod to Forest de Hagenau, near Paris, and rendezvous was made at 1030 near Bernay. The bombers aborted at 1055 and the 355th stayed with them until they crossed the coast.

F.O.544. Major Sluga led the 358FS out for its second mission of the day to chaperone three B-17s from the First Bomb Division on their way to bomb an oil dump near Brussels. The route was Orfordness to Dunkirk to the target at Bois de Houssiere and back over Schouwen Island. Bombing appeared excellent with many secondary explosions visible in the target area. The mission was strictly routine.

September 3

The 2ndSF went out and Sumner Williams, a 354FS pilot flying with the Scout Force, failed to return. Williams had mechanical problems on the way back and bellied in near Nantes. He evaded and returned about a week later.

Claims: None   Losses: 1 (pilot evaded)

September 5

F.O.550. Lieutenant Colonel Stewart led a ramrod to Karlsruhe. Following rendezvous at 1045 in the Vitry area, the group took the Second Division B-24s over the target at 1140 and back to Rheims by 1240. No fighters were seen and little flak was experienced until the target was reached. Everybody was back home by 1240.

While the 355th had an uneventful day, the new 479th went wild by destroying 58 aircraft to break the 355th's ETO record established on April 5. The record was short lived however, because the 56FG topped the new record with 60 on the same day.

September 8

F.O.556. Major Marshall led a ramrod to the Karlsruhe area. Up at 0902, the group picked up the bombers over Dieppe at 1011 and the target was reached by 1151. The bombing results appeared to be very good and the mission was relatively uneventful.

Lieutenants Wagner and Thompson escorted a straggler and ran low on gas so they landed in France before coming home the next day. Hovde had fuel problems and crashed during takeoff. Although "OLE III" was totally destroyed, Hovde walked away with only some bumps and bruises.

September 10

F.O. 561. Major Lenfest led a ramrod to the Ulm area to support First Force B-17s attacking fuel and ammo dumps plus tank and motor vehicle fabrication centers. Rendezvous with the B-24s was made over Berck sur Mer at 0914 and the target, obscured by overcast, was bombed at 1110.

On the way home, Brown and Betounes spotted an airfield near Frankfurt covered with He-60s. Brown destroyed six and Betounes damaged four before pulling away, then shot up a locomotive before rejoining the 354FS. Escort was sustained until the group reached Lille at 1330.

Lieutenant Pardee of the 358FS had an oil leak and landed in the Lille area, to return the next day.

Claims: 6 Destroyed   Losses: None

September 11

F.O. 563. Lieutenant Colonel Stewart led a ramrod to support Second Division heavies attacking the Misburg oil refineries. During the briefing, the Group Intelligence Officer, Danny Lewis, predicted a strong reaction from the Luftwaffe.

Following take off and formation, the 355th sighted the tail of the bomber stream over Ostend at 1030 and moved up the line to rendezvous with the lead boxes near Koblenz at 1120. The 355th escorted the bombers to Hanover and Misberg without incident, but near Kassel about 25 Me-109s "essed" across the top of the bombers in an American style formation and proceeded to bounce the bombers from four to six o'clock high.

Major Marshall, leading the 354FS at the seven o'clock position to the bombers, immediately split the squadron into two forces and attacked. The second section, comprised of Blue and Green flights, took on the top cover while Marshall led the Red and Yellow flights after the diving Me-109s. Brown ambushed three at low altitude and Marshall shot down two in a fight ranging from 25,000 feet to the deck. Marshall was scoring heavily on a third Me-109 before a heavy concentration of flak from a medium sized German town drove him away. Priest and Shultz each got singles while Peglar bagged another double to raise his total score to four air, one ground.

Maisch and Frost of the 358FS managed to pick off three more 109s before the rest got away. Maisch got a pair after jumping 20 Me-109s by himself, and Frost, on loan from the RAF, got one Me-109 in a separate action. While on the deck Frost damaged a DO-217 and another Me-109 on Kirchain airfield. Captain Morgan, a new 358 pilot and MTO vet, was hit by flak and spun in.

Lieutenants Johnston, McCurry, Bob White and then Schultz strafed the Marburg airdrome and destroyed two FW-190s and two JU-52s. On the second pass McCurry was hit hard by flak. McCurry bailed out but tragically slipped out of his parachute harness on the way down.

Zimmerman and Rafferty were caught in a heavy flak barrage over a small German town while coming home at low altitude and Rafferty spun in and blew up. Zimmerman was hit also but managed to limp back to Allied lines before crash landing.

Escort was broken off at 1330 near Zwolle and the group returned to Germany to look for more airfields. The 357FS destroyed or damaged 10 locomotives and damaged many boxcars and flatcars, while the 354FS and 358FS shot up flak towers and other targets of opportunity but no more aircraft were spotted.

Claims: 16 Destroyed   Losses: 3

September 12

F.O.565. Captain Mendenhall led a ramrod to Brux, Czechoslovakia after Marshall returned with fuel feed problems. Marshall returned for a fix and was off again only to be recalled by Stewart for an important briefing for the next day's mission.

Rendezvous with First Division bombers was made at 1045 north of Ludwigslust. At 1145 nearly 40 FW-190s, with 109s flying top cover, jumped the B-24s near Muritz Lake. Flying a "Company Front" formation, the FW-190s closed from seven o'clock to the bombers and split-S for the deck before the 355th could head them off. The 357FS caught the trailing elements and McHugh and Monahan shot down two and one, respectively. The rest of the squadron chased several long nose FW-190s but could not close.

During the chase, the 357th strafed Schwartz airfield and Chapman was hit by flak to become a POW. Lieutenant Cullerton destroyed seven on the ground, Juntilla got four and Haviland destroyed three before they pulled away from the field.

Ellison of the 354FS was last seen following an FW-190 through the bombers and Reed of the 358FS was last seen near the ground. Both remain MIA.

Several more gaggles were spotted near the bombers but broke when the group turned into them. Thompson and Vigna of the 358FS's Yellow flight caught up with a pair to shoot one down and damage the other. Each time the 355th reformed quickly to continue their escort duties and the Luftwaffe departed to search for easier prey.

At 1230 escort was broken off near Plauen and the group as down by 1430.

Claims: 18 Destroyed   Losses: 3

September 13

No mission was flown on the 13th but it was obvious to everyone on the base that something big was in the wind. Twenty-two Mustangs from the 4thFG and 361stFG were flown in early in the morning and their pilots were ferried back to their home bases.

Lieutenant Colonel Stewart and Major Franklin, from the 4th Group, had briefed the pilots the previous evening on a maximum effort mission code named "Frantic-7". The 355th was to escort three bomber groups to drop supplies to the Polish Underground, surrounded by German troops in the heart of Warsaw, and then take the bombers on to Russia.

A Command set of maps was issued to Stewart and Marshall and Master sets were given to Majors Lenfest, Sluga and Elder. The Command sets differed by the inclusion of Special Air Navigation Charts which included a one millionth scale map of Kiev to Berlin which was tied to fourteen individual 1:500,000-scale maps of the area. Special instructions were given to the pilots to leave their sidearms home, carry extra spark plugs for the engines, maintain good formations and leave any Jerry fighters encountered alone after one pass. Fuel discipline had to be tight to maintain a modest margin to find Piryatin.

The pilots were also instructed not to discuss politics, not to fraternize with the Russian women and just stay the hell away from any possible controversies with the Russian allies.

In addition to the pilots of the 355th, Major Lewis and Captain McMillan were scheduled to go on the mission as B-17 passengers.

After the build up to the mission, it was scrubbed due to severe weather in the target area.

September 14

Scrubbed again.

September 15

F.O.570. Stewart led the group off at 1001. The 4thFG escorted the First Wing while the 361thFG took the Second and Third Wings of Frantic to the rendezvous point.

On the way to relieve the 4th and 361st, the 355th was recalled between Emden and Bremen. The mission was cancelled when two of the three wings of Fortresses couldn't penetrate the thunderstorm wall near Berlin. The recall occurred at 1130 and all the boys were home by 1315.

September 17

F.O.575. The Shuttle Mission was put on temporary hold and the group was briefed for an area patrol in the Low Countries. Operation Market Garden, a massive airborne and armor attack designed to secure a Rhine crossing at Arnhem, required the full resources of the Eighth Air Force to support the effort.

Major Sluga led from 0714 to 1225. The 355th arrived over the assigned area at 0830 and swept the Brussels - Amsterdam -Ostend area to protect the southwest flank of the invasion. All the action with the Luftwaffe occurred much further to the northeast and the patrol was uneventful except for the destruction of several trains near Dorsten.

September 18

F.O.577. Major Marshall led the maximum effort ramrod, "FRANTIC 7 Dash One" to support the 95thBG, 100thBG and the 390thBG on their mission of mercy to Warsaw.

Stewart led the group on the take off but a bad generator forced him back shortly after crossing the Channel. Marshall, acting as the mission deputy at the head of the bastard Borax Squadron, pulled his squadron to the lead position and Major Lenfest assumed command of the 354FS.

Elder and Sluga led the 357th and 358FS as the group headed toward the rendezvous point near Koszalin on the Baltic Sea. About half way to Stettin, the bombers were picked up on C-channel and they reported they were running about 15 minutes late.

Rather than orbit around the rendezvous point for awhile and attract unwelcome attention, Marshall decided to throttle the group back a little to slow down and conserve fuel. At the next radio contact, the bombers indicated that they were now about 15 minutes early. Marshall had to quickly plot an intercept course to pick up the Forts on the other side of a large weather front between Stettin and Torun and still have enough fuel to complete the escort.

Additionally, the 355th no longer had the luxury of bypassing a couple of large flak concentrations and received a heavy and accurate barrage over Stettin. Several 358FS Mustangs were damaged and Hoffman was wounded in the arm but managed to complete the mission.

The group picked up the B-17s near Torun at 1145 hours. At 1253 hours, several small gaggles of Me-109s were spotted attacking the bombers. Mindful of dwindling fuel supplies, each of the squadrons dispatched flights to engage, drive them off and come back. Brown, leading Yellow flight of Marshall's Borax Squadron damaged one Me-109 and then picked off another with a 90 degree deflection shot. Brown then shot up some ground targets, including a Ju-87, before rejoining the squadron.

Elder and Kirby of the 357FS each destroyed a 109 while Michelena of the 358FS shot down another Me-109.

In the ensuing scrap, either Vigna or Peters was accidentally shot down by another 358FS pilot when he slipped in between the other 358th Mustang and the pursued Me-109. Both Peters and Vigna later turned up KIA.

At the target, the B-17s slipped down to about 14,000 feet to find a hole in the overcast over Warsaw. One B-17 was shot down by flak while another was crippled by fighters but 107 Forts managed to dump their loads of food and medical supplies over the city. Unfortunately, a large percentage ultimately fell into German hands.

A flight of Mustangs escorted one crippled big friend to an emergency landing at Brzesc while the rest of the group broke escort at 1345 hours to continue on to Piryatin. The 355th made the Piryatin area right at the estimated time of arrival but the pilots had a difficult time locating the small grass strip because of smoke and haze. All Mustangs except Peters and Vigna were safely on the ground by 1520.

About an hour after landing, Marshall flew to Poltava where most of the bombers were located. After planning the next day's mission with the bomber Task Force leader, Colonel Karl Truesdell, Marshall flew back to Piryatin. The complicated dispersal of bombers to Poltava and Mirgorod was dictated by the Luftwaffe's spectacular success on the first Shuttle Mission when most the B-17s were destroyed on the ground at Poltava.

Claims: 4 Destroyed   Losses: 2

September 19

F.O.577B. After briefing the group, Marshall took off to carry the operations order to Poltava and Mirgorod, then returned to lead the fighters on the second leg of their epic journey. The target for the day was the marshalling yard at Szolnok, Hungary. Several aircraft stayed in Russia because of various problems, but 56 Mustangs left Piryatin at 0953 hours. Major Hovde led the 358FS when Sluga's P-51 lost a generator.

Rendezvous with the bombers was made at 1330 near Horodenka, Poland and escort continued over Czechoslovakia, Rumania and Hungary. Little flak was encountered over the target and the bombing appeared to be excellent. Near Brod, Yugoslavia, the low group of bombers was bracketed by accurate flak but managed to keep everybody and continue on to Italy. The 355th broke escort between Brod and Doboy at 1400 and proceeded to Italy.

The force was scattered over three bases in Foggia and everybody was down by 1600 hours. The group pilots toured the local areas for the next two days.

September 22

F.O.577-C.   After briefing the pilots at three separate fields, Marshall led the 355th up at 0959 for the final leg home.

The bombers were picked up near Marseilles at 1325 and escorted to Auxerre. At 1550 escort was broken and Marshall brought the group back to Steeple Morden for a landing in near zero-zero visibility. All Mustangs landed safely by 1700 hours.

September 25

F.O.586.   Major Elder took 41 Mustangs to Koblenz on a ramrod to support two boxes of B-24s. At 1112 hours, the bombers were picked up near Liege and escorted to the target at 1138. Escort was broken near Ostend at 1330 hours and all Mustangs returned by 1425.

September 26

F.O. 588.   Lieutenant Colonel Stewart led a ramrod to Hamm. Forty-four P-51s made rendezvous at 1350 near Meppel and took the bombers over the target at 1425. No fighters were encountered and escort was broken at 1515 north of Ijmuiden.

The Second Scout Force made their operational debut out of Steeple Morden and led the way to sniff out weather and target info for the Second Bomb Division.

September 27

F.O.590.   Lieutenant Colonel Stewart led a ramrod to Kassel. The 355th provided penetration, target and withdrawal support to 156 bombers attacking locomotive fabrication targets.

Rendezvous with the bombers was accomplished at 0850 between Zwolle and Apeldorn with 45 Mustangs. The target area was reached at 0928 and shortly afterwards ten FW-190s were intercepted by elements of the 354FS. Henry Brown shot down two to raise his combined air/ground total to 27.7, making him the highest active scoring ace in the ETO. Deacon Priest got another FW-190 in the same fight.

After escort was broken at 1200, Red flight of the 354FS strafed an airfield near St. Vith. Stewart and Williamson destroyed a JU-88 and FW-190 respectively on what was believed to be the Eschwege airdrome.

Everybody came home safely but four bombers and a fighter from another group were seen to go down near the target area.

Claims: 5 Destroyed   Losses: None

September 28

F.O.591.   Lieutenant Colonel Stewart led a ramrod to heavily defended Merseburg. Third Division bombers attacked the synthetic oil plants and ammonia works and expected to receive a warm reception from Luftwaffe defenses.

Stewart led 42 Mustangs to their rendezvous with the bombers near Ghent at 1015 and escorted them to the target at 1210. Only a lone Me-163 was seen in the 355th area, but the flak was so thick "you could walk on it." Several other groups, including the new 479thFG encountered numerous German fighters and had good days. The 479thFG, led by the legendary Zemke, shot down 13 to bring their three day total to 42.

At any rate, the bombers flew a tight formation, the 355th provided close escort and Jerry stayed away.

Landfall out was made over Ostend at 1420 hours. Lieutenants Roberts and Douglass of the 358FS made emergency landings on the Continent and returned later. Douglass landed in a mine infested airfield near Montdidier and rolled to a stop eight inches away from a land mine!

All other pilots returned safely by 1500 hours.

September 30

F.O.592.   Lieutenant Colonel Stewart led a fighter sweep from Koblenz to Munster to an area south of Hersfeld. The 355th

132. Billy Hovde miraculously escaped disaster when "Ole III" lost power on takeoff, September 8. (Hovde)

133. Hendrickson's OS-U after running out of room; September '44. (Claar)

134. Rare escort to some Ninth Air Force B-26s somewhere over France. (Marshall)

135. Flight Lieutenant Warren Peglar debating relative merits of the Spitfire versus the Mustang with 354th FS CO Bert Marshall. Peglar just shot down his second double while on exchange duty with the Bulldogs. (Peglar)

136. The B-24 became a familiar sight when the 65th Fighter Wing (4th, 56th, 355th, 361st and 479th Groups) escorted the Second Bomb Division beginning September 1944. This Liberator belonged to the 392nd BG. (Wilkerson)

137. Crew chief Gerry Thompson has Marshall's WR-B ready for the shuttle mission to Russia. Lenfest's WR-F is seen next to the main gear of "Jane III." (Marshall)

138. "Loaners" from the 361st and 4th Groups enabled the 355th to put 72 birds in the air for the shuttle. (Marshall)

139. The last UK-to-Russia shuttle mission took off in typical English weather. (Hovde)

140. Williamson's WR-H, "Palma," after unsatisfactory performance with new 150-octane fuel during the shuttle takeoff. (Bennett, Williamson)

141. B-17s from the 100th Bomb Group carrying supplies to Warsaw. (Hart)

142. Soviet commander congratulating "Junior" Brown for his good day over Warsaw. His gun-camera film, in his left hand, contains record of one kill and two damaged. (Brown, Shiller)

143. Mission commander Bert Marshall with two Soviet pilots and an unknown American officer at Piryatin on September 18. (Marshall)
144. Future B-70 test pilot Al White and WR-S "Mary Lou" over England in September 1944. (Mendenhall, Bennett)
145. Gresham, Lenfest and Kirby look on as Sluga and Soviet officers hold a map. (Marshall)
146. Captain Walter Gresham's YF-T, "Trigger III," about September. Within a month the 358th FS would paint the white cowl band and rudder yellow, in the final markings change. (Gresham)
147. Squadron photo of the 357th in late 1944. (Williams, Hart, Robinson)

148. Lieutenant Colonel Gordon Graham, last wartime CO of the 354th FS. He assumed command of the squadron within three weeks of assignment to the group. (Graham)
149. Haviland's last OS-H, "Barbara," in late 1944. (Haviland, Torrey)
150. West Pointer Chuck Lenfest, stuck in the mud and captured trying to rescue Henry Brown, October 3, 1944. (Marshall, Lenfest)
151. Captain Bill Cullerton, ace and 357th top scorer, with OS-X, "Miss Steve," in September. Cullerton destroyed 13 German aircraft in two missions! (Cullerton)
152. Squadron photo of the 358th in the fall of 1944. (Williams)

153. Priest's WR-E, "Weepin' Deacon," bellied in somewhere in France after a dead-stick landing. (Brennan)

154. Sergeants Singleton and Moses in front of Moroney's OS-I, "Mary Jane," (Seidl)

155. This Second Scouting Force ship belonged to Cox and Hartsough (crew chief). Late summer or early fall, 1944. (Wilkerson)

156. Pilots of the Second Scouting Force in the fall of 1944. Most were "recycled" bomber pilots itching to fly fighters. (Dumas)

157. Crewmen Caldwell and Winterstine with John Wilkins in the new Second Scout Force. Wilkins latter bagged an Me-262 while flying out of Steeple Morden. (Caldwell)

158. Gordy Graham with the 354th FS mascot, Yank. Aces Graham, Haviland and Marshall all brought topflight pilot skills to the group from Training Command. (Sims)

159. Williamson's WR-A, "Palma II," in late 1944. (Marshall, Williamson)
160. Bert Marshall belly-landing "Jane IV" after getting worked over by flak. Taking two hits by 40mm, the group's air exec completed the last mission of his first tour with this hairy evolution on November 29, 1944. (Marshall)
161. Gordy Graham and WR-F, "Down for Double." (Marshall)
162. Billy Hovde's "Ole V" in early 1945, following write-off of "Ole IV" in a dead-stick landing. (Hovde)
163. Jim Jabara and WR-K, "Ceegar Kid." Jabara didn't get any air-to-air opportunities with the 355th but made up for it in Korea. (Bennett)
164. Woods and Marshall out in front of "Gremlin Villa" after the tough November 20 strafing show. (Decklar)
165. Good view of Graham's WR-F and the two Spitfire mirrors. (Galer)

had a freelance assignment to find and destroy Jerry but the Luftwaffe was uncooperative.

Landfall was made near Knocke at 1129, reached the Koblenz area at 1208 and patrolled until 1410 near Dummer Lake. Landfall out was made over Ijmuiden at 1515 and everybody came home by 1620.

Major Sluga and all remaining pilots left in Russia and Italy during the Shuttle came home to Steeple Morden.

Majors Marshall, Elder, Sluga and Lenfest were awarded the Polish Cross of Valor, Poland's second highest decoration, for their leadership roles during the Shuttle. Although not named in the original citation, Major Wilson was also awarded the Polish Cross of Valor for his role in the mission.

By the end of September, the following pilots previously reported Missing in Action had returned to England. All pilots who had evaded capture with the assistance of the Underground were transferred out of ETO combat operations.

Pilot	Squadron	MIA Date
Macurdy	358FS	01/29/44
Martin	357FS	01/29/44
Dufresne	357FS	02/11/44
Couture	354FS	06/07/44
Harrell	357FS	06/07/44
Donovan	358FS	06/08/44
Ruark	354FS	06/27/44
Costello	357FS	07/20/44
Taylor	354FS	08/03/44
Bernoske	357FS	08/08/44
Eshelman	357FS	08/12/44
Shade	357FS	08/14/44
Brien	358FS	08/18/44
Hurley	357FS	08/28/44
Smith	354FS	08/28/44
Hughes	358FS	08/28/44
Tolby	358FS	08/28/44
Duppstadt	358FS	08/28/44
Phillips	357FS	08/28/44
Williams	354FS	09/03/44

September closed with the miserable weather normally associated with the English Fall.

The month had been an interesting one, particularly the experience of the last Shuttle Mission. The Luftwaffe had shown much more resistance during the month than any other period following D Day. The 355th did not encounter Jerry nearly as much as several other groups, particularly the newer ones such as the 339thFG and the 479thFG. Additionally, the veteran 55thFG destroyed other 100 German aircraft during the first part of the month.

October 1

Hovde led the 358FS on a "Bomber Affiliation Mission" from 1452 to 1615. The squadron orbited the rendezvous point for 30 minutes but the "Bourbon Blue" bombers never showed for the fun and games. As the squadron reached the point of no return on fuel, a bomber formation was spotted about 20 miles away, heading north. Because of the fuel situation, Hovde led the 358FS back to Steeple Morden and everybody was down by 1735.

October 2

F.O.594. Major Marshall led a ramrod to support the Second Division strike at Hamm. Forty-four P-51s made both rendezvous and landfall over Egmond at 1230 hours and escorted the B-24s to Hamm. The formation was tight and the target appeared to be hammered at 1327.

The 357FS broke escort over the target and swept the area but saw no enemy aircraft. Landfall out was made over Egmond at 1444 and escort was broken at mid-Channel.

October 3

F.O.596. Major Elder led a ramrod to Gielbelstadt to support a Third Division strike on German radar facilities near Wurzberg. Thirty-seven Mustangs made rendezvous near Liege at 0956.

Following the bombing, Lenfest led the 354FS down to strafe a grass airfield near Nordlingen. Lenfest destroyed an FW-190 and Brown destroyed an Me-110 to raise his aggregate confirmed score to 28.7. Unfortunately, Brown was hit by flak and had to belly WR-Z in on a nearby field.

Lenfest landed close by in Marshall's WR-B to pick up Brown but stuck the Mustang in a mud hole while taxiing over. Al White also landed to pick up Brown but neither Brown nor Lenfest spotted White and headed for the woods to try to evade capture. The rest of the squadron buzzed Brown and Lenfest to try to get their attention to no avail. A disappointed Al White turned his Mustang into the wind and took off and Brown and Lenfest became guests of the Luftwaffe for the rest of the war.

Lieutenant Percival of the Scout Force did not return but was believed to be safe on the Continent.

In one short period the squadron lost the 355th's top ace, another ace and acting commanding officer of the 354FS and the only two group Mustangs equipped with the new K-14 gunsight. Marshall, the 354FS Commander and Acting Group Executive Officer, lost his deputy as well as his favorite Mustang.

Eighth Air Force Headquarters sent down a strongly worded order absolutely prohibiting any further rescue attempts and guaranteed a court martial for future attempts. As a result, the attempt was only made one more time, successfully, by a 4thFG pilot when Green picked up McKennon in the spring of 1945.

Major Gordon Graham, recently acquired by the 355thFG, transferred from Headquarters to the 354FS as Squadron Ops officer prior to assuming command of the squadron.

Claims: 2 Destroyed   Losses: 2

October 5

F.O.598. Major Marshall led a ramrod to escort Second Division B-24s attacking Lippstadt airfield. Future ace Gordon Graham made his first combat mission on Marshall's wing. Forty-seven 355thFG Mustangs picked up the B-24s over Egmond at 1055. Observed bombing results were excellent and the force turned for home at 1157. One B-17 was hit by flak near the target and went down in flames.

An Me-262 crossed over the bomber track at 30,000 feet and headed south near Apeldorn but no contact was made on either side.

Shortly afterwards, Lieutenant Juntilla of the 357FS experienced engine trouble and bellied his P-51 in to become a POW.

Escort was broken at 1300 between Egmond and Ijmuiden and everybody was on the ground by 1320.

Claims: None   Losses: 1

October 6

F.O.599. Lieutenant Colonel Stewart led a ramrod to Berlin for the first time in a long while. The group provided a 40-ship escort to B-17s attacking the Berlin Aero Engine Works.

The 355th picked up the Forts over Wesermunde at 1055 and escorted them to the target. Between the Initial Point and the target, approximately 100 Me-109s and FW-190s attacked the trailing boxes at 1215 hours. The point of attack was on a straggling box of B-17s behind the escorting 355thFG and the 4thFG, close to Berlin. The line abreast attacks took about 15 B-17s out of the box on the first pass. Stewart dispatched the 357FS and part of the 354FS to go back to assist the 4FG in breaking up the attack. The two enemy gaggles immediately split essed for the deck but not before Captain Lamer shot down two FW-190s and Colson got one more. The 4th picked up another three. Yellow nosed P-51s of the 361st also got into the scrap and scored on several Me-109s before they dove away.

Escort was continued until 1335 over Ijmuiden and the group was down by 1430.

During debriefing several pilots reported unmarked Mustangs firing at other P—51s near the target.

Claims: 3 Destroyed   Losses: None

October 7

F.O.600. Major Marshall led the 355th on a ramrod to Ruhland synthetic oil refineries. Fifty-four Mustangs were dispatched to support the B-17s and B-24s on this maximum effort strike. The group P-51s met the bombers over Nordheim at 1150 after orbiting 30 minutes. The 354th and the 358FS had an uneventful escort except for a futile chase of a couple of Me-262s. The two squadrons escorted the B-17s over the target and back before breaking escort over the Zuider Zee and south of Hanover, respectively.

The 357FS broke up an attack by approximately 75 FW-190s and Me-109s near Leipzig at 1310. Six B-24s were seen to go down or drop out of formation. Most of the gaggle dove for the deck before completing their stern attack, but Lieutenant Monohan managed to shoot down a trailing FW-190 before they got completely away. On the way back, Monohan found an unknown airfield and destroyed an Me-109 on the ground.

The rest of the 357FS rejoined the bombers rather than chase Jerry and finally broke escort at 1345 south of Hanover.

The Scout Force was bounced by 20 plus single engine fighters, including an Me-163, near Bielefeld. The Scout Force pilots escaped with no casualties and the German fighters made only one pass before heading for the deck.

Claims: 2 Destroyed   Losses: None

October 9

F.O.603.   Major Elder led the A Group on a ramrod to support bombers attacking the Geissen Controlling Station and marshalling yards near Ruhland.

Up at 1235, 25 Mustangs made rendezvous near Liege at 1350 with two wings of B-24s. Elder took his force over the target and back to Liege, where escort was broken at 1610. Bombing was done through 10/10 cloud cover and no enemy fighters were sighted.

Major Hovde led the B Group to escort the Third, Fourth and Fifth Wings of B-24s to the same target. The 27 P-51s of the B Group picked up their charges over Liege at 1415 and cruised over the target at 1505. Bombing was done through heavy cloud cover and escort was broken at 1615 south of Bruges. Both missions were uneventful and everybody was down by 1705.

October 12

F.O.1235A.   Major Sluga led the 355th on a ramrod to support Second Division Liberators on a raid on the Varrelbusch -Cloppenburg airdrome. Forty-nine Mustangs picked up the B-24s over Zwolle at 1110 and headed out over the Zuider Zee.

At 1120 two Me-262s made a pass on the Blue flight of the 354FS but scored no hits before departing with their 100-knot speed advantage. Just before the Me262s made their pass, a V-2 was spotted climbing above 30,000 feet before nosing over for England. Another V-2 was spotted by the Second Scout Force climbing from the Rheine area and a third rocket was seen climbing from the Leiden locale.

Three more Me-262s were seen north of Enschede but going too fast to engage. A couple of B-24s were blown up by flak over the target and no chutes were seen. Escort was broken at 1235 north of Egmond and everybody came home by 1340.

October 14

F.O.1238A.   Major Marshall led a ramrod to escort four boxes of B-24s to the Kaiserslautern Marshalling Yards. Fifty-three Mustangs made rendezvous with the Second Division at 1115 over the Channel. From the Initial Point, the B-24s bombed three separate targets between 1210 and 1250. Cloud cover varied from 7/10 to 10/10 over the targets and escort was broken at 1410 over Ostend. Flak was heavy to moderate and one B-24 went down near the Meuse river on the way in. No enemy air activity was experienced and all ships were home by 1500.

October 15

F.O.1240A.   Major Sluga led a ramrod to the Cologne marshalling yards. The rapid German retreat from the Western Front made the rail and road network increasingly important targets.

Rendezvous was made at 0917 near Brussels and the black and white tailed B-24s were escorted to the target. The Libs were flying a pitiful formation but German fighters failed to take advantage of their opportunity. Following bombs away at 0944, escort was broken over Charleroi at 1100. The mission was strictly routine.

October 17

F.O.1245A.   Major Elder led a ramrod to the Cologne area from 0813 to 1210. Rendezvous with Second Division B-24s was made at 0917 near Brussels and the bombers were escorted over the target area at 0944. Escort on this routine mission was broken near Charleroi at 1100 and everybody was home by 1210.

October 18

F.O.1246A.   Major Sluga led a ramrod to escort Third Division B-17s to Kassel and Minden. Forty-seven out of the 55 Mustangs dispatched made rendezvous near Namur at 1038 and the target was reached at 1115.

Shortly after the bombing, three unusual contrails were spotted climbing from 12,000 feet to 50,000 feet before disappearing. Flak was heavy but no fighters were encountered although three Me-262s were seen well below the bombers.

Lieutenant Lonkausky of the 357FS was hit by flak near Cologne and seen to bail out near the deck.

Escort was broken at 1321 over Malmedy and everybody was back by 1450.

Claims: None   Losses: 1

October 19

F.O.1249A.   Captain Mendenhall led a ramrod to the Mainz area to support Second Division B-24s striking the Gustavsburg Diesel Engine Works. The group put 52 fighters in the air by 1045 and 49 made rendezvous over Brussels at 1140.

The target was bombed at 1245 and escort was broken over Ostend at 1400. Although several Me-262s were spotted by the B-24s, no contact was made. One B-24 was seen to belly in south of Brussels.

October 22

F.O.1254A.   Major Elder led a ramrod and fighter sweep to the Hanover area from 1155 to 1635. After picking up the lead box of B-24s over Zwolle at 1329 the 355th escorted them over the target and back to the Munster area where escort was broken at 1440. The solid cloud cover cut the planned sweep short and the Mustangs rejoined the bombers. After landfall over Ijmuiden at 1500, the group left the bombers and returned home.

Shortly after landing, Captain Norman McDonald was killed when another 354FS Mustang accidently collided with his bird while taxiing. The other pilot was not hurt.

Claims: None   Losses: 1

October 23

Marshall turned over the reins of the 354FS to Graham and became full time Group Executive Officer. In the next week Cummings would leave the 355th for good and Stewart would assume command.

October 26

F.O.1264A.   Lieutenant Colonel Marshall led a ramrod to Minden. Forty-six P-51s met the Second Division B-24s over the west coast of the Zuider Zee at 1340.

The mission was pretty routine until the Initial Point when three Me-262's came out of cloud cover at five o'clock to the Libs and made a "roller coaster" pass through one box. Marshall's Red flight dropped their tanks to bounce but the jets split-S and dove away. One B-24 was seen smoking, but stayed in formation. The 355th broke escort over the Channel at 1537 and returned to base.

Marshall entered the base hospital shortly after landing, to remove splintered nose cartilage from college football injuries, and didn't get back on flying status until November 9.

October 30

F.O.1273A.   Major Elder led a ramrod to Hamburg. The 355th put 69 birds in the air to escort Second Division B-24s on a maximum effort strike at the oil refineries. Rendezvous was made over Zwolle at 1235 hours and 28,000 feet.

The B-24s flew a miserable formation, the target was obscured by 10/10 cloud and fortunately, no Jerry fighters showed to pick on the straggling Liberators. Hamburg was bombed through the overcast and the escort was contintued to 1355.

Spencer and Lake of the 357FS landed in Belgium and came home the next day. All other Mustangs were back by 1501.

November 1

F.O.1278A.   Major Hovde led a ramrod to support a strike against the Gelsenkirchen synthetic oil refineries. Up at 1208, the group made contact with Second Division heavies west of Egmond at 1315 hours. In addition to their normal loads, the 143 bombers also dropped 1000 leaflet bombs at 1340 hours.

An Me-262 made a diving attack on a group of Mustangs behind the 355th between Coesfeld and Nordhorn at 1408, shooting down one. The pilot of the Me-262 outdistanced 30 to 40 trailing P-51s and P-47s, but made the serious error in judgment of turning back too soon and was quickly shot down.

Several rocket contrails were seen about 20 miles east of the target. Escort was broken at 1452 south of Egmond on the return track.

November 2

F.O.1281A.	Major Elder led a freelance support to First and Second Division bombers attacking Merseburg. The 355th put up 56 Mustangs to try to take full advantage of the opportunity to roam at will, unfettered by close escort responsibilities. The group took off at 1012, made rendezvous west of Merseburg at 1216 and provided area support north of the Merseburg area and the main bomber track.

Shortly before reaching the target, the 357FS and part of the 354FS headed off several Me-262s coming down from Berlin and pursued when they broke for the deck. The 357th lost the jets but spotted some FW-190s and Me-109s which were landing at an airdrome near Wernigerode. At the same time the 358FS engaged six Me-109s attacking one box of B-17s at 1250 near Merseburg. The 109s shot down a B-17 while Mikalauskas and McElroy came away with one Me-109 destroyed and one damaged.

Priest and Woolard of the 354FS each shot down an Me-109 near Naumburg after their flight attacked 25 plus Me-109s queing up for a pass on some B-17s.

In the same time frame, the 357FS had a field day. In addition to Elder, Wilkes, Moroney and Cullerton shooting down five more Jerry fighters near Naumburg, the squadron destroyed another 25 fighters on the ground near Wernigerode. Cullerton and Elder had their best day getting a total of eight and six respectively. Erickson destroyed four on the ground while Dufresne, Miller, Williams and Moroney each claimed two apiece.

Lieutenants Cavender and Engelbreit each got one on the ground also, but Engelbreit got hit hard by flak and had to belly his "Spook III" in near the airdrome.

Zimmerman had coolant or oil pressure problems and bailed out over occupied territory in Holland. Both pilots turned up POW. All the rest of the group returned by 1530.

Claims: 33 Destroyed	Losses: 2

November 4

F.O.1286A.	Major Sluga led a ramrod to Misburg to support Second Division B-24s hitting the oil refineries. The group expected more determined resistance following the previous mission and put 60 P-51s up just in case. Rendezvous was made at 1135 southwest of Hamburg and the force dropped their loads at 1206. Flak was heavy and one B-24 went down near Hanover.

The 354th broke into several Me-262s poised to hit some unidentified Mustangs but the Germans casually dove away and quickly outran their pursuit. The encounter occurred between Hildesheim and Minden.

Jackson of the 354FS strafed three barges near Minden, damaging all three but the mission was otherwise uneventful.

November 5

F.O.1288A.	Captain Williamson led a ramrod to Karlsruhe from 0907 to 1325 hours. The Second Division attacked Karlsruhe, Frankfurt, Ludwigshafen, Kaiserslautern and Hanau. Fifty-four Mustangs met the B-24s off Dover at 0955 and escorted them to the target and back to Charleville before breaking escort at 1310. The group came out over Calais at 1325.

Some Me-262s were seen in the vicinity of Nancy but not engaged and everybody was down by 1425.

November 6

F.O.1291A.	Major Sluga led a ramrod to the Minden area to attack the locks, canal and aquaducts. Forty-five 355th Mustangs made rendezvous with several combat wings of B-24s at 1005 near Zwolle. The target was bombed at 1040 and escort was broken at 1203 north of Ijmuiden.

Priest and Woolard beat up several rail cars and a locomotive on the way back, but the mission was otherwise boring.

November 8

F.O.1296A.	Lieutenant Colonel Stewart led a ramrod back to Merseburg. Fifty Mustangs met First Division B-17s over the Zuider Zee at 1015 and the target was bombed at 1107.

Two Me-262s attacked one box of bombers near Dummer Lake but no results were observed and the jets quickly left the area. The 355th covered the bombers on the withdrawal until escort was broken over the Zuider Zee at 1330.

November 9

F.O.1299A.	Major Wilson led A Group on a ramrod to the Metz area from 0823 to 1230. Rendezvous was made northeast of

Laon at 0945 and the bombers were escorted over the target at 1058. Escort was broken at 1125 near Douai and the fighters were back by 1230.

Captain Mendenhall led B Group on a sweep to the Metz - Aschaffenburg area. They strafed road and rail targets in that region for the first time since the memorable day of August 28 when the group lost an all time high of eight Mustangs and two pilots.

An airfield was spotted near Mittenberg and one pass was made by the 354FS. Lieutenant Hull's Mustang was clobbered and he bellied it in. There were no aircraft on the field and the Mustangs continued looking for other targets. Several barges, locomotives, rolling stock, armored vehicles and trucks were destroyed around Badenhausen, Waldeschaff and Aschaffenburg. Lieutenant Todd limped back at 150 knots to friendly territory in a flak crippled bird and six 354FS pilots landed on the Continent before coming home the next day.

Lieutenants Todd, Wood, Spencer, Jackson, McLear and Johnson made landings at bases other than Steeple Morden.

Claims: None   Losses: 1

November 10

F.O.1301A.   Captain Colson led a ramrod to support B-24s attacking Langendiebach, near Frankfurt. Rendezvous was made near Liege at 1131 and the target was bombed at 1300. Ten tenths cloud covered the route most of the way and bombing results were not observed. Escort was broken at 1400 hours south of Liege.

November 11

F.O.1306A.   Captain Mendenhall led 37 Mustangs on a ramrod to Bottrop. Second Division B-24s, on their way to hit the synthetic oil plants, were met at 1055 south of Egmond and escorted to the target.

The 355th also picked up the Fourth Combat Wing when the 4th Group missed their rendezvous. The B-24s of the flew excellent formation so the escort task was easy. Enemy fighters were reported around the Zuider Zee but not encountered and escort was broken at 1253 west of Egmond.

Minchew, Long and Nelson (357FS) plus Rodebaugh and White (354FS) landed at St. Trond. All others returned home by 1345.

November 16

F.O.1314A.   Captain Bille first led a ramrod to Aachen and then a sweep of the area following bombs away. Forty-six P-51s of the 355th met Second Division bombers over Louvain at 1230 and stayed with them until 1310 when escort was broken over Namur.

The 355th encountered snow squalls and intermittent showers in the Greszen and Marburg area but destroyed seven locomotives, damaged three and shot up more than 43 goods wagons.

Lieutenant Woolard was hit by 20mm flak near Berleburg. Woolard rolled over on his back and bailed out of his burning P-51 from 2,000 feet. Woolard was captured and later killed by artillery fire after escaping prison camp with Lenfest in April 1945.

Landfall out was made over Knocke at 1445. Haraburda, Roberts and Masters landed in France but everybody else was home by 1530.

Claims: None   Losses: 1

November 18

F.O.1317A.   Major Sluga led a strafing mission to Leipheim from 1012 to 1610. Forty-six white nose Mustangs of the 355th joined the red nose 4thFG, now led by Kinnard, on a joint effort to destroy Me-262s on Leipheim airdrome.

The two groups reached the target at 1240 and remained in the area for an hour. The 355th provided top cover for the 4th until they finished strafing. Two 4th Group Mustangs were seen to collide and one crashed northeast of the field. After the 4th finished, they pulled up to provide top cover while the 355th went in. In addition to claims for 14 Me-262s destroyed on the ground, the 355th also destroyed eight locomotives, nine tank cars, thirty troop cars and several buildings plus gun emplacements. Those pilots claiming two Me-262s included Long, Haviland, Fortier and Todd. Duffy, Wood, Beatty, Wilson, Max and Colson claimed one apiece.

The group withdrew at 1335 and returned home on the deck and came out over Calais around 1520.

Claims: 14 Destroyed   Losses: None

November 20

F.O.1320A. Lieutenant Colonel Marshall led a fighter sweep to the Trier - Frankfurt - Kassel - Osnabruck area. Solid cloud cover obscured the ground from take off at 1005 until the target area was reached at 1210. The group let down through a hole in the undercast somewhere between Bonn and Koblenz and proceeded to look for targets of opportunity.

The 358FS looked over an airfield near Zulpick, found nothing and proceeded to strafe rail targets nearby. Lieutenant Haraburda was shot down and killed by light flak near the rail station.

The 357th and 354FS strafed rail and road traffic around Koblenz and encountered extremely heavy concentrations of flak in several areas. In fact, the flak was the heaviest encountered by the group during the war. To make the situation even worse, the ceiling was low and the German flak gunners had perfect altitude infomation.

All squadrons turned for home before 1300 hours after raising hell with a variety of ground targets including locomotives, rail cars, trucks, half tracks, barracks and soldiers. All traffic in the target area appeared heading in a southwesterly direction.

On the way back, Lieutenant White's engine failed over the North Sea. Several 357FS pilots orbited the area but White never was seen again.

Claims: None   Losses: 2

November 21

F.O.1323A. Lieutenant Colonel Stewart led a ramrod to support B-17s attacking Merseburg from 0935 to 1510. The bombers were picked up at 1007 over the Channel and escorted to the target by 1203. Several jet contrails were observed near the target but no combat ensued.

Escort was broken south of Ostend at 1410 and everybody was down by 1510.

November 25

F.O.1333A. Major Elder led a ramrod and area support to bombers attacking Merseberg synthetic oil plants. Rendezvous was made at 1110 over Geizen. The 357th and 354FS broke escort after the target was reached and strafed rail and road targets of opportunity.

The 358FS escorted the bombers back to Malmedy at 1445 and then dropped down to the deck to destroy a train on the way home.

November 26

F.O.529B. Major Sluga led the 355th on a ramrod to Hanover from 1005 to 1445. Forty Mustangs picked up the B-24s at 1120 east of Ijmuiden and escorted them to the target.

Between 1235 and 1243 several waves of 30 to 40 single engine German fighters attacked the escorted B-24s. The first wave was engaged by the 354th and 357FS with claims of 17 destroyed for no loss, fighters or bombers. While the rat race was in full progress, the second and third waves of FW-190s and Me-109s struck and several B-24s went down in spite of the 358FS and the Second Scout Force efforts to blunt this attack. The 358th destroyed four with no losses to raise the group total to 21, while the 2ndSF added five more.

High scorers for the 355th included Frank Masters with three. McLear, Priest, Hauver, Max, Moroney and Haviland scored two apiece while Mellen, Duffy, Molnar, Barab, Lyons and Beckman nailed singles.

Priest's and Haviland's doubles raised their air victory totals to the ace level of five and six respectively, and made them the group's fourteenth and fifteenth air aces.

Lieutenant Whalen of the Second Scout Force got three FW-190s while Lieutenant Ceglarski and Captain Whitlow each shot down one. Whalen's triple raised his score to four and made him the top scorer for the 2ndSF. Legend has it that Whalen calmly lit up a cigarette while pursuing his last victim over Hamburg and earned the nickname "Gooney". Captain Stauder of the 2ndSF was last seen just after the fight ended and nobody saw him again.

Escort was broken at 1310 over Dummer Lake and the group headed out over the North Sea. While over the North Sea, Kelley collided with Barab and both aircraft blew up. No chutes were seen and neither turned up after the war.

Claims: 26 Destroyed   Losses: 3

November 27

F.O.1343. Major Wilson led a ramrod to Bad Kreuznach from 1025 to 1445. Rendezvous was made with Second Division

B-24s at 1150 west of Dummer Lake and escorted over the target at 1225. The target was obscured by clouds so bombing results were not observed. Many stragglers were seen on the way back and the group broke up into flights to provide needed escort and the last Mustang touched down at 1445.

November 29

F.O.1348A. Lieutenant Colonel Marshall led the A Group after Stewart aborted. The 355th provided escort to B-24s attacking Altenbecken and Hanover. Rendezvous was made over Dummer Lake at 1200 and the group proceeded to Hanover before orbitting back to the Dummer Lake area.

Following escort duties, Marshall took the A Group down to strafe near Leer and Sogel at 1400. While Marshall was strafing a troop train, a second train pulled out of another siding and put a heavy concentration of fire into Marshall's Mustang. With Priest looking him over and keeping close tabs on the smoking P-51, Marshall limped back to Steeple Morden with over 200 holes and no hydraulics for his third belly landing.

Major Kirby led the B Group to provide complete escort duties to B-24s attacking Altenbecken. Take off was at 1049 and rendezvous was made over the Zuider Zee at 1200 hours. The B-24s were escorted over Altenbecken where they bombed through the clouds at 1253. No opposition was encountered and escort was broken over Ijmuiden.

November 30

F.O.1354A. Major Elder led the A Group on a freelance support to Merseburg from 1018 to 1600. Although 30 Mustangs took off, eleven returned early for various mechanical related reasons and only 19 made rendezvous at 1138. As no other group had yet made contact, Nuthouse requested that the A Group maintain close escort with the lead wing of B-24s from Ostend through the target. At 1200 hours the A Group was released from close escort and Elder's Mustangs swept ahead to scout the penetration route. Nothing of interest was spotted and the A Group turned for home at 1457 east of Brussels.

Major Sluga took the B Group out to provide close support to third Division B-17s attacking Merseberg. They picked up the 13th and 14th Wings over Brussels at 1138. Merseburg was bombed at 1325 and escort was broken south of Koblenz at 1430.

December 2

F.O.533B. Major Wilson led a rodeo from Kassel to Munster. The 355th took off at 1034, made landfall over the Hague at 1125 and swept the assigned route under guidance from Nuthouse. Bandits were reported in several areas but thick, layered cloud formations prevented contact. The 355th turned for home at 1415, crossed out over the Hague at 1445 and landed by 1525.

December 4

F.O.1370A. Lieutenant Colonel Stewart led a free lance from 1037 to 1610 with 30 Mustangs forming the A Group. Rendezvous with the B-24's was made near Brussels at 1140. They swept ahead of the bombers at 30,000 feet and orbited over the target area until the bombers dropped their loads. The A group then swept the withdrawal route until 1440 when they turned for home near Namur.

Captain Bille led a ramrod to Bebra. The B Group escorted the strung out bomber force from Brussels to Bebra and back to Namur where they joined the A Group and returned home together. Both efforts were entirely uneventful.

December 5

F.O.1374A. Lieutenant Colonel Stewart led the A Group off the runway for a free lance support to the bombers heading for Berlin, but aborted shortly after take off. Major Hovde assumed the lead and took 23 Mustangs to the rendezvous point with B-17s over Zwolle. They escorted the Fortresses to a point short of the target and then swept ahead to Berlin to look for trouble.

As the Third Division B-17s approached Berlin, Hovde spotted about 70 FW-190s forming up ahead of the bombers and called Moon Elder to bring the B Group forward to help out. Elder was too far away so Hovde took his little band down to attack. In the next couple of minutes they scored 13-0-7 for no loss and completely broke up the attack. Hovde personally destroyed five and shared another with Alexander when he ran out of ammo. Alexander scored another single and Lieutenant Baker shot down two. Duffy and Silva from the 354FS got one apiece while McElroy and Robert Brown added one each to the 358FS total. While the German gaggle was completely disorganized Hovde's small force broke for the deck and escaped.

In two short minutes Hovde doubled his air score, became the 355th's second double air ace, eclipsed Woody's group record score of April 24 and won the DSC for breaking up the attack against formidable odds. Not a single bomber was attacked as a result of the A Group's effort.

B Group arrived shortly after the scrap was over and raised hell with Hovde for not leaving any. Elder led the B Group on the continued escort until 1230 near Hannover and then came home.

Lieutenant Williams of the B Group lost oil pressure on the way home, between Berlin and Dummer Lake for unknown reasons and bailed out to become POW.

Claims: 13 Destroyed   Losses: 1

December 6

F.O.1383A.   Major Elder led the A Group on a free lance support to Bielefeld while Major Sluga led the B Group on a ramrod to the same target. The B Group made rendezvous at 1105 west of Zwolle, and escorted the Second Division bombers over the target at 1150. Escort was broken at 1325 north of Amsterdam.

The A Group stooged around the assigned rendezvous point west of Bielefeld for 40 minutes but did not see their assigned B-24s so they picked up the unescorted first Combat Wing over the target. The mission was uneventful and the A Group broke escort over Egmond at 1315.

Both Elder and Sluga commented officially on the difficulties of proper escort when the bombers were late and flying poor formations.

Lieutenant Colonel Marshall assumed command of the group while Stewart was away for the next two weeks. Marshall finished his first tour of combat operations with his belly landing on 29 November and was getting ready to go home on 30 day leave with Kinnard. Priest, Williamson and Al White were also getting ready to go back to the States.

December 9

F.O.1397A.   Captain Fortier led a ramrod after Major Kirby aborted over the Channel. The 355th made rendezvous at 1137 southeast of St. Dizier and escorted the First Division B-17s to the Stuttgart area. The Fortresses bombed Boblingen airdrome at 1230. The mission was uneventful and escort was broken at 1414 near Laon.

December 10

F.O.1404A.   Major Bille led the A Group on a free lance while Captain Mendenhall led the B Group on a ramrod. Both forces supported Second Division Liberators attacking Bingen.

The A Group made rendezvous at 0955 over Ghent and covered the B-24s to the target. Bingen was bombed at 1050 through heavy cloud cover and the force turned for home. Lieutenant Ivey, of the 354FS, lost all oil pressure and bailed out between Minden and Allied lines to become POW. Escort was broken at 1145 near the Meuse River.

The B Group furnished penetration, target and withdrawal support for the third box of B-24s. The only difference between the two 355th efforts was a strict escort directive for the B Group, while A ranged ahead of the bomber stream on both the penetration and withdrawal routes.

December 11

F.O.1408A.   The 355th supported the Second Combat Wing of B-24s on a ramrod to Hanau. Sluga led A and Kirby took B to the rendezvous point southeast of Brussels at 1130. The 358FS investigated contrails near Mannheim at 1135 but they turned out to be B-17s.

Both A and B escorted the bombers over the target and back to Karlsruhe. Escort was broken at 1300 and everyone but Kemper was home by 1450. Kemper had mechanical problems but made it safely to Legacy and returned the next day.

December 12

F.O.1412A.   The mission was a ramrod and the assignment for the 355th was to escort the first four combat groups over the targets in the Hanover-Munster area and back along the withdrawal route. Major Mendenhall, then Williamson, took the A Group and patrolled the north side of the bombers while Captain Dissette led B on the close escort.

Rendezvous was made north of Eisenach at 1140 and the bombers reached the target by 1158. V-12 rockets were spotted at Malmedy, Rotterdam, Kassel and Siegen on the way in.

On the way back, McElroy took Blue flight of the 358FS down to escort stragglers and picked off two trains on the deck. Art Curran destroyed an unidentified twin engine aircraft near Gotha.

The group broke escort near St. Vith at 1353.

Claims: 1 Destroyed   Losses: None

December 15

F.O.1422A. Major Hovde led a sweep to provide general support to First and Second Division bombers attacking targets in Paderborn, Hanover and Munster. Landfall was made at 1040 somewhere near Zanvoort at 24,000 feet. Nuthouse sent Falcon and Bentley (354th and 358th) Squadrons to patrol the Paderborn-Munster area, while Custard (357th) made rendezvous with the bombers at 1200 over the Initial Point.

The 357th came out at 1320 over Noordval. The 354th and 358th came back over Den Helder at 1300. Everybody came home except Alexander of the 358th. He lost his coolant around 1215 and bailed out north of Munster to become a guest of the Germans.

Claims: None   Losses: 1

December 18

F.O.1430A. Lieutenant Colonel Stewart led a free lance patrol to the Hamm and Ludensheid area from 1100 to 1520. A solid undercast made landmark identification impossible and the group proceeded to Cologne after landfall near Ostend at 1150. After an uneventful patrol around the Ruhr, the 355th left the area at 1415 at 37,000 feet and landfall was made over Ostend at 1440.

December 23

F.O.1443A. Major Sluga took the A Group on a ramrod to Dahlen for a completely uneventful escort. They remained in the target area from 1305 to 1350 and came home without incident.

Major Wilson took 28 Mustangs of the B Group on a free lance support to the Trier area to support strikes by First, Second and Third Division bombers on tactical targets. They ran a shuttle service to Malmedy, St. Vith and Trier finally breaking escort at 1320 near Liege.

The Scout Force spotted 30 Me-109s heading east at 1235 plus another 15 FW-190s near the target area at 1240. The Focke Wulfs bounced the two Scout Force pilots but the Mustangs escaped. Several large explosions, believed to be fuel or ammo, were observed in the target areas.

Lieutenants Goth and Heaton crashed their Mustangs while taking off in the terrible weather, but both sustained only minor injuries.

December 24

F.O.1446A. After waiting two hours, 65 Mustangs took off at 1428 for a fighter sweep to the Cologne-Munster area. Major Elder led the A Group and Major Graham led the B Group. The mission was essentially the same except for a ten minute separation between the two forces.

One lone chute was spotted near Walcheran Island at 1540 on the way in.

The 355th was vectored to Amsterdam, Aachen, Munster and out over Dunkirk at 1650.

Steeple Morden was completely socked in and most of the 355th landed at Warmingford and Wattisham. The pilots were brought back by trucks for turkey dinner but left afterwards to return to their ships. All Mustangs came home early Christmas Day.

December 25

F.O.1415A. Major Hovde led a ramrod to an area east of Trier. Forty-four Mustangs took off from various fields at 0815 and made rendezvous with the bombers over Walcheren Island at 1037.

Southwest of Koblenz, approximately 75 FW-190s and 15 Me-109s attacked the high squadron of B-24s from six o'clock. Major Graham and Lieutenant Hauver of the 354FS caught the tail end of the string to shoot down two FW-190s, an Me-109 and probably destroy another FW-190.

Vic Iglesias and Monahan of the 357FS picked up two more FW-190s and Iglesias shot one down near Koblenz. Monahan was last seen by Iglesias on the tail of an FW-190 on the deck and never heard from again.

The 355th quickly reformed around the B-24s and provided close escort during withdrawal. Hovde later pointed out in debriefing that no other Mustang group provided escort to the B-24s after the bounce and most chased the Jerry fighters without returning.

Claims: 4 Destroyed   Losses: 1

December 28

F.O.1458A.   The 355th flew a ramrod to support B-24s attacking marshalling yards at Neunkirchen and Hamburg. Major Graham led the A Group and Major Sluga led the B Group.

The 355th made rendezvous over Ostend and provided escort to the target and back to Charleroi. The target was bombed at 1240 and escort was broken at 1325.

A blue Spitfire flew along the withdrawal route from 1315 to 1325. It took violent evasive action when approached and the pilots suspected that it may have been a captured ship flown by a German pilot.

Major Mendenhall led an eight ship escort to three B-24s with "R-4" on their fuselages. Rendezvous was made at 1225 over Luxembourg and the Liberators were escorted to the front line area. The B-24s and the Mustangs cruised around the target for about 45 minutes and turned for home at 1430. Lieutenant Stanton's engine failed between Brussels and Antwerp but he bellied in successfully and came back the next day.

December 29

F.O.1463A.   The 355th split into A and B Groups to provide both free lance and ramrod support to bombers attacking northeast of Luxembourg. Stewart led the free lance while Elder led the close escort.

Rendezvous was made at 1140 near Ghent and the escort was continued over the target and back to Liege by 1310. The B Group returned to Malmedy to cover rear boxes of B-24s and escort was broken by 1357.

The A Group broke escort to sweep an area east of Frankfurt. One flight strafed the Lauterbach area and destroyed several trains.

December 30

F.O.1467A.   Lieutenant Colonel Stewart led a free lance to the Frankfurt - Mannheim area from 1010 to 1545. The 355th arrived in the Frankfurt area at 1210 and swept Ludwigshafen, Mannheim, Kassel and Karlsruhe at altitudes ranging from 19,000 to 28,000 feet. They finished at 1345 west of Strasbourg and returned home.

December 31

F.O.1471A.   Major Hovde led the A Group to Hamburg. Twenty-six Mustangs departed Steeple Morden at 0832 and picked up Third Division Forts over Borkum Island at 26,000 feet. Despite smoke pots and heavy flak, the target was clobbered at 1240. Although several flights of FW-190s were seen landing near Minden, the A Group was low on fuel and passed up the bounce. They broke escort over Cuxhaven at 1245 and headed home.

Major Elder led the B Group to Misburg and made rendezvous over Cuxhaven at 1045. Fifteen miles west of Wilhemsburg, Blue and Green flights of the 354FS bounced 20 FW-190s. The FW-190s shot down a B-17 while Major Graham and Lieutenant Hauver shot down two and one FW-190, respectively. Hauver became the 355th's 16th air ace while Graham raised his total to three. The remaining Jerry fighters split-S for the deck.

The rest of the B Group stayed with the bombers and another large gaggle of German fighters moved on to look for easier pickings. Escort was broken at 1235 over Dummer Lake and everyone came home by 1400.

Claims: 3 Destroyed   Losses: None

SUMMARY OF COMBAT OPERATIONS, 1944

The 355th ended 1944 with 590 confirmed victories (in third place behind the 4th and the 56th Fighter Groups), and the highest number of confirmed victories in the Eighth Air Force since the end of March, 1944.

The white nose Mustangs had also established a well deserved reputation for providing excellent close escort to the B-17s and B-24s of the Eighth Air Force. They frequently passed up opportunities to raise their victory scores while sticking to the prime mission — protecting the bombers.

COMBAT OPERATIONS DIARY
1945

January 1

F.O.1476A. Just prior to briefing, a struggling Fort from nearby Bassingborne crashed and exploded near the 354FS' D Flight area. Crew Chief Bob Marzo was seriously wounded in the explosion but was pulled away by Ray Katzensky and Mort Braun and rushed to the base hospital. Both men were awarded the Soldiers Medal for their heroic action.

Major Wilson led a ramrod to escort First Division Forts attacking oil targets in Derben. About 20 minutes after R/V, near Lenzen, two Me-262s bounced one of the trailing flights of group but dove away before engaging. Two more Me-262s attacked the bombers between Lenzen and Derben but also broke away when the 355th Mustangs turned into them.

Near Stendal unusual flak, described as a large white flash, followed by dense smoke, was seen in the bomber formation but no bombers were seen to go down. The mission was otherwise uneventful.

January 2

F.O.1479A. Major Kirby led the A Group on a ramrod to the rail and marshalling targets at Remagen. Following a 0930 take off, the A Group picked up the bombers at 1107 over the Zuider Zee and took them over the target at 1202. Escort was broken at 1243 near Charleroi.

Major Sluga took the B Group to Dummer Lake and picked up the Second Division at 1202. Escort was broken near Charleroi at 1245.

Eight other 355th ships escorted a photo recon Mosquito to Bud Kreuzenach and all ships were home by 1345.

January 3

F.O.1485A. Major Hovde took 25 birds on a ramrod to the Hamburg - Neunkirchen area. The A Group met with the Second Division at 1045 over Metz. They bombed through 10/10 cloud cover and returned to icy runways after breaking escort near Sedan.

Captain Duffy took the B Group and picked up the B-24s over Metz also. The mission was uneventful except that Lieutenant Schmidt of the 357FS had to bail out due to coolant loss near Charleville at 1225. He hitched a ride back to the base next morning.

Captain Seely of the 358FS belly landed at Steeple Morden due to unknown causes but sustained only minor injuries.

January 5

F.O.1491A. Major Graham led 56 Mustangs on a ramrod to Kirn, Oberstein and Cochem. The 355th picked up the Second Division Liberators near Namur at 1130. Nuthouse requested help for a straggler and Graham sent the 357FS to escort the straggler plus investigate bandits reported near Aachen. No bandits were spotted and one element took the wounded Big Friend back to Allied territory. Escort was continued over the targets and back to Arras by 1335. The bomber escort Mustangs were down by 1455.

Several other Mustangs from the 354FS escorted a P-38 on a photo recon mission from 1132 to 1510. They made landfall over Westmund at 1230 and escorted the PRU Lightening to Dortmund, Krefeld and Geilenkirchen. Haze and smoke partially obscured the target area and the escort turned for home at 1400. Landfall out was made at 1440 over Hammstede and all eight Mustangs were home by 1510.

January 7

F.O.1499A. Major Kirby and Major Sluga led the 355th A and B Groups on a ramrod to Achern and Rastatt. Kirby's A Group picked up Second Division Liberators southwest of Brussels at 1115. The B-24s were ten minutes late but the fighters found them and provided escort to the target area where they were again separated by a thick front at 1205. The group orbited the target area until 1300 but did not re-establish contact again. They turned for home and made landfall over Knocke at 1350.

Sluga's B Group was directed by Nuthouse to pick up a lonely box of B-24s and made rendezvous at 1115 over Lille. At 1215 the B Group penetrated a thick front near Saarebourg and lost the Liberators. They continued to orbit the target area and picked up another batch of B-24s as they emerged from the front at 1300 hours. The black tailed B-24s were escorted until 1330 near Givet and everybody was down by 1457.

January 8

F.O.1503A. Major Hovde led an area support to the Trier area. Forty-four Mustangs arrived over Trier at 1030 and patrolled at 27,000 feet as far east as Frankfurt. Nuthouse vectored the 355th toward Mainz to investigate reported enemy fighters but none were found.

They left the Mainz area at 1145, withdrawing along the bomber route, and covered some Third Division B-17s on the way home. All fighters were down by 1310.

January 13

F.O.1513A. Major Graham led a ramrod from 1108 to 1540. The 355th picked up four boxes of B-24s at 1230 near Cambrai and escorted them to the Rudesheim rail bridge. The target area was reached at 1405 and a recall order was received as the bombers dropped their loads through 6/10 cover.

All group fighters landed at fields other than Steeple Morden due to extremely bad weather conditions over the base. Lieutenant Ksanznak spun out near Melbourne and was killed in the crash.

Claims: None   Losses: 1

January 14

F.O.1515A. Major Wilson led a ramrod to Hallendorf on the first of three separate missions that day. Thirty Mustangs picked up Second Division bombers at noon and escorted them to the target area. At 1340, they picked up more B-24s near Brunswick and escorted them to the Dutch Coast when escort was broken at 1500. They swept the Zwolle area, shot up several locomotives and other road targets and then returned home.

Bud Fortier took fifteen 354FS Mustangs to Cologne to escort First Division B-17s. They arrived in the Koblenz area at 1234 and swept from Koblenz to Siegen to Cologne at 30,000 feet. Nuthouse reported bandits west of Bonn but the 355th didn't find any.

Unknown to Fortier at the time, those fighters escorting the Third Division B-17s in the Berlin area were having a field day. The 357thFG bounced approximately 200 fighters of JG 300 and shot down 56 for the loss of three to set the ETO record for a single group.

Major Elder led the third effort on the day from 1235 to 1620. The mission was a sweep and Elder took his twelve Mustangs over Munster at 1400 and then to Meppen. At 1430 the 355th sighted ten Me-109s climbing to engage from 10,000 feet. Lieutenant Mills shot down two Me-109s while Elder, Woods and Decklar each nailed one before the rest dove away. Shortly afterwards, Nuthouse vectored them to an area southwest of Dummer Lake where the 12 Mustangs engaged 13 FW-190s. Eight long nose FW-190s were quickly shot down for no losses. Graham and Kemper each shot down a pair, while Decklar and Mills added singles to their earlier scores.

Gordon Graham's double made him the group's 17th air ace and one of the fastest to achieve the total of five air victories. In order, only Marshall, Olson and Brown achieved "acedom" with fewer missions.

Claims: 11 Destroyed   Losses: None

January 15

F.O.1519A. The 355th provided area support to bombers attacking the jet fighter base at Lechfeld.

Major Sluga led 26 Mustangs of the A Group while Major Graham led 27 Mustangs of the B Group from 0954 to 1230. The group met the bombers short of Lechfeld at 1225 and provided escort while the bombers bombed the airdrome. The planned strafing attack on Lechfeld was called off because of 10/10 cloud cover and a low ceiling. Instead, the two forces visited their old stomping grounds of Oberpfaffenhofen and Landsberg to come away with claims of 12-0-19. All the twin engine aircraft on **Landsberg** were painted black and believed to be Me-262s. The group left the area at 1330 and landed at 1535.

High scorers for the day were Delhammer with three and Falvey with two. Graham, Wilson, Fortier, Lake, Fussell and Gore each claimed one destroyed apiece.

Claims: 12 Destroyed   Losses: None

January 16

F.O.1521A.   Major Elder led a ramrod to Ruhland and it turned out to be one of the hairiest missions of the war for the 355th. Rendezvous was made with the B-24s at 1041 northeast of Zwolle. The target was bombed at 1115 and escort was broken over Strasbourg at 1345.

The weather, which was marginal at take off, went from bad to unbelievable and all the fighters were directed to land at Goxhill. Elder requested permission to take the entire group to Serenade on the continent but was told to try for either Manston or Goxhill. As a result five aircraft were lost after running out of fuel. Three bailed out and two made dead stick landings. Billy Hovde survived a miraculous crash when his Mustang stalled out on a dead stick final as a result of a B-24 cutting him out of the pattern. He spun out from 150 feet, completely demolishing "OLE IV" but walked away with bruises and one deep gash in his back. All pilots returned to Steeple Morden the next day.

Claims: None   Losses: 5 Mustangs, No pilots

January 17

F.O.1525A.   Stewart led a free lance to the Paderborn area with the new Executive Officer, Lieutenant Colonel William Gilchrist, flying his wing. Gilchrist took over after Marshall went home on leave and was flying Cummings' OS-V on his first mission.

The group arrived in the Munster area about 1155 and patrolled to Kassel to Eisenach to Hanover to Kassel and back to Hanover. They dropped down to strafe rail traffic between Ulzen and Salzwedel, claiming eleven locomotives and more than 43 freight and tank cars.

Several dummy aircraft were spotted on airfields near Salzwedel and Lemwerden, but no strafing was done. The 355th left the Bremen area on the deck at 1430 and came home by 1555.

January 20

F.O.1535A.   Major Wilson led a sweep from the Ruhr to Frankfurt. After making landfall near the Hague at 1032, they reached Dummer Lake at 1130. While the 354FS provided top cover, the 357th and 358FS strafed between Minden and Stadhagen. A flak train with 40mm guns was spotted near Minden so they avoided it and shot up 32 other less heavily defended locomotives. Twenty of the locomotives were parked on a siding near Diepholz but didn't have their boilers operating so few explosions were noted.

Lieutenant Masters of the 358th caught some 20mm flak near Minden and bellied in to become POW.

Claims: None   Losses: 1

January 21

F.O.1539A.   Captain Peterson led six 358FS Mustangs on a photo recon mission to the Politz area to check out the refineries. They arrived over Politz at 1325 and made two passes through heavy flak to take their pictures.

On the way home, two Me-262's bounced northeast of Steinhuder Lake at 1430. The jets made several firing passes but failed to score. They cornered Roscoe Allen but he managed to out turn the pair and the jets broke away at 1440. Allen landed in France and returned the next day.

The rest of the group provided penetration, target and withdrawal support to Heilbraun. The mission was completely uneventful and escort was broken at 1340 hours southwest of Nancy.

January 28

F.O.1563A.   Major Hovde led a boring ramrod to Dortmund. Rendezvous with the B-24s was made at 1047 over Den Helder and escort was maintained until 1320 over Ijmuiden. Four bombers were seen spinning down over Dortmund and two went down over the target due to flak but the bombing results appeared to be good. No fighters seen but the flak was intense.

January 29

F.O.1566A.   The 355th provided escort to several Second Division Liberators boxes from 1023 to 1525.

Lieutenant Colonel Stewart led A Group to escort the B-24s from Zwolle to Steinhuder Lake. Nuthouse released the A Group from escort duty at 1230 and gave them permission to free lance. They patrolled Hanover, Hamburg, Lubeck, Kiel, Bremen and Emden before leaving at 1400.

Just before turning home, Lieutenant Prothro reported rising engine temperatures and dropped below the undercast to try to reach allied lines. He was hit by flak near Geldern and badly burned before bailing out to become POW.

Major Elder led B Group and provided close escort all the way to the target at Bielefeld and back to the Zuider Zee at 1400.

Claims: None   Losses: 1

January 31

F.O.1573.   Major Haviland led the A Group off the ground in severe weather but was forced back due to fuel feed problems. Captain Minchew assumed the lead until the 355th was recalled by Nuthouse ten miles inland from Egmond.

Major Sluga led the B Group until they were also recalled at 1030 near Egmond.

February 3

F.O.1586A.   On a ramrod to Magdeburg and Berlin, the A Group was led by Lieutenant Colonel Stewart while Major Haviland led B. Sixty five P-51s took off but three came home early.

Stewart's A Group made landfall over Ijmuiden at 1025 and took the lead box of B-24s from the Zuider Zee, over the target at Magdeburg and back to Ameland where the escort was broken at 1330. Major Sluga took part of the A Group and swept the southern flank of the bomber track to Berlin. On the way back they dropped to the deck near Hamburg and strafed. Lieutenant Cummins of the 358FS was hit by flak while strafing an armored train near Ulzen and killed when his Mustang crashed and burned.

The 2ndSF spotted 30 to 40 Me-410s on the deck near Stendal at 1047 but Stewart chose to keep his force with the bombers.

The B Group picked up their B-24s over the Zuider Zee and headed for Magdeburg. Custard Green flight dropped down to strafe after the target was bombed at 1240. Near Celle they strafed an unidentified airfield obscured by a thick haze, damaging several JU-88s, and then strafed five buildings which resulted in heavy explosions.

Hoffman and Donothan landed on the continent after Hoffman's ship was damaged by flak. Both came home later that day.

Claims: None   Losses: 1

February 6

F.O.1595A.   The 355th escorted Second Division B-24s to Magdeburg from 0917 to 1400. Captain Gresham led the A Group while Major Wilson led the B Group.

The A Group made rendezvous over Ijmuiden at 1015 and the B Group joined them over the Zuider Zee about 15 minutes later. Part of the A Group swept on ahead to Steinhuder Lake, then over Magdeburg, Leipzig, Stendal, Berlin and back to Magdeburg to pick up the Libs as they came off the target. The rest of the 355th provided close escort all the way until escort was broken over Dummer Lake at 1230. Landfall out was made at 1314 over Ijmuiden at 14,000 feet.

February 9

F.O.1605A.   With Stewart at the head of the group, the 355th provided area support to Third Division B-17s. Following landfall north of Egmond at 1054, the group swept along the southern flank of the bomber track until they reached the Magdeburg and Leipzig area at 1140.

The group split up to patrol from 26,000 feet all the way to the deck where several enemy aircraft were encountered in the air and on the ground.

The 354FS scored first around 1210 when Jim Duffy blew up an FW-190 stooging around Berlin. He became the group's 18th ace and raised his combined air/ground total to ten.

A flight of the 357FS bounced some Me-109s and FW-190s near Brandenburg where Lyons shot down an Me-109 and Ludeke destroyed an FW-190.

The Second Scout Force turned in a good day's work over Magdeburg when they attacked a large force of Me-109s at 15,000 feet. Lieutenant Colonel John Brooks earned a DSC for leading his flight into the lead elements of the first 50 ship formation and personally destroyed two Me-109s. Whalen shot down a pair to raise his total to six and become the Second Scout Force's only air ace. The large German force reacted strongly but appeared disorganized after Whalen and Brooks nailed the leaders. Some of the Me-109s broke for the deck while others appeared to dogfight among themselves. In the confusion, the Scout Force's small band quietly slipped away.

Stewart took the rest of the 357FS down to strafe Kothen, Mensdorf, Burg and Brandenburg airdromes. Although the aircraft were well dispersed the squadron came away with claims of 2-0-9. Stewart and Forehand each claimed a JU-88 destroyed.

Lieutenant Taylor of the 358FS was hit by flak while strafing a locomotive near Halberstadt and died from injuries sustained during a crash landing at Liege.

After a busy day of strafing rail and road targets the group came out over Egmond at 1330.

Claims: 9 Destroyed   Losses: 1

February 10

F.O.1609A. Major Elder led a fighter bomber ramrod in which the 355th Group escorted the B-24s while carrying parafrags under one pylon and a wing tank under the other. The group rendezvoused south of Den Helder at 1215 and provided escort until the target area was reached at 1247. Because the cloud cover over the target area reached 32,000 feet, Nuthouse ordered the group to abandon the strafing mission and return to base.

On the way back, Lieutenant Stalcup had to bail out over the North Sea due to mechanical problems, about 30 miles short of England, and drowned in the ice cold water before Air Sea Rescue could reach the scene.

Claims: None   Losses: 1

February 11

F.O.1612A. Major Elder led a fighter bomber sweep to a truck park area near Steinhuder Lake. Forty-eight P-51s arrived over Dummer Lake at 1005 and let down through a solid overcast.

Rail traffic was practically nil in the area so the three squadrons bombed and strafed targets of opportunity around Celle, Ulzen and Quakenbruck area.

Landfall out was over Zandvoort at 1137.

February 14

F.O.1622A. The group went to Magdeburg and the 355th split into three forces to support the B-24s. Stewart led the A Group, Gresham led B and Wilson led the Security Force from 1007 to 1555. The A and B Groups rendezvoused with the B-24s over Ijmuiden around 1130 while the Security Force escorted the Second Scout Force to the Dresden area.

Wilson took one flight down to strafe west of Magdeburg where Wilson's ship was hit hard by a flak train. Wilson struggled back to Belgium but his Mustang went out of control on final approach and he was killed in the crash. Wilson was one of the original group pilots that started combat with the 355th. He was very well liked and respected so the loss was a blow to everyone who knew him.

Claims: None   Losses: 1

February 16

F.O.1631A. Major Sluga led a free lance support to the Munster and Hanover area. The 355th took off at 1053 and reached the patrol area around Paderborn at 1249. The target area was patrolled until 1315 when Nuthouse sent them over to Osnabruck to pick up some stray bombers. The 355th escorted some Third Division B-17s until 1445 when escort was broken over the Zuider Zee.

February 20

F.O.1642A. Lieutenant Colonel Elder led a free lance support to the Second Division B-24s attacking Nurnburg. Landfall was made at Ostend at 1047 and the group arrived south of Stuttgart at 1148. They were recalled about the same time and came back out over Ostend at 1320.

February 21

F.O.1647A. The group went on a ramrod to Nurnburg from 0906 to 1505. Lieutenant Colonel Graham led the A Group while Captain Bille assumed the lead of B. Both A and B Groups met the B-24s in the Brussels area between 1015 and 1020. The B Group stayed with the bombers all the way, while A strafed from Ansbach to Coburg, Gotha and Jena.

Graham's force clobbered a train near Wunzburg before turning for home. Costigan of the 354FS was hit hard by flak near Ansbach, pulled up to 1500 feet and then nosed into the ground before he could bail out.

B Group made Landfall at 1440 over Ostend and everybody but Costigan was back by 1505.

Claims: None   Losses: 1

Colonel Stewart was transferred to the 4th Group at Debden where be became Commanding Officer. On same day, Kinnard and Marshall returned from the States from their 30-day leaves, along with Al White.

Kinnard became the Group's third Commanding Officer, Marshall assumed the responsibility of Group Operations Officer and Gilchrist continued as Group Executive Officer.

February 22

F.O.1650A.   Major Kirby led the A Group on a ramrod while Captain Dissette led B. The two Forces met the B-24s over the Zuider Zee and took the bombers to the marshalling yards northeast of Einbeck by 1314.

A tremendous explosion was observed in the Northeim marshalling yards following the 491st BG's run. After relief from escort duties, both A and B dropped down to strafe airdromes and road traffic between Furstenau and Quackenbruck.

Lieutenant Kemper of the 354FS was hit by flak near Quakenbruck at 1355 and bellied in near Dummer Lake. Bob White destroyed two Me-410s and damaged an FW-190 on Harsleben airdrome, while the Scout Force picked up two more on the ground. Forty plus German aircraft were observed on Halberstadt airdrome but everybody was too low on fuel to stick around and do something about it.

The group came out over Egmond at 1445.

Claims: 4 Destroyed   Losses: 1

February 23

F.O.1654A.   The 355th provided free lance support to B-17s attacking targets in the area. The A Group, led by Graham, picked up the bombers over Ijmuiden and provided general support to the target area.

They left the bombers at 1130 and Graham led the 354FS down to strafe the Neuburg airdrome for claims of 3-0-8. Lieutenant Bob White survived a spectacular low altitude bailout near Ingolstadt after getting hit by flak over the airdrome to become POW.

The B Group picked up the bombers southwest of Dummer Lake and swept ahead of the bomber track to Zwikau, Nurnburg and Regensburg. The 357FS strafed some German airfields near Munich and came away with claims of 5-0-6.

Landfall out for both A and B Group was over Dunkirk around 1348.

Claims: 8 Destroyed   Losses: 1

February 24

F.O.1658A.   Captain Bille led a free lance support along the Hamburg, Brunswick and Dummer Lake line. The 355th crossed over at 1042 north of Egmond and patrolled until 1315. Nothing of interest was spotted even though Nuthouse sent the group chasing several unidentified bogies. Landfall out was made over Egmond at 1415.

February 25

F.O.1662A.   Major Kirby led a strafing mission to an area east of Fassburg. Following take off at 0800, 45 355th Mustangs made landfall over Ijmuiden at 0905.

At 1000 hours, the 355th came down through an overcast to strafe targets of opportunity. More than 40 JU-188s, plus 40 more U/I twin engine aircraft were spotted on Fassburg but intense flak moved them away to other areas surrounding the airdrome. Lieutenant Long claimed a JU-188 before pulling away.

Lieutenant Tolby shot up one Me-109 on the ground, got separated from the rest of the 358FS and bounced 20 more 109s on the way home. He picked off one under the overcast and quickly pulled up into the clouds to escape the rest.

The rest of the 355th had a field day shooting up rail and road traffic. Claims included eight locomotives and 18 goods wagons destroyed, plus 62 rail cars and 116 trucks destroyed or heavily damaged.

Claims: 3 Destroyed   Losses: None

166. OS—S and Garlich on the way out, March 1945. (Weidmann)

167. Seidl and Wright working on Cullerton's OS-X of the 357th FS. (Seidl)

168. Graham and Fortier's ships moving at Steeple Morden, late 1944. (Bennett)

169. Clay Kinnard looks over the route and tail markings of the Libs the 355th will escort, while Nicholson fiddles with the board. (Decklar, Vickery, Galer)

170. The last Malcolm hood bird in the 355th was WR-V, "Dutchess of Manhattan." The pilot was Bob White, future X-15 test pilot and vice wing commander of the 355th in Thailand. (Vickery)

171. YF-G, "Gynn Lynn," and Wagner showing typical flak gunner's view of the Mustang. (Hart, Sluga)

172. Captain Hank Bille in OS-K, "Prune Face." Bille was the 355th's last ace, scoring a double on April 20, 1945 to raise his score to six air, four ground. (Bille, Hart, Haviland)

173. 354th Intelligence Officer Sims receiving "Distinguished Order of the Purple Heart" for injuries sustained during collision with a door during a blackout. (Mendenhall, Sims)

174. Major Bud Fortier's unnamed WR-N at Steeple Morden, early 1945. (Mendenhall, Bennett)

175. Lieutenant Bill Whalen's WR-A after a crash-landing in bad weather on December 11. Whalen scored one victory with the 4th FG and five with the 2nd Scout Force to become the only weather scout ace. (Decklar)

176. A 91st BG Fortress from nearby Bassingbourn crashed and exploded near Williamson's WR-A on January 1, 1945. Sargeants Katzensky and Braun received the Soldier's Medal for the rescue of badly wounded crewchief Marza. (Galer, Braun, Baldwin)

177. Kinnard getting his local base transportation tuned up. (Minchew, Kinnard, Sims)
178. Todd, Molnar, Kemper, Beeler, Goth, Pearson, Stanton, Dick White, Silva and Duffy goofing off in English weather, early 1945. (Silva)
179. Everett Stewart's last 355th Group Mustang in January 1945. Note the extended white cowl and red border. This P-51 was given to Gordy Graham in late February. (Stewart)
180. Norm Jackson running up the throttle before releasing the brakes. (Bennett)
181. Carl Decklar's WR-H, "Dot Darlin." He scored three aerial victories, all in 1945. (Decklar)

182. Duffy explains the situation to Kinnard. Note the new-model G-suit. (Galer, Hart)
183. Captain Ed McNeff, a very capable 357th pilot, made a spectacular one-wheel landing on March 24, 1945. (Bille, Ramsdell, Drake)
184. The ubiquitous Jeep bringing 357th pilots out to the hardstand for another mission. (Weidmann, Badavas)
185. Glantz talking it over with Joe Mellen. The Mustang is WR-C, "Lil Lila Lee," in care of Julius Moseley. (Silva, Mellen)
186. Marshall, Kinnard and Al White returning to Steeple Morden for their second tour, February 1945. (Kinnard)

187. Duran Vickery rolling in WR-M, "Alabama Bound," during early winter, 1945. (Vickery)

188. Major Bud Fortier in WR-N. (Fortier, Duffy)

189. Lieutenant Colonel Sluga's YF-L, "Slugger," just before his last mission, March 21, 1945. Hit by flak near Salzbergen, Sluga hit the silk for the third and last time, becoming a POW (Sluga, Hart)

190. Marshall and crew chief Thompson's "Jane VI," badly damaged by anti-strafing poles and flak on March 22, 1945. (Marshall)

191. Delhammer's OS-B, "Super Gal II," early in the new year. (Delhammer)

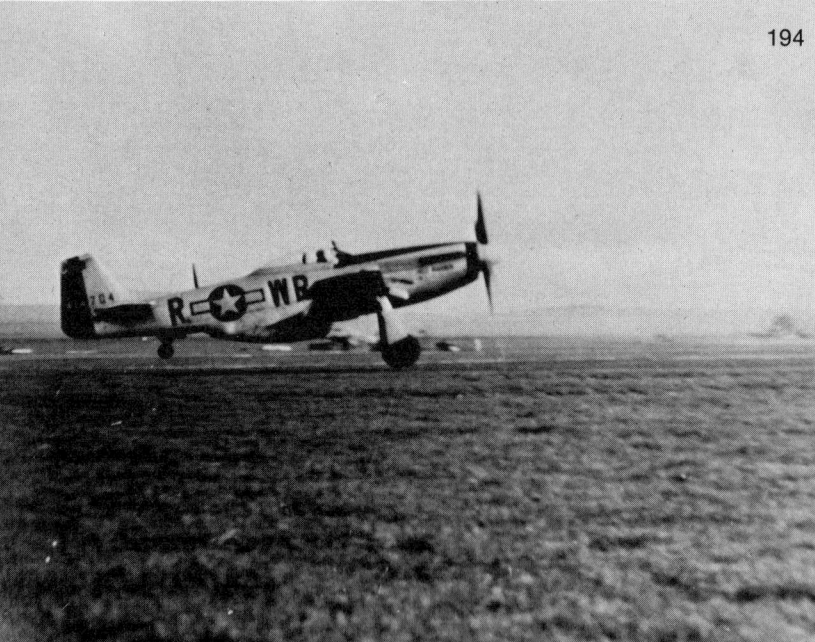

192. Lieutenant Bill Whalen was the only Scout Force pilot to achieve ace status, claiming six air and two ground by February 1945. (Dumas)

193. Chuck Hauver made ace on his last mission, flying WR-R, "Princess Pat," on December 31, 1944. (Sims, Hauver)

194. Hauver's WR-R just after he left the 355th Group to return home. (Bennett, Galer, Vickery)

195. Captain Jim McElroy on YF-S, "Big Stoop III," shortly after becoming the 358th's last air ace on February 27, 1945. (Hovde)

196. Hovde and crew chief Downing. Russian translation: "Major Hovde" on nose lettering remains from the shuttle mission. (Hovde)

197. Lieutenant Colonel "Moon" Elder scrutinizing Mitchell's handiwork, February 1945. (Hart)

198. Captain Jim Duffy, high-scoring 354th ace, and WR-Y, "Dragon Wagon," in 1945. (Duffy, Fortier)

199. Clay Kinnard leading the 355th out to cover the Rhine crossing, March 24. (Kinnard, Hess)

200. Aircraft of the 357th FS forming up for another long-range penetration. (Hart, Brennan)

February 26

F.O.1665A. The group flew a ramrod to Berlin from 1023 to 1630. Sluga led A Group while Graham led B. Both elements of the 355th made rendezvous with Second Division bombers north of Lingen at 1130 and escorted them to the target. Berlin was bombed through an overcast and escort was broken by B Group at 1455 west of Dummer Lake, while A Group stayed with the bombers until they reached the Zuider Zee at 1531.

Lieutenant Hardee of the 357FS spun in, crashed near the base in bad weather, and died from his injuries the next day.

Claims: None Losses: 1

February 27

F.O.1670A. The group flew a Ramrod to Halle and strafed on the way back. Kinnard led the A Group at the head of the 358FS and Elder led the B Group. Both forces had to orbit the rendezvous point for about 30 minutes before the B-24s showed up.

Rendezvous was made southeast of Namur and escort was continued through the target and back to Metz by 1515. While B Group continued to provide close escort, Kinnard led the 358FS down to strafe south of Plauen. Lieutenant McElroy picked up a lone DO-217 near Plauen at 1345 and shot it down to become the 355th's 19th air ace. The ceiling was down to 200 feet so the squadron pulled off the deck to return home.

Landfall out for A Group was near Ostend at 1542 and all Mustangs were back by 1640.

Claims: 1 Destroyed Losses: None

February 28

F.O.1675A. The group provided ramrod support to bombers attacking Siegen. The A Group, led by Captain Gresham, and B Group under the command of Lieutenant Colonel Graham, made rendezvous with B-24s over Ostend at 1432. A Group provided escort over the target and back to Charleroi where the bombers were left at 1540.

Graham's force strafed the railway line from Schweinfurt to Neustadt and shot up trains and road traffic before turning for home.

March 1

F.O.1678A. The group flew a Ramrod to Ingolstadt with Kinnard at the head of A Group while Sluga took B.

B Group provided close escort all the way to the target while Kinnard's bunch swept from the rendezvous point over Metz to the Amberg-Regensburg area. Several trains, trucks and flak towers were destroyed by the A Group before turning for home at 1450. The trains included flat cars carrying unassembled Me-109s and FW-190s.

Sluga's B Group engaged six Me-262s at 1320 near Ingolstadt. Lieutenants Beatty and Wilkens of the 358th and Second Scout Force, respectively, each shot down one of the jets while the rest dove away.

Jack Beckman was hit by flak while chasing one of the diving Me-262s and seen to bail out, but was never seen again.

The weather was awful over England and a total of 18 of the group Mustangs made emergency landings all over the Continent.

Claims: 2 Destroyed Losses: 1

March 2

F.O.1683A. Lieutenant Colonel Graham led a Ramrod to Magdeburg. The 355th made rendezvous with B-24s at 0930 over the Zuider Zee and escorted them to the target by 1040.

Lieutenant Allen of the 358FS had to abort at 1010 because of oxygen failure and turned for home. On the way down from 21,000 feet, he spotted fifteen bomb laden Me-109s heading southwest from Dummer Lake about 6000 feet below him and bounced. The Me-109s had light blue wing tips and dragon-like insignia on the fuselage. Allen started shooting from the six o'clock position, but none of the Me-109s even attempted to drop their bombs. Allen came away with claims 5-2-0 after running out of ammo.

The rest of the group had an uneventful day and broke escort over the Zuider Zee at 1236.

Claims: 5 Destroyed Losses: None

March 3

F.O.1690A. The group provided another ramrod support back to Magdeburg with Captain Minchew leading A and Captain Fortier leading B.

Both A and B Groups met the B-24s over the Dutch coast and took them to Magdeburg. The A Group swept ahead until 1020 when they engaged three Me-262s. Lieutenant Lyons managed to damage one before the jets outran them. Both A and B Groups orbited the target area until the bombers dropped their loads and then turned for home, making landfall over Egmond at 1155.

Ten more jets attacked the B-24s in the vicinity of Arend See and got away before the 355th had a chance to position for a bounce. Several B-17s and B-24s were observed to go down near Magdeburg and Brunswick.

March 4

F.O.1697A. Lieutenant Colonel Sluga led a ramrod to Biebelstadt but the mission was recalled just short of the target because of towering thunderstorms in the target area.

The group picked up the B-24s west of Charleville at 0900 and became part of an assorted menagerie of B-17s, B-24s, P-47s and other P-51s as Nuthouse vectored them around thunderstorms. Somewhere between Strasbourg and Stuttgart the mission was recalled and the 355th broke escort west of Metz.

March 5

F.O.1704A. Captain Dissette led a free lance sweep from 0745 to 1315. Fifty-eight group Mustangs made landfall at 0936 north of Cuxhaven and arrived in the area northeast of Hamburg at 1000 hours. Nuthouse vectored the 355th to various points near Hamburg, Hagenau, Ulzen, Steinhuder Lake and Hannover, but no enemy fighters were seen or encountered. The last flight left the Dummer Lake area at 1120 and the group made landfall north of Egmond at 1220.

March 8

F.O.1721A. On the ramrod to Betzdorf and Siegen, Captain's Gresham and Duffy led A and B Groups.

The A Group made rendezvous north of Zwolle at 1254 with the lead box of B-24s, while Gresham's B Group picked up the second box in the same general area. The target was bombed at 1358 and escort was broken over Charleroi at 1505.

One shot up Liberator with a white horizontal bar on a green rudder was picked up over Herford and escorted to the English coast.

March 10

F.O.1731A. The group flew a ramrod to support B-24s attacking the Schildesche rail viaducts. Rendezvous with the bombers was made over Liege at 1045. The A Group, led by Captain Fortier and B Group, led by Captain McElroy, took their charges to the target which was bombed through 10/10 cloud cover. Escort was broken southwest of Liege at 1315.

March 11

F.O.1738A. Kinnard led a ramrod to Kiel. Rendezvous was made over the North Sea at 1230 and the target was bombed through solid overcast at 1320. Extremely large bursts of white flak were observed several thousand feet above the formation while over the target, but no damage was done.

Escort was broken northwest of the Teschelling Islands at 1435.

March 12

F.O.1742A. Elder and Marshall led the 355th A and B Groups on a ramrod to the port area of Swinemunde.

Landfall and rendezvous was made over Nordstand at 1050 and the B-24s were escorted to the target area by 1205. Elder's Mustangs left the bombers over the target to make an uneventful sweep to the Berlin area before turning for home and crossed out north of the Hague at 1340.

Marshall's B Group continued close escort around the target and back until they reached Heligoland Island at 1355 where the rest of the 355th turned for home.

Mills, Vickery and Langley made landings in Belgium and returned the next day.

March 14

F.O.1752A. Major Kirby took the 355th on a fighter sweep through an area from Marburg to Mulhausen to Hildesheim and over to Kassel. The group crossed the bomber track south of Koblenz at 1415 and let down to sweep their assigned area. Nuthouse reported jets in the Ruhr area but no enemy fighters were spotted so the group turned for home at 1605.

March 15

F.O.1761A. The group put up 51 Mustangs for a ramrod to the Berlin area. First the A Group, led by Kinnard, picked up the bombers over the Zuider Zee at 1300. They covered the southern flank of the bomber force all the way to Berlin and back to Steinhuder Lake where escort was broken at 1530.

Marshall's B Group picked up the same force of B-24s over the German border at 1310 and provided round trip close escort until the Zuider Zee was reached at 1620.

Lieutenants Long of the 358FS and Dressler of the 357FS were hit by flak near Hanover and struggled eastward to belly land behind Russian lines. Both returned in early April.

Claims: None   Losses: 1 Mustang   No pilots

March 17

F.O.1774A. Lieutenant Colonel Kinnard and Captain Fortier led A and B Groups on a ramrod to Munster. Rendezvous was made at 1308 over the Zuider Zee and bomber escort was provided over Munster and back to Egmond where the bombers were left at 1520.

March 18

F.O.1779A. Captain's White and Gresham led A and B Groups of the 355th on a ramrod to targets near Berlin. Gresham's ships picked up B-24s at 1035 over Zandvoort several minutes after Al White's A Group rendezvoused over Alkmaar.

White took his 22 Mustangs out in front of the bomber track over Dummer Lake and swept ahead to Hanover then on to the target area of Hennigsdorf. The B-24s and Gresham's force were met north of Berlin where A Group rejoined the parade before turning for home.

Both forces broke escort near Zwolle and returned home by 1525.

March 19

F.O.1785A. The 355th provided ramrod support to B-24s attacking Neuburg, with Captain McElroy leading A and Major Kirby heading up B Group.

Kirby's B Group picked up the B-24s southeast of Metz at 1325 and McElroy's P-51s joined them over Saarburg at 1345. While A Group provided close escort, Kirby's force roamed from 12,000 to 20,000 feet to provide area support.

Captain Spencer of the 354FS bounced an Me-262 over Gelchsheim airdrome and opened fire from extreme range. The Me-262 raced away but was seen to crash and burn over Kitsingen airdrome at 1645.

Both A and B Groups broke escort west of the Rhine and made landfall over Knocke at 1705.

Claims: 1 Destroyed   Losses: None

March 20

F.O.1794A. Lieutenant Colonel Kinnard led a ramrod to Hamburg to support Third Division B-17s. The 355th made rendezvous at 1532 over the Belgian border and reached the target at 1549.

Shortly before bombs away, six Me-262s were engaged and two of the jets made repeated and persistent attacks on the 358FS's Peterson and Roberts. Both managed to avoid the passes by turning inside the jets.

Eight to ten Me-262s, believed from Nordholtz airdrome, attacked the bombers singly from various directions and altitudes. Two B-17s were seen to be hit hard by 30mm cannon fire and blow up. Elements from all three squadrons chased individual jets but were unable to close with them, even with altitude advantages.

The 355th regrouped west of the target area and escorted the B-17s back to Juist, where escort was broken at 1706.

March 21

F.O.1801A. Lieutenant Colonel Sluga led the first mission of the day when he took the group out to provide penetration support to the bombers attacking Horsten and Salzbergen airfields. The 355th rendezvoused over Egmond at 0925 and provided close escort to the targets. The 354FS stayed with the bombers while the 357th and 358FS proceeded along the bomber route to the target. They orbited the airdome at 5000 feet while they waited for the bombers to drop their loads. At the same time the heavies were dropping their loads, some 9AF Mustangs strafed the field, and one was seen to crash and explode during his run.

By the time Sluga led his force across the field, the Jerries were totally alert and caught Sluga with a burst of flak in his wing. Sluga regained altitude and started back home but "Slugger" caught fire and Sluga had to go over the side for the third time in his career to become POW.

No enemy aircraft were seen and everybody else rejoined the bombers until escort was broken at 1105 over Egmond.

Claims: None   Losses: 1

F.O.1806A. Lieutenant Colonel Marshall led a ramrod to the Muldheim area with 35 Mustangs for the second mission of the day. The 355th picked up the bombers over Schouen Island at 1720 and 24,000 feet. Muldheim was bombed at 1800 and escort was broken at 1825 northeast of Antwerp. Except for a rocket contrail seen at 35,000 feet over the Hague, the mission was entirely uneventful.

March 22

F.O.1810A. Both A and B Groups provided ramrod support to Second Division B-24s attacking Kitzingen airdrome.

Captain Bille's B Group provided close escort on penetration, target and withdrawal after making rendezvous north of Verdun at 1130. A heavy concentration of bombs was observed on the airfield as well as large secondary explosions, believed to be oil storage dumps. Bille's 28 Mustangs broke escort over Aachen at 1450 and returned home with unfired guns.

Marshall's A Group also made rendezvous at 1130 and provided penetration support until 1200. They departed the bombers at noon and swept ahead to the target. They strafed Memmingen, Wurzburg and Kitzingen to destroy 12 Me-262s, He-111s, FW-190s and Me-109s, plus damage nine more. Lieutenant Dave Tuholski was hit by flak over Wurzburg and bellied his burning P-51 in at the edge of the field where he was rescued by German troops. Captain Silva claimed three and F/O Falvey picked up two for the high scores.

Anti-strafing poles, at least 20 feet tall and heavy flak made strafing particularly hazardous. Marshall was again clobbered by flak and bellied "JANE VI" in at Steeple Morden for his fourth belly landing of the war.

Claims: 12 Destroyed   Losses: 1

March 23

F.O.1819A. Captain Dissette led a fighter sweep from 0839 to 1340. Twenty-six P-51s of the 355th patrolled the Bremen -Hannover - Kassel - Giessen area after making landfall over Den Helder at 0943.

Nuthouse vectored Dissette up and down the Rhine but nothing of interest was encountered except some red nosed Mustangs and Thunderbolts near Frankfurt. The group left the area at 1210 and crossed out over Schouen Island at 1245.

March 24

The 355th flew three separate missions to provide top cover for the Rhine Airborne invasion. The patrol area was bounded by Furstenau, Osnabruck, Munster and Bergstein.

F.O.1828A. Lieutenant Colonel Elder led the early mission from 0556 to 1110. Landfall in was made at 0703 over Egmond and the uneventful patrol was broken at 0950. The 357FS and 358th crossed back over at Egmond at 1015.

F.O.1828A. Lieutenant Colonel Kinnard led 28 P-51s on the second patrol from 1007 to 1601. Nuthouse vectored the group all over the patrol area but the only German fighters spotted were already being chased by other Mustang groups. The 355th departed the patrol area at 1450, crossed over Egmond at 1510 and touched down by 1601.

F.O.1828A. Captain Minchew led the last patrol after leading 23 Mustangs away from the base at 1457. They patrolled from 20,000 feet to 15,000 feet to Kassell to Hamm and Minden before leaving the area at 1750. An unidentified aircraft was seen to blow up over Rheims at 1630 but the patrol was otherwise uneventful.

March 26

F.O.1843A. Lieutenant Colonel Marshall led a ramrod to Merseburg after receiving the field order at the same time as the scheduled takeoff. The mission was fouled up from the beginning and stayed that way. After making landfall over Boulogne, Nuthouse reported the B-24s to be near the rendezvous point 150 miles to the east.

Marshall quickly plotted an intercept course but miserable weather precluded any hope of contact so the group swept Gotha and Erfurt instead. After an uneventful sweep they made landfall over Walcheren Island at 1445 and were down by 1545.

March 28

F.O.1849A.   Lieutenant Colonel Graham led the group on a ramrod to Berlin. Forty-nine P-51s met First Division B-17s at 0845 southwest of Bonn. The B-17 boxes were scattered, not in proper order and flying poor formation, so the briefed escort was impossible. Nuthouse vectored the 355th to various points on the bomber track until they finally settled on the last three boxes and stuck with them from 1000 hours to noon. At 1200 hours, escort was broken southwest of Kassel and landfall was made at 1245 over Overflakke.

March 30

F.O.1863A.   Graham took 47 Mustangs on a ramrod to Wilhemshaven. After making rendezvous north of Groningen at 1315, they supported the B-24s through the target and back to Juist where they broke escort at 1413.

Graham went back to the Danish peninsula and continued to patrol. Unfortunately, they had orders not to strafe the area and had to pass up many trains and trucks before turning home for good at 1605.

March 31

F.O.1874A.   The 355th provided close escort to B-24s attacking Nienhagen with Lieutenant Colonel's Kinnard and Elder at the head of A and B Groups.

Rendezvous occurred at 0815 over Egmond and A Group escorted the bombers until shortly before the target. Several Me-262s were spotted and chased near the Initial Point but not caught. The A Group returned to escort duties until landfall over Egmond at 1043.

The B Group had an uneventful escort from Zwolle to the target and back to Egmond at 1045.

The Second Scout Force successfully engaged several Me-262s and Me-163s near Brunswick. Castleberry destroyed one Me-262 and Dick Nyman scored heavily on another but only claimed it as damaged.

Claims: 1 Destroyed   Losses: None

April 2

F.O.1882A.   Lieutenant Colonel Graham and Captain Dissette led A and B Groups on a ramrod which was recalled due to weather.

The A Group made rendezvous over the North Sea and swept ahead to patrol from Husum to Schleswig to Rensberg and Flensberg before recall at 1630.

The B Group met the bombers at 1455 and provided escort until recall at 1605. A B-24 with a yellow tail and black vertical stripes fired several times at 355th Mustangs but no one was hurt.

April 3

F.O.1887A.   The 355th went on a ramrod to Kiel with Marshall at the head of A and Bille leading B. They met the Third Division B-17s at 1645 west of Heligoland and escorted them to the target. Kiel was bombed through breaks in the cloud cover at 1725 and escort continued until 1830. No enemy fighters were seen and landfall was made over Ording at 1805.

April 4

F.O.1896A.   The 355th flew a free lance support to Parchim, Perleburg and Kaltenkirchen airdromes. First Kinnard, then Duffy led the A Group while Elder led B.

Both forces made landfall north of Egmond at 0806 hours and arrived in the target area around 0915. While waiting for the bombers, Duffy's 25 Mustangs patrolled from 9,000 to 24,000 feet and Elder's force split to work the north and south areas separately.

Before the bombing, one flight of 354FS P-51s dropped below a 1000 feet ceiling cloud base to look over Ludwiglust airdrome and were surprised by several long nose FW-190s. Lieutenant Goth was killed in a head on pass and Truell crashed and exploded when he tried to split-S too close to the ground. Gray was hit by flak near the airdrome and seen to crash and explode south of

Ludwiglust at 0900. Three losses on this day made April 4, 1945 the second worst day for losses for the 354FS during the war. Al White shot one of the FWs down before the fast moving Germans climbed back into the clouds.

Another flight of the 354th strafed some sea planes on the way out. John Molnar destroyed two while Hixson destroyed one and Bancroft damaged a couple. The A Group made landfall north of Egmond at 1145.

The B Group encountered and bounced four long nosed FW-190Ds near Leipzig and quickly shot down three. Long shot down two while Cullerton got a single. Cullerton's kill raised his air total to five and made him the group's 20th air ace although he was already one of the 355th's top strafers at this time.

Shortly afterward, Cooper damaged a strange but impressive fighter with two in-line engines, one pushing and the other pulling. The fighter was later identified as the new DO-335. Riffle also damaged a twin jet AR-234 as the B Group turned for home.

German aircraft were also spotted at Rechlin, Hagenou and Dedelstord airdromes on the way back but everybody was too low on fuel to do anything about it.

Claims: 7 Destroyed   Losses: 3

April 5

F.O.1903A.   Major Kirby led 50 P-51s on a ramrod to Eger. Because of very bad weather only one squadron made rendezvous with the Second Division bombers.

Following rendezvous at 1050 the escort was continued under extremely poor visibility conditions over the target and back until 1150 when they lost contact with the B-24s. They swept along the withdrawal track until landfall over Zeebrugge but did not make contact again.

Other elements of the group were vectored by Nuthouse toward the bombers but they failed to make contact. One flight scouted Neuberg, Ottingen and Ingolstadt airdromes looking for jet fighters. More than 80 aircraft were spotted but no jets were seen.

McDonnell of the 354FS was hit by German flak after straying too close to Buren, at 1440 hours, while coming back from an emergency field. He crashed and burned near a canal in Holland.

Claims: None   Losses: 1

April 6

F.O.1909A.   Captain Gresham led 40 Mustangs on a ramrod to Stafzfurt. The group made landfall north of Knocke and rendezvous with the B-24s south of Aachen. Following rendezvous at 0824, the bombers dropped their loads at 0945 and escort was broken at 1110 at Rheine. Landfall out was made south of Knocke and everybody was down safely by 1245.

April 7

F.O.1914A.   The A and B Groups of the 355th provided ramrod support to B-24s attacking Duneberg and Krummel. Lieutenant Colonels Kinnard and Graham led A and B respectively and rendezvous for both forces took place over the Zuider Zee between 1125 and 1138.

Six Me-262s and an HE-280 attacked the B-24s short of the Initial Point at 1250. Numerous FW-190s and Me-109s joined the attack during the bomb run. The tactics of the German fighters were to attack in several small groups from five to seven o'clock high, on the trailing boxes then sweep below and hit the lead squadrons in a climb.

The presence of the 479th Group on the opposite side of the bomber track from the 355th created heavy congestion at the point of attack and the two groups had problems staying out of each other's way.

Despite the problems of air traffic control around the bombers, Kouche and Finnesey of the 358FS damaged two ME-262s, Mellen and Beeler of the 354FS each destroyed an FW-190D and Vineyard shot down an ME-109K. The 357FS scratched when Forehand shot down an Me-109 and Reiff, Griswold and Hartzog shared an Me-262.

During the penetration a P-51 with German markings was observed, a B-24 was seen to shoot down an Me-262 and a 56th Group Jug shot down an Me-109. At the target, an FW-190 shot down two B-24s and was in turn shot down by them.

The group made landfall north of Husum over the Danish coast and broke escort over the North Sea. Mills and Plowman disappeared while penetrating cloud cover on the way home and were never heard from again.

Claims: 5 Destroyed   Losses: 2

April 8

F.O.1918A. The 355th provided ramrod support to the fourth box of B-24s attacking Roth airdrome. Lieutenant Colonel Marshall's A Group made rendezvous at 1125 over Dornstadt. The target was bombed at 1220 and escort was broken at 1240 west of Neustadt.

Marshall's force then swept south to the Oberphaffenhofen and Augsburg area where Graham and Decklar caught and nailed three Me-109s over Oberphaffenhofen. Cullerton detached his flight and led them down to strafe Ansbach Airdrome where Weidmann destroyed one Me-109 and damaged another, but both he and Cullerton were hit hard by flak. Cullerton bailed out of his burning P-51 and landed OK but was captured later by the SS. His captor shot him in the stomach and left him to die, but Cullerton was saved when some civilians took him to a hospital and doctor's care. Weidmann made an emergency landing at field A84 on the continent. The rest of the A Group left the area at 1330 and made landfall over knocke at 1440. Captain Dissette's B Group made rendezvous south of Koblenz near Mainz and escorted the B-24s over Roth at 1220. After breaking escort near Koblenz, Lieutenant Brown of the 358FS destroyed two twin engine aircraft on an unidentified field near Neustadt.

Excellent bombing was observed at Roth with all the bombs hitting south of the runway, causing two large secondary explosions. Me-262s were sighted in wooded dispersal areas on Landsberg and Memmingen airdromes and significant concentrations of light flak guns were also observed around all the airfields.

Claims: 4 Destroyed   Losses: 1

April 9

V.O.1929A. Lieutenant Colonel Graham led a ramrod to Memmingen to strike at the Me-262s spotted on that field the day before. Nuthouse advised Graham that Memmingen and other airdromes could be strafed after the bombers were through.

Rendezvous was made at 1630 in the vicinity of Strasbourg and the target was bombed from 1721 to 1725. Graham then took the 354FS down to strafe Memmingen airdrome. Although no jets were destroyed, they came away with claims of 7-0-1. Graham destroyed two HE-111s while Langley, Barnhart, Al White, Jabara and Falvey each destroyed one.

The other two squadrons continued escort until 1815, near Ludwigshafen. Two flights of the 358FS went back to strafe Hailfingen airdrome and came out with claims of 7-0-5. Bill Lynch destroyed an HE-111 and an Me-110 while Fees, Patrinely, McCollom and Lanier each destroyed an Me-110. Patrinely and Knutty shared another Me-110.

Claims: 14 Destroyed   Losses: None

April 10

F.O.1936A. Major Kirby and Lieutenant Colonel Graham led A and B Groups of the 355th on a ramrod to Rechlin airdrome. The two forces made rendezvous north of Terschelling with the 20th Combat Wing of B-24s.

Captain Gresham spotted an Me-262 near Lubeck at 1425 and chased him for 25 minutes before closing enough to register hits on the right engine. The Me-262 managed to get away so Gresham's flight turned back and rejoined the group at 1510 near Wittenburg.

Rechlin was bombed at 1500 and several flights each from A and B Group dropped down to strafe while the rest of the 355th continued close escort. The strafers worked over Rechlin for abouty 40 minutes and claimed 17-0-22. There were all kinds of aircraft on the ground including captured B-24s and P-38s, Me-109s, Me-410s, HE-111s, JU-52s, JU-188s, JU-88s and DO-217s. Those claiming doubles included Graham, Jabara, Falvey, Fletcher, Garlich and Watkins. Hixson, Stanton, Galer, Misner, Burnet and Kirby each claimed singles.

On the way home one B-17 was seen burning east of Ludwiglust and another was spotted in similar trouble northeast of Stendal. Escort was broken at 1635 and everybody landed by 1730.

The 339th scored 105, the 78th picked up 52 and the 56th contributed another 45 destroyed to contribute to the record total of more than 280 German aircraft destroyed in one day. The day's total shattered the tally of 177 set on 9/5/44.

Claims: 17 Destroyed   Losses: None

April 11

F.O.1944A. The group provided ramrod cover to Regensburg with Captain Dissette leading A and Captain Al White leading B. Rendezvous was made over Koblenz at 1203, the target was bombed at 1334 and escort was broken over Frankfurt at 1445. After an uneventful mission, the A Group came out over Knocke at 1545 while B Group made landfall over Blankenberg at 1608.

The 339th ignored the no strafing directive by 8th Fighter Command to claim 118 and raise their two day total to 223 German aircraft on the ground. For one day they became the leading strafing group in the ETO.

April 13

F.O.1962.   Lieutenant Colonel Kinnard led a ramrod to Hagenow airdrome. The 355th picked up the sixth box of First Division Forts north of Heligoland around 1505.

As landfall was made near Husum, Marshall alerted Kinnard over the R/T that he could see 50 plus German aircraft on Husum airdrome. Following bombs away and withdrawal, Marshall led the 354FS away from the bomber stream southwest of Hanover and returned to Husum.

The 354th destroyed the flak positions on the first run and made seven passes on the field to claim 37-0-17. At least 35 individual fires were counted so the total claims for destroyed aircraft were probably conservative. Those claiming three or more destroyed included Mellen (5), Vickery (5), Marshall (4), Silva (3) and Duffy (3). The total bag for the day was the highest individual squadron total for the war in the 355th but, even more importantly, there were no losses.

The 358th and 357th Squadrons strafed Schleswig, Flensburg and Leck airdromes to record combined claims of 32-0-14. Twelve of the claims for damaged aircraft were brand new HE-111s parked wing tip to wing tip on Leck Airdrome. The 357th hammered the 111s but none of them would burn so they went to Schlewsig to help out the 358th. The two squadrons pounded the airdrome for claims of 29-0-1. Those claiming two or more included Kinnard (2-1/2), Gore (2-1/2), Tullock (4), Cooper (3), Nicodemus (2), Garlich (2), Iglesias (2) and Finnesey (2). Warner Schlect, a 358th pilot, was shot down by flak and crash landed successfully west of Rendsburg airdrome.

Curran led Green flight of the 358th down to shoot up Flensburg on the way home and destroyed an FW-190 to give him two for the day. Parks destroyed another one and also blew up an Me-109.

In all, the 355th destroyed 69 and damaged another 31 to set a new group record. The 354thFS came back in perfect formation but buzzed the field to let the ground crews know that they had a good day. The group was back in the ground scoring lead for the duration.

The 56thFG scored 90 and Lieutenant Murphy set a new record with 10 on the ground. The 56th now had a solid lead over the 4th in the race for top honors.

Claims: 69 Destroyed   Losses: 1

April 16

F.O.1997A.   Lieutenant Colonel Elder led a ramrod to Traunstein, first to escort the Second Division Libs, then to strafe the target after the bombing. The bombers were met over Trier at 1405 and escort was carried to the target and back to Gunsbert around 1555. Ten Me-262s were reported north of Munich but were not spotted so Elder took his 62 Mustangs southeast of Regensburg for some strafing. Elder's 357FS strafed three fields in the region of Linz for claims of 29-0-36 for the loss of two. Lake was seen to spin in and explode over Eferding and Long was forced to crash land just short of the Russian lines to become POW. Those claiming three or more included Elder (4), Bille (4), Frank Elliot of the 2ndSF (3) and Cooper (3).

Dissette led the 358FS to Straubing for claims of 18-0-6 for the loss of four pilots and five Mustangs. Lynch and McCollum bellied their ships in to become POW although Lynch later escaped. Dissette and Rogers were shot down and managed to evade capture. Donathan was severely wounded in the leg but managed to belly in on the friendly side of the front line and recovered from his wounds. Those claiming three or more on Straubing were Marsh (5), Seeley (4), McCollom (4) and Lynch (3).

Graham led the 354FS over Eger and Gog to add to the group tally. The squadron claimed 23-0-6 with top honors going to Graham (3), Mellen (3) and Fletcher (3).

The 355th left the target areas around 1700 and crossed out over Ostend at 1840. While the group had set a new 355th record for a single day, it was far be low strafing totals recorded by the 4th, the 353rd and the 78th.

Under the command of John Landers, the 78thFG claimed over 160 German aircraft destroyed on the ground to set the ETO record for a single day. The total was reduced 30 plus to 125 but the record stood. Captain Ammon of the 339thFG destroyed 11 to set the final ETO record for individual strafing kills.

Claims: 70 Destroyed   Losses: 6 (2 pilots evaded)

April 17

F.O.2006A.   Lieutenant Colonel Graham led a ramrod to Knocehlavy, Czechoslovakia. The group put 52 P-51s in the air, made contact with their assigned B-24s over Wurzburg at 1410 and reached the target at 1503. Most of the 355th stayed with the bombers until they reached Pulda at 1605, when they departed for home.

Flights from the 354th, 357th and 358FS hit the deck to look for juicy targets but did not find any. Gresham destroyed an HE-177 on Cheb airdrome and damaged three that wouldn't burn. McNeil of the 357th destroyed an unidentified twin on Eger and damaged an Me-109. Graham and O'Neil damaged three Me-262s which also wouldn't burn and got the hell out after the first pass over Pilzen.

All other airdromes looked over by 355th pilots had been thoroughly worked over by other groups. At Pilzen, Budajovice, Eger and Marienburg Airdromes, only 27 out of the 172 observed aircraft were not burning or burned out hulks. After the mission, Clay Kinnard remarked, "Sure like to shoot up airplanes but hate to lose good guys at this stage of the game."

Claims: 2 Destroyed   Losses: None

April 18

F.O.2017A.   Lieutenant Colonel Gilchrist led a boring ramrod to the Zweisel and Passau marshalling yards. After arriving at the rendezvous point at 1245, the group swept to Nuremburg and back to Mannheim before they met their tardy B-24s at 1300. The target was bombed at 1400 and results appeared to be good. Escort was broken at 1503 over Grailsheim.

April 20

F.O.2039A.   Lieutenant Colonel Kinnard led on an area support to Second Division bombers in the Prague area. After making landfall over Schowen Island at 0950 they arrived over Prague at 1127.

Kinnard spotted dust rising from Letnany airdrome but the German fighters stopped their engines as the 355th approached. Kinnard craftily circled away from the area for about fifteen minutes and then took the 357th and 358FS in low. They caught about 12 Me-109s forming up over the airdrome and claimed 8-0-4 for no losses. In the encounter, both Kinnard and Bille shot down two while Seeley, Parks and Iglesias got singles. Lieutenants Snook and Knutty shared the last one. Later, Seeley's and Park's kills were awarded as "probables." Captain Bille's pair raised his air total to six and made him the group's last air ace in the last combat action for the 355th FG during World War II.

The 354thFS swept the Pilzen - Munich area from 1120 until reforming around Prague at 1345.

Although the airfields at Hostivice, Kbely and Letnany had more than 230 aircraft, including Me-262s, the group was forbidden to strafe. The German pilots, described as "agressive but inexperienced" would probably have lived had they not taken off to challenge the 355th over Letnany. More than a few pilots, including Kinnard, wished that they had chosen to stay on the ground at this stage of the war.

The 355th Mustangs came out over Schowen Island at 1522. Except for Barnhart and Kaplan, who landed on the Continent, all the pilots were down by 1605.

Claims: 8 Destroyed   Losses: None

April 21

F.O.2084A.   Lieutenant Colonel Marshall and Captain Duffy led A and B Groups of the 355th on a ramrod to the Regensburg - Salzburg area. Both sections were guided by Nuthouse to rendezvous from 0940 to 1044 near Frankfurt. Continuous and heavy cloud formations caused the bomb groups to split up while climbing to alititude. Marshall and Duffy split the group into eight ship sections to cover all the various unescorted B-24 formations.

The escort altitudes ranged from 7,000 to 18,000 feet in the Frankfurt to Regensburg trip. Only excellent work by Nuthouse made rendezvous and escort practical. One B-24 was seen to go down over Regensburg at 1028, the target was bombed at 1030 and escort was broken over Wurzburg at 1115.

April 25

F.O.2084A.   Majors Fortier and Gresham led the last ramrod of the war for the 355th Fighter Group. The mission to support the Second Bomb Division over Hallein, Germany was totally uneventful except for flak over the target.

Rendezvous was accomplished at 0920 over Wittlich, southwest of Weisbaden, and the target was reached at 1056. The bombers unloaded at 24,000 to 26,000 feet and appeared to clobber the rail yards. Escort was broken at 1220 over Dormstadt.

Quite a few German aircraft were observed on the Erding and Genacker airdromes plus several Me-262s on an autobahn north of Munich. The no strafing rule was in effect however, and the group came home with unfired guns on the last mission of the war.

201. Stewart and WR-S "Sunny VII" in February 1945. Shortly after this photo was taken, Stewart moved on to the 4th FG while Kinnard took over the 355th. (Marshall)

202. Silva's WR-B, "My Catherine S" in the spring of '45. (Silva)

203. Walt Gresham, 358th FS Operations Officer, 1945. (Hovde, Gresham)

204. Kawa and Bille in OS-K, "Prune Face," near the end of the war. (Bille, Weidmann)

205. Gordy Graham leading the 354th troops in the spring of 1945. WR-F, "Down for Double," was inherited from Ev Stewart in February. (Graham)

206. Gerry Thompson, crew chief of WR-B, putting the final checks in the cockpit before another mission. (Thompson)

207. Wiedmann running carbon deposits out of OS-H in friendly skies. (Wiedmann)
208. Misner lost power while bringing Cullerton's OS-X in on final. Watkins was later given the repaired ship as OS-N and renamed it "Fickle Fanny." (Marshall)
209. OS-K being prepared for another Bille ride in 1945. (Wiedmann)
210. Duran Vickery and WR-L, "Ann Anita." (Vickery)
211. Duffy on the wing of "Dragon Wagon" around the first week of April. (USAF)
212. Kinnard's WR-A soaking up rare English sunshine. Note new rocket launchers under the wings. (Galer)

213. The last OS-R of John Elder, 357th CO, just before the April 16 mission when he added four more to his total score on the group's biggest day. (Hart)
214. Marshall's "Jane VI" bellied in after severe flak damage on March 22's strafing mission. The left horizontal stabilizer is also gone. (Dumas)
215. Duffy's "Dragon Wagon" rolling out of the 354th area. (Galer)
216. General Spaatz presents Brooks, 2nd Scout Force CO, with the DSC for outstanding leadership over Magdeberg on February 9. (Marshall)
217. Kinnard, Spaatz, Gilchrist, Doolittle and Stewart at Steeple Morden in late March. (Marshall)

218. Weidmann looking over a very close brush with death in April 1945. German flak was the dominant risk to 355th pilots at this time. (Weidmann)

219. Hall, Marshall, Stewart, Auton and Spaatz enjoy "Little Yank" at Station F-122. Note the diversity of non-regulation foot-war. Proof that RHIP! (Marshall)

220. Watkins flying the restored OS-X, "Miss Steve," after Cullerton jumped out of another '51 on April 8. (Weidmann)

221. Galer in "Cherraine," coded WR-Q. (Galer)

222. Sergeants Braun, Thompson, Katzinski, Bruno and crew chief Gerry Thompson in front of WR-B. Thompson often "loaned" the 354th ship to Marshall but didn't always get it back in good condition. (Thompson)

223. Second Scout Force exec, Frank Elliot, shooting the bull with his crew after the April 16 strafing mission. (Hart)

224. Lieutenant Roscoe Allen nailed five with two probables on March 2, but his combat film was fogged so the claims were disallowed. A real heart-breaker. (Hovde)

225. Vic Iglesias destroyed four confirmed in OS-A, "Jersey Bounce," including perhaps the last Me-109 claimed by the group, on April 20. (Weidmann)

226. Bert Marshall, 355th air exec, and WR-B, "Jane VII," in mid-45. (Marshall)

227. Crew chief Billy Mitchell and squadron commander John Elder in front of OS-R. The 357th insignia "Licking Dragon" lives today on 357th TFS A-10s.

228. Marshall and Ranger brother-in-law, Joe Hilsman, going for a ride in the base two-seater. (Hilsman)

229. By September Bert Marshall was group CO. He jokingly commented that he had more concern teaching a few 355th fighter pilots how to fly the B-26 than combat against the Luftwaffe. (Marshall)

230. The last and only "Jane" to survive the war. Number VII getting the once-over by 404th FG pilots in Straubing, Germany. (Houston via Ethell)

231. Duffy leading Fortier for a joyride near V-E Day. (Duffy, Gess, Fortier)

232

233

234

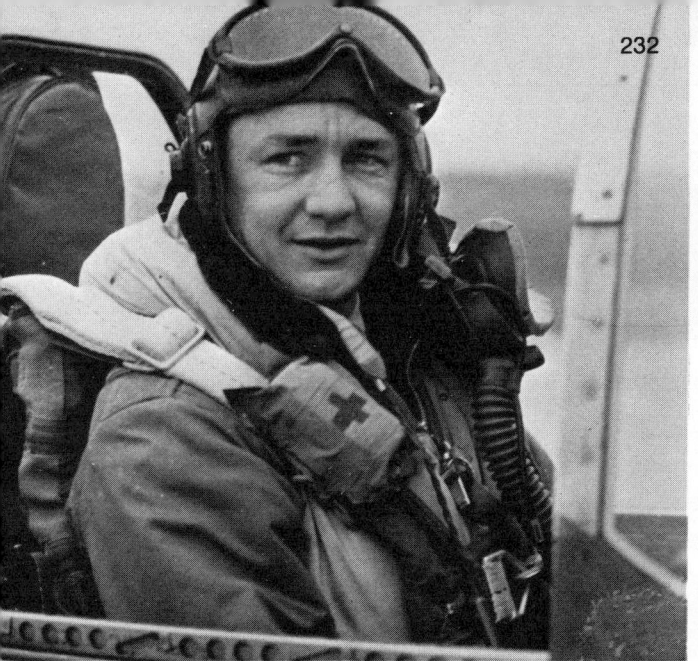

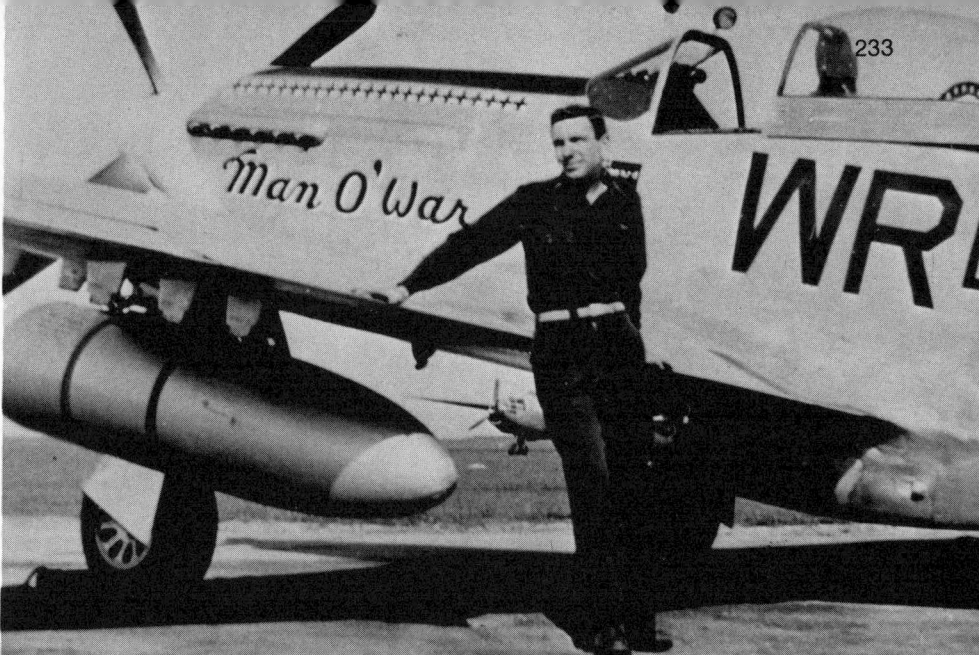

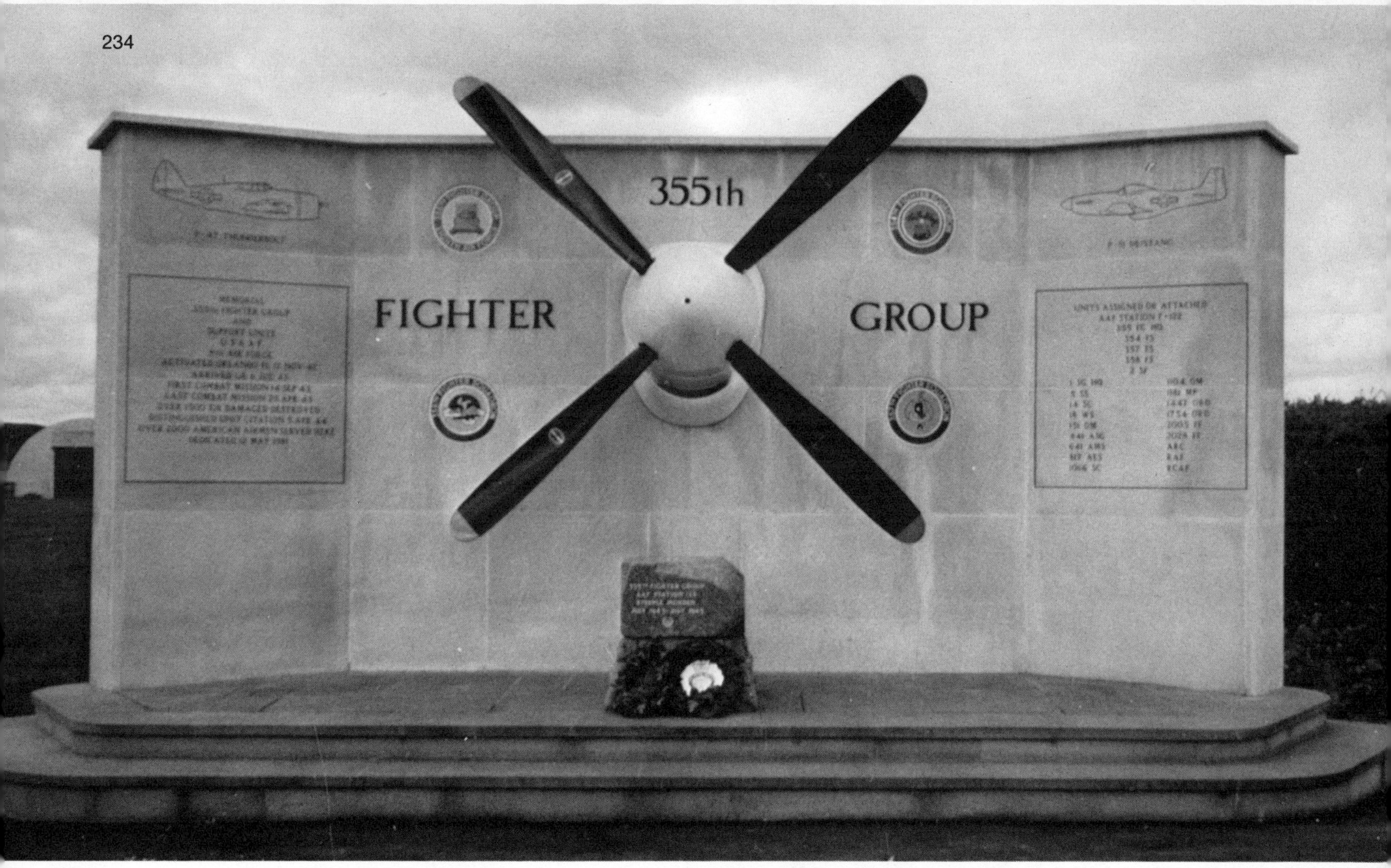

232. Bill Gilchrist, 355th air exec, in 1945. (Dumas)

233. Lieutenant Langley leaning on Kinnard's last "Man O' War." (Kinnard, Vickery)

234. The familiar white nose of a 355th Mustang is mounted on this memorial at Steeple Morden, England. Dedicated in May 1980, this striking testament is lasting tribute to the men of the 355th who died in WW II. (Graham)

235. The 355th's second war came 30 years after the first. This F-105D, "The Ripper," flew with the 354th TFS out of Takhli, Thailand, in 1970. (USAF)

236. Reformed late in the Indochina War and redeployed with A-7As, the wing flew the Corsair II until 1976. (USAF)

237. Just like old times — almost. The 355th returned to Republic aircraft over 40 years after receiving P-47s. Now flying the Thunderbolt II at Davis-Monthan AFB, Arizona, the wing has maintained combat readiness in far-flung places. This A-10 carried Maverick missiles and Rock Eye bombs during a flight in Korea during 1977. (USAF)

SUMMARY OF COMBAT OPERATIONS, WW II
SEPTEMBER 14, 1943 - APRIL 25, 1945

The 355th Fighter Group ended the war with an interesting and unique record as the third highest scoring group in the Eighth Air Force and the top strafing outfit. While four 8th AF fighter groups finished ahead of the 355th in total air-to-air victories (56th, 357th, 4th and 352nd), none surpassed the 355th in terms of harrassment of the German war machine on the ground and only two had higher losses to German flak.

Following the end of hostilities the United States Army Air Force re-evaluted the position of awarding ground scores on an equal basis with air to air victories in aces' totals. The author has no quarrel with the decision but would like to point out at least two major results of bringing fighter aircraft to ground level.

First, the fighter aircraft of the Allies, particularly the far-ranging Mustangs and Lightnings, contributed substantially to the total disruption of German transportation. While the Germans were successful in their efforts at dispersing a major segment of their industrial base to make it less vulnerable to strategic air attacks, the offsetting penalty was increased reliance on road, rail and barge transport to support logistics requirements. Fighter pilots shot up everything in sight and imposed severe restrictions on movements of men and material.

Second, and crucial to the Allied air offensive in the west, was the harrassment of the German Air Force on the ground. In the words of General Adolf Galland, chief of the Luftwaffe fighter arm; "Regarding your question about the effects of ground strafing of the 8th and 9th AF fighters. Yes indeed, the fighter pilots, fighter operations and logistics as well as the ground support did suffer very seriously under these actions. Trev (Constable) has repeatedly described how important it was that the US escort fighters were allowed and ordered to change more and more from the defensive protection role to the active offensive one. By doing so, important Luftwaffe operational mistakes in the Battle of Britain were avoided. Based upon my own "combat advises"(which were modified or supplemented according to the operational air situation at least once a month), our Fighter Divisions did make all efforts to assemble strongest "combat formations" consisting of several fighter wings in order to attack the big bomber formations with a local and temporary air superiority. The offensive tactics and especially the advanced strafing of the US fighters did make this intention more and more difficult, and finally impossible. As a natural consequence the morale of the German fighter pilots was increasingly affected and degraded, when they were already attacked in taxiing, take-off, or in climbing and assembling. Mostly this was the case below and in advance of the patterns of the big USAAF incursions. Therefore, we were forced to base the fighter wings either more to the north or the south, respectively, and to take off earlier for climbing and assembling. External jettison tanks were needed (Goring tried in vain to limit the dropping only to extreme emergency situations); also, our own temporary very successful assault fighters (**Sturmjager**) tactics with our own fighter cover were more and more handicapped by the US fighters. The strafing of our fighter bases induced the fighter groups and squadrons to move to semi-prepared airfields and strips. This was a real difficult job considering the complexity of all necessary services. The dispersion of the planes on these airfields and a maximum camouflage there was also becoming mandatory.

"All these facts resulted in higher efforts, extended time for the assembly of strong fighter combat units in sufficient altitude. Very often the offensive aggresivity and the strafing of the US fighters prevented the intention of the Luftwaffe fighters and their guiding fighter divisions. As a consequence the morale of the German fighters in general (only a few cases were the exception) decreased from day to day, permanently. The time to split "S" and dive down (**Abschwung**) was present. The best answer and countermeasure would have been to have the Me-262 flown only by the best fighters we had at that time."

(Quoted with permission from General Galland and Colonel Toliver from correspondence dated 28 March, 1984. The author gratefully acknowledges their consideration and thoughtful replies).

Whether fighter pilots credited with destruction of five or more aircraft on the ground in German skies should be accorded the designation of ace is not for this author to decide. Unquestionably, they deserve all the praise they can get for a crucial job well done and my hat is off to each and every one.

355th Fighter Group Statistical Summary

Aircraft

Unit	German Aircraft Destroyed			355th Fighter Group Losses				
	Air	Ground	Total	Air	Flak	Ops	Unk	Total
355 HQ	16.0	18.5	34.5	0	2	0	0	2
354 FS	133.0	197.0	330.0	8	20	22	5	55
357 FS	110.5	173.5	283.5	10	30	21	4	65
358 FS	80.5	117.5	198.0	10	27	14	7	58
2 SF	12.0	4.0	16.0	0	0	2	1	3
Total	**352.0**	**510.5**	**862.5**	**28**	**79**	**59**	**17**	**183**

Pilots

Unit	Lost in Action				Returned		
	POW	KIA	MIA	Total	Evaded	Rescued	Total
355 HQ	1	0	0	1	1	0	1
354 FS	18	24	6	48	6	1	7
357 FS	21	27	3	51	11	3	14
358 FS	18	28	3	49	8	1	9
2 SF	0	1	2	3	0	0	0
Total	**58**	**80**	**14**	**152**	**26**	**5**	**31**

POST V-E DAY

After the Germans surrendered on May 8, 1945, the 355th settled into a semi-state of peacetime activities. On July 3, 1945, a group of 355th personnel left Steeple Morden by motor convoy as an advanced party to prepare for the move to Gablingen, Germany. By July 18, most of the 355th Fighter Group had made the move and the 355th became part of the Army of Occupation.

On April 15, 1946, the group moved again to Schweinfurt, Germany. On August 1, 1946, the 355th transferred without equipment or personnel to Mitchell Field New York, and the 358thFS was redesignated the 56th Reconnaissance Squadron. The 355th Group, including the 56th RS was inactivated on November 20, 1946.

Although the 354th and 357th Fighter Squadrons were reactivated on September 11, 1954, and redesignated as Fighter-Intercepter Squadrons, the 355th Fighter Group was not reactivated until August 15, 1955. In 1955, the 355th was comprised of the 354th FIS, the 357th FIS and 469th FIS and stationed at McGhee-Tyson Airport in Knoxville, Tennessee.

The 355th Fighter Group was reactivated at George AFB, California on April 13, 1962, and redesignated the 355th Tactical Fighter Wing on July 8. The 355th TFW consisted of the 354th, 357th, 421st and 469th Tactical Fighter Squadrons, flying Republic F-105s.

The 355th Tactical Fighter Wing started flying combat operations from both Kadena AFB, Okinawa and Korat RTAFB, Thailand on March 6, 1965. Over the next several years the 355th turned in a superb combat record while operating from Kadena AFB, Korat RTAFB and Takhli RTAFB.

The Wing participated in every major air strike against North Vietnam until reassignment and inactivation on October 6, 1970. In the Vietnam conflict, the 355th destroyed 28 MiGs and damaged nine, plus six helicopters. The Wing flew 101,304 sorties and dropped more than 202,000 tons of bombs while suffering the highest number of losses, 136 POW/MIA pilots, of any other air unit in the same period.

A measure of the 355th's effectiveness was the award of five Presidential Unit Citations and four Air Force Outstanding Unit Awards during the 1965 to 1970 period.

Additionally, Major Merlyn Dethlefsen of the 354th Tactical Fighter Squadron was awarded the Congressional Medal of Honor for bravery "above and beyond the call of duty" over Thai Nguyen on March 10, 1967.

The 355th TFW was reactivated on July 1, 1971, and equipped with the Vought A-7D. The unit assigned to the 355th TFW included the 11th Tactical Drone Squadron, the 33rd Tactical Fighter Squadrons. On May 18, 1972, the 358th Tactical Fighter Squadron was reactivated and joined the Wing once again.

Elements of the Wing mobilized to Korat RTAFB, Thailand, in October 1972 to fly the A-7D to participate in air strikes and search and rescue missions. By January 27, 1973, every pilot in the 354 TFS had flown a combat mission and by April the Squadron had flown 1,209 combat sorties. Most of the missions were precision strike missions but also included escorting Mekong River convoys. The incredible accuracy of the A-7D enabled the 354 TFS to perform outstanding service in the close ground support role and make them the favorite of the forward air controllers. In the six months prior top reassignment in the States, the 354 TFS racked up an impressive record in North Vietnam, Laos, Cambodia, and South Vietnam while flying 2,517 combat sorites. In addition to the superb tactical capability that the A-7D possessed, it also proved to be a survivor as only one 354 TFS pilot was lost in this last combat duty for the 355th.

At the time of this writing, the 355th is now a Tactical Fighter Training Wing stationed at Davis-Monthan AFB in Tucson, Arizona. Since Vietnam the control of the Wing transferred from the Strategic Air Command to the Tactical Air Command and shed the A-7D for the newer Fairchild A-10 Thunderbolt II. After forty years the 355th is flying the Thunderbolt again and remains one of the most distinguished units to ever fly combat for the United States Air Force.

THE SECOND SCOUTING FORCE

The Second Scouting Force was attached to Station F-122 (Steeple Morden) in the summer of 1944 and flew Mustangs drawn from the 355th Fighter Group T/O. While the P-51s were maintained by each of the three group squadrons, the fighter pilots assigned to the Scouting Force included not only 355thFG pilots but also other volunteer pilots from the rest of the 65th Fighter Wing. The lead pilots were volunteers from the Second Bomb Division who had completed their tours as B-24 drivers and wanted to fly Mustangs.

The concept of the Scouting Force was largely formed and promoted by Colonel Bud Peaslee and spawned from the idea that more up to date weather reports from aircraft flying in front of the bomber force would probably be a very effective way of improving mission results.

Peaslee got the official word to proceed in July and formed the First Scouting Force. Their first mission to Munich was out of Steeple Morden on July 16, 1944.

In parallel with Peaslee, Lieutenant Colonel John Brooks, III also conceived better ways to improve target and weather intelligence. Early experiments included the use of B-24s (too slow and vulnerable), Mosquitos (fast enough but still vulnerable) and finally war weary P-47s. The P-47s not only assisted in formation assemblies, but were also sent ahead to scout route and target weather.

An attempt was made to use existing fighter groups to perform the same function. The result was largely unsatisfactory because the average fighter pilot did not fully understand the operational problems of bombardment groups in the conduct of their (bomber) missions.

Peaslee activated the First Scouting Force on July 12, 1944 and Brooks was assigned to observe the 1st Division Operations in August, 1944. After his appointment as Commander, Second Scouting Force-Steeple Morden, Lieutenant Colonel Brooks began building his team. He selected Major Frank Elliot as his deputy and recruited several other bomber pilots (Whitlow, Ziegler, Counselman, Bertleson, Weber, Edmonson, Moore) to act as lead pilots.

Major Elliot had the distinction of having more flying time than anybody on the base and Captain Bob Whitlow, ex-West Point tackle and classmate of Billy Hovde, was probably the largest Mustang pilot in the ETO.

The 355th Fighter Group supplied several fighter pilots, including Sumner Williams, Richard Dillon, Floyd Taylor and James Kilmer to the new force as well as several others. Other groups in the Wing also supplied experienced fighter pilots to act as escorts to the lead bomber pilots in their new Mustangs.

All the bomber pilots flew about 20 hours in the 355thFG AT-6 in order to transition to the P-51. After about 15 to 25 hours in the Mustang, including formation and further transition training, the bomber pilots were ready for their operations.

During training however, Lieutenant Jim Bertleson was killed in a flying accident when his AT-6 spun in near Steeple Morden on September 11, 1944. Captain Ziegler had a mid-air collision and suffered a broken arm. After a long stay in the hospital he was sent home.

The first mission for the new Scout Force was to Hamm on September 26, 1944. While the primary function of the Scouts was to report weather conditions, they also provided valuable service in other ways. Several times during the war the Second Scout Force also reported large concentrations of German fighters to the 355th. Nor did they shy away from German fighters even when greatly outnumbered.

On November 26, 1944 the 2ndSF took 12 ships to scout Misburg and Bielefeld. Four ships went down to check out Bielefeld while the remaining eight stayed out in front of the Misburg force. Near Hannover approximately 200 FW-190s were observed approaching the bombers. The large German force split into several smaller forces of 50 to 75 ships and attacked in waves. One by one, the squadrons of the 355th Fighter Group took on the attacking gaggles of enemy fighters. By the time the last wave of German fighters started their attack, all the 355thFG Mustangs were fully occupied. Bob Whitlow led the eight ship Scout Force into the scrap and took on the last wave. In a running gun battle, the Scouts shot down five plus several damaged and a probable and broke up the German attack. Lieutenants Bill Whalen and George Ceglarski nailed three and one while Whitlow got the last one. Captain Stauder did not return from the mission and nothing was heard from him again.

On February 9, 1945 the badly outnumbered Scouts again engaged a superior German fighter force near Magdeburg and came away with four scalps for the loss of none. Brooks earned a DSC for leading the aggressive attack on the 50 plus Me-109s and destroying two, while Whalen also shot down two to raise his total to six in the air and become the Scouts' only ace.

The Second Scout Force proved invaluable to the Second Division bombers, not only for scouting target conditions but also for timely information regarding route information such as paths through severe weather and concentrations of German fighters. They were not only able to provide alternate routes through or around heavy weather but also provided the 355th with the tools to provide more effective escort. The Scout Force developed and maintained an excellent relationship with the 355th Fighter Group and contributed significantly to the group's success as a premier escort organization.

The Second's colors were white nose, green cowl band (upper), white cowl band (lower), and white rudder. The 355th Mustangs assigned to the Scouts also had a black horizontal bar above the WR, OS or YF squadron identification letters of the 354th, the 357th and the 358th Squadrons, respectively.

POSTSCRIPT

Any organization is only as good as its leaders, and the 355th Fighter Group was blessed with many such as William J. Cummings, Everett W. Stewart, Claiborne H. Kinnard, Bert W. Marshall, Gordon M. Graham, Edward W. Szaniawski, John L. Elder and Emil L. Sluga. These men, and others, set the pattern of sucess enjoyed by the 355th.

It is fitting to mention the 355th Fighter Group Association. Begun as the brainchild of the late Gordon Hunsberger, with the ardent support of people like Robert E. Kuhnert, Douglas B. Warden, Henry D. Wertz, Harrison T. Price and others, the association took off to become perhaps the finest example of any organization of its kind.

Finally, the author, Bill Marshall, has modestly said about his book, "It's a story written by an engineer with no talent nor skill in writing, and is the end result of a strong compulsion to know more about this facet of my dad's life."

Bill's dad, the late fighter ace Bert W. Marshall, was the most respected and loved pilot who flew with the 355th. This book, a labor of love, respect and admiration for his father, is a fitting tribute.

William J. Hovde
Colonel, USAF (Ret)

APPENDIX A

Claims and awards for German aircraft destroyed

The lists presented below in Tables A, B and C are a result of extensive research involving the 355th Group History, the 354th, 357th and 358th Fighter Squadron Histories, the United States Air Force Study Number 85 and the United States Army Air Force Victory Credits Board. There are many contradictions and omissions in the comparison of the above documents. The author found USAF #85 to be extremely accurate however, with one exception and three open questions. Neither the exception nor the questions affect the Aces list and USAF #85 is used as the official source for all air victory **awards** presented in Table B -"Awards".

Although several contradictions exist concerning the ground scores officially awarded as a result of Eighth Fighter Command's final Victory Credits Board, dated September, 1945, the ground scores contained in that report or prior official Victory Credits Board documentation was used as the basis for final awards.

Two notable exceptions include the final ground tally awarded to the author's father, Bert W. Marshall, and to one of the 355th's top strafers, William J. Cullerton. In the case of Marshall, whose ground scores were listed under "Marchall" instead of "Marshall" (same serial number, etc.), his final tally of 7 air, 4 ground was reduced to 7 air, 3 ground even though he had the official documentation for 4 confirmed ground scores on April 13, 1945. The author has no idea what subsequent review of gun camera film occurred or what judgements passed between April and September, 1945. Therefore, the final review stands and his score was reduced accordingly. In the case of Bill Cullerton the final official 8th Air Force ground score was 21 ground. Conversations with Bill indicated that he had never claimed more than fourteen or fifteen on the ground and subsequent review of the group histories confirmed his statement. After thorough research of the microfilm, the author uncovered a double entry by the 8th for his fantastic day on November 2, 1944 in which he destroyed two in the air and six on the ground. The Eighth Fighter Command credited Bill with exactly 12 ground scores on the same day. Accordingly, his ground score was reduced from 21 to 15, which corresponds to his records and the 355th Fighter Group records.

The claims list presented in Table A -"Claims" is a complete tally of claims made by the pilots at debriefing and forwarded on to higher command for final review and award. The reviewing authority was Eighth Fighter Command through September, 1944. Thereafter, the reviewing authority was the Second Division, to which the 65th Fighter Wing (4th, 56th, 355th, 361st and 479th Fighter Groups) was attached for operations control. Some scores were reduced and some increased.

The list in Table B -"Awards" is a complete list of awards for air and ground scores as determined by USAF #85 and the USAAF Victory Credits Board, respectively, and explained above.

The list in Table C-"Aces" is a compilation of pilots whose combined air and ground scores totaled five or more aircraft destroyed. Although the Air Force withdrew the designation for pilots who achieved "Acedom" via ground scores, it is the author's wish that all the 355th pilots in that category receive credit for a very dangerous undertaking.

The scores, air and ground, of the Second Scout Force are also included in the lists to reflect their contribution to the battles of the 355th.

The list is as complete and accurate as the author could make it but also includes some decisions based on careful evaluation of conflicting data. For any errors of omission or commission, the author humbly apologizes.

TABLE A-Claims

Date	Pilot Name	Unit	Air	Ground
43-10-04	Ekstrom, Carl F	358	1.00	
43-10-20	Myers, Raymond B	358	1.00	
43-11-05	Sweat, Charles H	354	1.00	
	Sluga, Emil L	358	1.00	
43-11-07	Olson, Norman E	357	1.00	
43-11-13	Neal, Thomas J	354	1.00	
	Vincent, Roland L	354	1.00	
	Olson, Norman E	357	1.00	
43-11-29	Woertz, Jack R	358	1.00	
43-12-01	Bernoske, Robert	357	1.00	
	Johnston, Ben D Jr	357	1.00	
	Ekstrom, Carl F	358	1.00	
	Macurdy, Harold H	358	1.00	
43-12-30	Murdock, Raymond F	354	1.00	
44-01-21	Duffy, James E Jr	354	1.00	
	Wilson, John H	357	1.00	
44-01-29	Macurdy, Harold H	358	2.00	
44-02-05	Olson, Norman E	357	2.00	
44-02-11	Burroughs, Vernon A	357	1.00	
	Szaniawski, Edward W	357	2.00	
44-02-20	Olson, Norman E	357	1.00	
	Dickson, James B	358	1.00	
44-02-21	Elder, John L Jr	357	1.00	
	Johnston, Ben D Jr	357	1.00	
	Olson, Norman E	357	1.00	
44-02-22	Hovde, William J	358	1.00	
	Kenny, Paul H	358	1.00	
44-03-02	Blair, Charles W Jr	358	1.00	
	Dudley, Lawrence M Jr	358	0.50	
	Fussell, Roscoe J	358	0.50	
	Gresham, Walter V Jr	358	1.00	
	Hoffman, Harold J	358	1.00	
	Myers, Raymond B	358	1.00	
44-03-06	Barger, Clarence R	354	0.33	
	Fortier, Norman J	354	0.33	
	Koraleski Walter J	354	2.33	
	Easterly, William S	357	1.00	
	Hill, Byron L	357	1.00	
	McCasland, Darwin D	357	1.00	
	Dickson, James B	358	1.00	
	Stewart, Everett W	HQ	1.00	
44-03-08	Barger, Clarence R	354		3.00
	Brown, Henry W	354		1.50
	Johnston, Curtis G	354		0.50
	Sweat, Charles H	354		1.00
	Norman, Robert L	357	1.00	
	Dix, Gerald J	HQ	1.00	
44-03-16	Duffy, James E. Jr.	354	1.00	
	Koraleski Walter J.	354	1.00	
	Lenfest, Charles W.	354	1.50	
	Morris, Ray S.	354	1.00	
	Neal, Thomas J.	354	2.50	
	Bille, Henry S.	357	0.33	
	Burroughs, Vernon A.	357	1.00	
	Colson, Carl C.	357	1.00	
	Kirby, Henry H.	357	0.33	
	MacFarlane, Walter E.	357	0.33	
	DeGeorge, John J. Jr.	358	1.00	
	Dickson, James B.	358	1.00	

			Claims	
Date	Pilot Name	Unit	Air	Ground
	Gresham, Walter V. Jr.	358	1.00	
	Kenney, Paul H.	358	1.00	
	Rosenblatt, Charles J.	358	1.00	
	Stewart, Everett W.	HQ	1.00	
44-03-18	Brown, Henry W.	354	1.00	
	Lenfest, Charles W.	354	0.50	
	Mendenhall, Lee G.	354	0.50	
	Neal, Thomas J.	354	1.00	
	Hovde, William J.	358	2.00	
	Stewart, Everett W.	HQ	1.00	
44-03-27	Crossen, Morris C.	357	1.00	1.00
	Reedy, Irving	357	0.50	
	Wilson, John H.	357	0.50	1.00
44-03-28	Culp, Harold E.	354		0.50
	Johnston, Curtis G.	354		1.00
	Minchew, Leslie D.	354		0.50
	Morris, Ray S.	354		1.00
	Neal, Thomas J.	354		0.50
	Burroughs, Vernon A.	357		1.00
	Butler, Reed B.	357		2.00
	DeMers, Raymond	357		1.00
	Hill, Byron L.	357		2.00
	Hillman, Howard K.	357		1.00
	Johnston, Ben D. Jr.	357		3.00
	Olson, Norman E.	357		1.00
	Packard, Hudson F.	357		1.00
	Schoenfeldt Edward E.	357		1.00
	Sturm, Jack D.	357		2.00
	Szaniawski, Edward W.	357		4.00
	Hovde, William J.	358		1.00
	Dix, Gerald J.	HQ		0.50
44-03-29	Brown, Henry W.	354	1.00	
	Kinnard, Claiborne H. Jr.	354	1.00	
	Koraleski, Walter J.	354	1.00	
	Lenfest, Charles W.	354	1.00	1.00
	Burroughs, Vernon A.	357	2.00	
	Elder, John L. Jr.	357	1.00	
	Johnston, Ben D. Jr.	357	2.00	
	Kaminski, Rudolph B.	357	1.00	
	McCasland, Darwin D.	357	1.00	
	Ramsdell, Fred L Jr.	357	1.00	
	Stewart, Everett W.	HQ	2.00	1.00
44-04-05	Benson, Arvid E.	354		1.00
	Boulet, William P.	354		2.00
	Brown, Henry W.	354	0.70	
	Duffy, James E. Jr.	354	0.20	
	Houston, Byron G.	354		3.00
	Johnston, Curtis G.	354	0.20	
	Kinnard, Claiborne H. Jr.	354	1.00	4.00
	Koraleski, Walter J.	354	1.20	
	Kurtz, Robert G.	354		1.00
	Lenfest, Charles W.	354	0.50	
	Mendenhall, Lee G.	354		3.00
	Morris, Ray S.	354		2.00
	Williamson, Brady C.	354	1.70	
	Woody, Robert E.	354	1.50	
	Butler, Reed B.	357		1.00
	Hill, Byron L.	357		1.00
	Kaminski, Rudolph B.	357		1.00
	Packard, Hudson F.	357		1.00
	Beckman, Jack M.	358		2.00
	Dissette, Lawrence J.	358		3.00
	Dudley, Lawrence M. Jr.	358	1.00	1.00
	Gresham, Walter V. Jr.	358		2.00

Date	Pilot Name	Unit	Claims Air	Ground
	Hoffman, Harold J.	358		2.00
	MacConkey, Jack S.	358		2.00
	McElroy, James M.	358		1.00
	Myers, Raymond B.	358		3.00
	Peterson, Noble E.	358		1.00
	Reed, Joe E.	358		2.00
	Rosenblatt, Charles J.	358		2.00
	Cummings, William J.	HQ		2.00
44-04-08	Brown, Henry W.	354	0.50	
	Kurtz, Robert G.	354	0.50	
	Minchew, Leslie D.	354	1.00	
	Elder, John L. Jr.	357		2.00
	Kirby, Henry H.	357		2.00
	McCasland, Darwin D.	357		1.00
	Olson, Norman E.	357		1.00
	Szaniawski, Edward W.	357	1.00	
	Wilson, John H.	357		1.00
	Harrington, James C.	358	0.50	
	Hovde, William J.	358	1.00	
	Sluga, Emil L.	358	1.50	
44-04-10	Austin, James P.	354		1.00
	Duffy, James E. Jr.	354		1.00
	Kinnard, Claiborne H. Jr.	354		1.00
	Kurtz, Robert G.	354		1.00
	Woody, Robert E.	354		1.00
44-04-11	Brown, Henry W.	354	1.00	1.00
	Brown, Richard	354		1.00
	Houston, Byron G.	354		1.00
	Jacobson, Donald J.	354		1.00
	Johnston, Curtis G.	354		3.00
	Schutt, Ralph C.	354		1.00
	Easterly, Williams S.	357		1.00
	McCasland, Darwin D.	357		2.00
	Schoenfeldt, Edward E.	357		1.00
	Dudley, Lawrence M. Jr.	358	1.50	
	Fussell, Roscoe J.	358	1.00	1.00
	Gresham, Walter V. Jr.	358	1.00	
	Martyn, Donald M.	358	0.50	
	Myers, Raymond B.	358	1.00	
	Reed, Joe E.	358	1.00	
	Sluga, Emil L.	358	1.00	
	Stewart, Everett W.	HQ	2.00	
44-04-13	Barger, Clarence R.	354		2.00
	Brown, Henry W.	354		2.00
	Brown, Richard	354		2.00
	Browning, Robert A.	354		1.00
	Duffy, James E. Jr.	354		2.00
	Kinnard, Claiborne H. Jr.	354		4.00
	Morris, Ray S.	354		2.00
	Williamson, Brady C.	354		2.00
	Woody, Robert E.	354		1.00
	Bille, Henry S.	357	1.00	
	DeMers, Raymond	357		0.33
	Hillman, Howard K.	357	1.00	
	Kerch, Joseph F.	357		0.33
	Norman, Robert L.	357		0.66
	Sturm, Jack D.	357	1.00	0.50
	Szaniawski, Edward W.	357	1.00	0.66
	Wilson, John H.	357	1.00	0.50
	Myers, Raymond B.	358	1.00	
44-04-15	Elder, John L. Jr.	357	1.00	
	MacFarlane, Walter E.	357		1.00
	Beckman, Jack M.	358		1.00
	Dissette, Lawrence J.	358		1.00

Date	Pilot Name	Unit	Claims Air	Ground
	Kenney, Paul H.	358		1.00
	MacConkey, Jack S.	358		1.00
	McElroy, James N.	358		5.00
	Myers, Raymond B.	358		1.00
44-04-19	Woody, Robert E.	354	1.00	
	Fussell, Roscoe J.	358	1.00	
	Meteyer, Thomas O.	358	1.00	
44-04-20	Browning, Robert A.	354		1.00
	Houston, Byron G.	354		1.00
	Kurtz, Robert G.	354		2.00
44-04-24	Boulet, William P.	354	3.00	
	Brown, Henry W.	354	2.00	
	Fortier, Norman J.	354	1.50	
	Kucheman, Henry J.	354	3.00	
	Woody, Robert E.	354	4.50	
	Bille, Henry S.	357	1.00	
	Butler, Reed B.	357	0.50	
	DeMers, Raymond	357	3.00	
	McNeff, Edward P.	357	0.50	
	Wilson, John H.	357	1.00	
	Dix Gerald J.	HQ	1.00	
44-04-29	Brown, Henry W.	354	1.00	
44-05-01	Dissette, Lawrence J.	358	1.00	
44-05-04	Martyn, Donald M.	358	1.00	
44-05-13	Brown, Henry W.	354	1.00	
	Fortier, Norman J.	354	2.00	
	Martin, William D.	354	1.00	
	Morris, RaY S	354	2.00	
	Perry, Emil F.	354	2.00	
	Dix, Gerald J.	HQ	2.00	
44-05-21	Englebreit, Joseph C.	357	0.50	1.00
	King, Myles	357		2.00
	MacFarlane, Walter E.	357	0.50	1.00
44-05-22	Dix, Gerald J.	HQ	1.00	
44-05-24	Perry, Emil F.	354		1.00
	Foster, Thomas J.	357	1.00	
	Myers, Raymond B.	358	1.00	
44-05-28	Eshelman, Francis L.	357	1.00	
	MacFarlane, Walter E.	357	1.00	
44-05-30	Donavan, David A.	358	1.50	
	Robinson, Allan T.	358	1.00	
	Santos, Albert R.	358	2.00	
44-06-06	Benson, Arvid E.	354		1.00
	Fortier, Norman J.	354	1.00	
	Graham, Clarence H.	354		0.50
	Marshall, Bert W. Jr.	354	1.00	
	Morris, Ray S.	354	0.50	
	Perry, Emil F.	354	1.00	
	Taylor, Floyd K.	354	0.50	0.50
	Bernoske, Robert	357	1.00	
	Cotter, John A.	357	1.00	
	Fuller, Leonard B.	357	1.00	
	James, Wayne W.	357	2.00	
	Kelley, Frederick W.	357	2.00	
	Dix Gerald J.	HQ		1.00
44-06-08	Brien, Cleveland J. Jr.	358	0.50	
	McGinty, William J.	358	0.50	
44-06-20	Graham, Clarence H.	354	1.00	
	Hoffman, Garlyn O.	354	1.00	
	Huish, Heber M.	354	0.50	
	Kucheman, Henry J.	354	1.00	
	Marshall, Bert W. Jr.	354	2.00	
	Martin, William D.	354	2.00	
	Taylor, Robert G.	354	1.00	

			Claims	
Date	Pilot Name	Unit	Air	Ground
	Williams, Summer C.	354	0.50	
	Wright, Gilbert S.	354	2.00	
	Buckles, Clifford R.	357	0.50	
	Fuller, Leonard B.	357	0.50	
	Minchew, Leslie D.	357	1.00	
44-06-21	Bernoske, Robert	357	1.00	
	Chapman, John M.	357	1.00	
	Haviland, Fred R. Jr.	357	1.00	
	Salinsky, Charles J.	357	1.00	
44-06-24	Cross, Richard G. Jr.	354		1.00
	Ellison, James C.	354		2.00
	Hulderman, Robert F.	354		1.00
	Martin, William D.	354		2.00
	Morris, Ray S.	354		3.00
	Perry, Emil F.	354		2.00
	Trembarth, Floyd W.	354		1.00
	Crandell, Jack L.	357		2.00
	Forker, George W.	357		3.00
	Haviland, Fred R. Jr.	357		3.00
	McHugh, Phillip M. N.	357		1.00
	McNeff, Edward P.	357		1.00
	Salinsky, Charles J.	357		3.00
	Spencer, Harold W.	357		2.00
	Kinnard, Claiborne H. Jr.	HQ		3.00
44-07-05	Hulderman, Robert F.	354		0.50
	Schwab, Warren A.	354		1.00
	Kinnard, Claiborne H. Jr.	HQ		0.50
44-07-07	Betounes, Samuel G.	354	0.50	
	Cross, Richard G. Jr.	354	2.00	
	Perry, Emil F.	354	1.00	
	Taylor, Robert G.	354	0.50	
	Cotter, John A.	357	1.00	
	Fuller, Leonard B.	357	1.00	
	Haviland, Fred R. Jr.	357	2.00	
	McNeff, Edward P.	357	1.00	
	Minchew, Leslie D.	357	3.00	
	Kinnard, Claiborne H. Jr.	HQ	3.00	
44-07-08	Bradley, Robert T.	354		1.00
	Cross, Richard G. Jr.	354		0.50
	Fortier, Norman J.	354		0.50
	Graham, Clarence H.	354		1.00
	Jackson, Nobert P.	354		1.00
	Kucheman, Henry B.	354		2.00
	Martin, William D.	354		1.00
	Morris, Ray S.	354		2.00
	Williams, Sumner C.	354		2.00
	Forker, George W.	357		1.00
	McHugh, Phillip M. N.	357		2.00
	Strachan, Robert W.	357		1.00
	Covault, Vern W.	358		1.00
	McGinty, William J.	358		1.00
	McNally, Russell I.	358		1.00
	Michelena, Ralph L.	358		1.00
	Pardee, Harry W. Jr.	358		1.00
44-07-13	Hendrickson, Edwin M.	357	1.00	
44-07-19	Folger, John M.	354	1.00	
	Covault, Vern W.	358	1.00	
	Duppstadt, Arthur G.	358		2.00
	Hovde, William J.	358	1.00	
	McElroy, James N.	358	1.00	
	Thompson, Robert M.	358	1.00	
44-07-20	Fortier, Norman J.	354	1.00	
	Peterson, Noble E.	358	1.00	
	Peters, Robert O.	358	3.00	2.00

				Claims
Date	Pilot Name	Unit	Air	Ground
44-07-21	Thompson, Robert M.	358	1.00	
44-07-24	Fortier, Norman J.	354		1.00
	Hoffman, Garlyn O.	354		1.00
	Patterson, Gilbert T.	354		1.00
	Cotter, John A.	357		1.00
	Gilleland, Alvah G.	357		1.00
	Blaylock, Donald C.	358		1.00
	Dillon, Richard M.	358		1.00
	Douglass, Ward H.	358		1.00
	Hovde, William J.	358		2.00
	Maisch, Joseph J. Jr.	358		1.00
	McNally, Russell I.	358		1.00
	Peterson, Noble E.	358		1.00
44-07-28	Marshall, Bert W. Jr.	354	1.00	
	McElroy, James N.	358	2.00	
44-08-01	Dillon, Richard M.	358	1.00	
44-08-03	Lenfest, Charles W.	354	1.00	
	Peglar, Warren B. (RCAF)	354	2.00	
	Cotter, John A.	357	1.00	
	Haviland, Fred R. Jr.	357	1.00	
	Minchew, Leslie D.	357	1.00	
44-08-06	Lenfest, Charles W.	354	1.00	
	Marshall, Bert W. Jr.	354	1.00	
	Martin, William D.	354	1.00	
44-08-11	Peglar, Warren B. (RCAF)	354		1.00
44-08-14	Elder, John L. Jr.	357		1.00
	Forker, George W.	357		1.00
	Shade, William A.	357		1.00
44-08-15	Gresham, Walter V. Jr.	358	1.00	
44-08-16	Bille, Henry S.	357	2.00	
	Crandell, Jack L.	357	1.00	
	Cullerton, William J.	357	2.00	
	Elder, John L. Jr.	357	2.00	
	Lamer, Charles W.	357	1.00	
	Michels, Kenneth M.	357	1.00	
	Spencer, Harold W.	357	2.00	
44-08-26	Cullerton, William J.	357		1.00
44-09-10	Brown, Henry W.	354		6.00
44-09-11	Brown, Henry W.	354	3.00	
	Johnson, Frederick W.	354		1.00
	Marshall, Bert W. Jr.	354	2.00	
	McCurry, Charles R.	354		1.00
	Peglar, Warren B. (RCAF)	357	2.00	
	Priest, Royce W.	354	1.00	
	Schultz, Floyd W.	354	1.00	0.50
	White, Robert M.	354		1.50
	Williamson, Brady C.	354		1.00
	Frost, Lionel S. (RAF)	358	1.00	
	Maisch, Joseph J. Jr.	358	2.00	
44-09-12	Cullerton, William J.	357		7.00
	Haviland, Fred R. Jr.	357		3.00
	Juntilla, J. O.	357		4.00
	McHugh, Phillip M. N.	357	2.00	
	Monahan, Harold L.	357	1.00	
	Thompson, Robert M.	358	1.00	
44-09-18	Brown, Henry W.	354	1.00	
	Elder, John L. Jr.	357	1.00	
	Kirby, Henry H.	357	1.00	
	Michelena, Ralph L.	358	1.00	
44-09-27	Brown, Henry W.	354	2.00	
	Mann, Herbert R.	354		0.50
	Priest, Royce W.	354	1.00	
	Williamson, Brady C.	354		1.00
	Stewart, Everett W.	HQ		0.50

Date	Pilot Name	Unit	Claims Air	Claims Ground
44-10-03	Brown, Henry W.	354		1.00
	Lenfest, Charles W.	354		1.00
44-10-06	Colson, Carl C.	357	1.00	
	Lamer, Charles W.	357	2.00	
44-10-07	Monahan, Harold L.	357	1.00	1.00
44-11-02	Priest, Royce W.	354	1.00	
	Woolard, Marion L.	354	1.00	
	Cavender, James V. Jr.	357		1.00
	Cullerton, William J.	357	2.00	6.00
	Dufresne, Roland J.	357		2.00
	Elder, John L. Jr.	357	1.00	5.00
	Englebreit, Joseph C.	357		1.00
	Erickson, Joel E.	357		4.00
	Miller, Kenneth J.	357		2.00
	Moroney, Edward J.	357	1.00	2.00
	Wilkes, Henry S.	357	1.00	
	Williams, Benjamin G.	357		2.00
	Mikalauskas, Kenneth E.	358	1.00	
44-11-18	Duffy, James E. Jr.	354		1.00
	Fortier, Norman J.	354		2.00
	Todd, Theodore P.	354		2.00
	Wood, Thomas L.	354		1.00
	Colson, Carl C.	357		1.00
	Haviland, Fred R. Jr.	357		2.00
	Long, Thurman C.	357		2.00
	Max, Joseph H.	357		1.00
	Nelson, James E.	357		1.00
	Wilson, John H.	357		1.00
	Beatty, Wendell W.	358		1.00
44-11-26	Ceglarski, George W.	2SF	3.00	
	Whalen, William E.	2SF	1.00	
	Whitlow, Robert V.	2SF	1.00	
	Duffy, James E. Jr.	354	1.00	
	Hauver, Charles D.	354	2.00	
	McLear, Robert M.	354	2.00	
	Mellen, Joseph E.	354	1.00	
	Molnar, John E.	354	1.00	
	Priest, Royce W.	354	2.00	
	Barab, Bernard R.	357	1.00	
	Haviland, Fred R. Jr.	357	2.00	
	Lyons, William S.	357	1.00	
	Max, Joseph H.	357	2.00	
	Moroney, Edward J.	357	2.00	
	Beckman, Jack M.	358	1.00	
	Masters, Frank R.	358	3.00	
44-12-05	Duffy, James E. Jr.	354	1.00	
	Silva, Stanley H.	354	1.00	
	Alexander, Arthur K.	358	1.50	
	Baker, Ray G.	358	2.00	
	Brown, Robert H.	358	1.00	
	Hovde, William J.	358	5.50	
	McElroy, James N.	358	1.00	
44-12-12	Curran, Arthur R.	358		1.00
44-12-25	Graham, Gordon M.	354	1.00	
	Hauver, Charles D.	354	2.00	
	Inglesias, Victor D.	357	1.00	
44-12-31	Graham, Gordon M.	354	2.00	
	Hauver, Charles D.	354	1.00	
45-01-14	Decklar, Carl E.	354	2.00	
	Graham, Gordon M.	354	2.00	
	Kemper, George A. Jr.	354	2.00	
	Mills, Newell F. Jr.	354	3.00	
	Wood, Thomas L.	354	1.00	
	Elder, John L. Jr.	357	1.00	

Date	Pilot Name	Unit	Claims Air	Ground
45-01-15	Falvey, Harold W.	354		2.00
	Fortier, Norman J.	354		1.00
	Graham, Gordon M.	354		1.00
	Delhamer, Robert W.	357		2.00
	Lake, Joseph E.	357		1.00
	Allen, Roscoe	358		1.00
	Fussell, Roscoe J.	358		1.00
	Gore, Victor E.	358		1.00
	Wilson, John H.	HQ		1.00
45-02-09	Duffy, James E. Jr.	354	1.00	
	Forehand, Willard F.	357		1.00
	Luedeke, Edward P.	357	1.00	
	Lyons, William S.	357	1.00	
	Stewart, Everett	HQ		1.00
	Brooks, John A. III	2SF	2.00	
	Whalen, William E.	2SF	2.00	
45-02-22	White, Robert, M.	354		2.00
	Ceglarski, George W.	2SF		2.00
	Whalen, William E.	2SF		2.00
45-02-23	Graham, Gordon M.	354		1.00
	Mann, Herbert R.	354		1.00
	Mills, Newell F. Jr.	354		1.00
	Vickery, Duran M.	354		1.00
	Walsh, Robert J.	354		1.00
	Elder, John L. Jr.	357		1.00
	Garlich, Robert L.	357		1.00
	Hardee, Sellers S.	357		1.00
	Riffle, Elmer H.	357		1.00
	Schmidt, George C.	357		1.00
45-02-25	Long, Thurman C.	357		1.00
	Tolby, William W. Jr.	358	1.00	1.00
45-02-27	McElroy, James N.	358	1.00	
45-03-01	Beatty, Wendell W.	358	1.00	
	Wilkens, John K. Jr.	2SF	1.00	
45-03-02	Allen, Roscoe	358	5.00	
45-03-14	Rodebaugh, Charles R.	2SF	1.00	
45-03-19	Spencer, Charles H.	354	1.00	
45-03-22	Decklar, Carl E.	354		0.50
	Falvey, Harold W.	354		2.00
	Fletcher, Jack M.	354		1.00
	Gadpaille, Warren J.	354		1.00
	Jabara, James	354		1.00
	Silva, Stanley H.	354		3.00
	Todd, Charles G.	354		1.00
	Tuholski, David C.	354		1.00
	Vineyard, Paul W. Jr.	354		0.50
	White, Richard M.	354		1.00
45-03-30	Cullerton, William J.	357		1.00
	Knight, Harold I.	357		1.00
	Kirby, Henry H.	HQ		2.00
45-03-31	Long, Thurman C.	357		3.00
	Castleberry, Marvin H.	2SF	1.00	
45-04-04	Decklar, Carl E.	354		1.00
	Hixon, Thomas R.	354		1.00
	Molnar, John E.	354		1.00
	White, Alvin S.	354	1.00	
	Cullerton, William J.	357	1.00	
	Long, Thurman C.	357	2.00	
	Riffle, Elmer H.	357	1.00	
	Weidmann, John J.	357		2.00
45-04-07	Beeler, Glen D.	354	1.00	
	Mellen, Joseph E.	354	1.00	
	Vineyard, Paul W. Jr.	354	1.00	
	Forehand, Willard F.	357	1.00	

Date	Pilot Name	Unit	Claims Air	Claims Ground
	Griswold, Walter L. Jr.	357	0.33	
	Hartzog, James P.	357	0.33	
	Reiff, William	357	0.33	
45-04-08	Decklar, Carl E.	354	1.00	
	Graham, Gordon M.	354	2.00	
	Weidmann, John J.	357		2.00
	Brown, Robert H.	358		2.00
45-04-09	Barnhart, Philip W.	354		1.00
	Falvey, Harold W.	354		1.00
	Graham, Gordon M.	354		2.00
	Jabara, James	354		1.00
	Langley, Donald B.	354		1.00
	Pearson, Richard P.	354		1.00
	White, Alvin S.	354		1.00
	Fees, Edwin W.	358		1.00
	Knutty, Harold P.	358		0.50
	Lanius, John H.	358		1.00
	Lynch, William J.	358		2.00
	McCollom, Francis N.	358		1.00
	Patrinely, Costa C.	358		1.50
45-04-10	Falvey, Harold W.	354		2.00
	Fletcher, Jack M.	354		2.00
	Galer, Donald	354		1.00
	Graham, Gordon M.	354		2.00
	Hixon, Thomas R.	354		1.00
	Jabara, James	354		2.00
	Stanton, O. N.	354		1.00
	Burnett, Willmont T.	357		0.50
	Cooper, Randolph W.	357		0.50
	Garlich, Robert L.	357		2.00
	Watkins, D. P.	357		1.00
	Kirby, Henry H.	HQ		1.00
45-04-13	Barnhart, Philip W.	354		1.00
	Beeler, Glen D.	354		1.00
	Duffy, James E. Jr.	354		3.00
	Falvey, Harold W.	354		2.00
	Galer, Donald	354		1.00
	Jabara, James	354		2.00
	Kaplan, Albert B.	354		1.00
	Kazacka, Arthur G.	354		1.00
	Langley, Donald B.	354		2.00
	Mellen, Joseph E.	354		5.00
	Mincemeyer, Allan J.	354		1.00
	Pearson, Richard P.	354		1.00
	Sarver, Frank A.	354		1.00
	Scheid, Adolph J.	354		1.00
	Silva, Stanley H.	354		3.00
	Vickery, Duran M.	354		5.00
	Westerveld, Robert	354		1.00
	Cooper, Randolph W.	357		3.00
	Garlich, Robert L.	357		2.00
	Iglesias, Victor D.	357		1.00
	Curran, Arthur R.	358		2.00
	Fees, Edwin W.	358		0.50
	Finnesey, Robert V.	358		2.00
	Gore, Victor E.	358		2.50
	Knutty, Harold P.	358		2.00
	Lacazette, Mario	358		1.00
	Leaf, Leroy R. Jr.	358		1.00
	Lister, Walter B.	358		1.00
	Nicodemus, Ralph J.	358		2.00
	Parks, Robert F.	358		1.00
	Patrinely, Costa C.	358		0.50
	Rouleau, Louis J. Jr.	358		1.00

			Claims	
Date	Pilot Name	Unit	Air	Ground
	Schlect, Warner J.	358		1.00
	Tulloch, John Jr.	358		4.00
	Kinnard, Claiborne H. Jr.	HQ		2.50
	Marshall, Bert W. Jr.	HQ		4.00
45-04-16	Duffy, James E. Jr.	354		1.00
	Fletcher, Jack M.	354		3.00
	Fortier, Norman J.	354		1.00
	Galer, Donald	354		2.00
	Graham, Gordon M.	354		3.00
	Heaton, Robert L.	354		2.00
	McLear, Robert L.	354		1.00
	McLeod, Michael J.	354		1.00
	Mellen, Joseph E.	354		3.00
	Molnar, John E.	354		2.00
	Sanders, Donald J.	354		1.00
	Scheid, Adolph J.	354		1.00
	Todd, Charles G.	354		2.00
	Beise, Marlin E.	357		1.00
	Bille, Henry S.	357		4.00
	Colson, Carl C.	357		2.00
	Cooper, Randolph W.	357		3.00
	Elder, John L. Jr.	357		4.00
	Elliot, Frank (2SF)	357		3.00
	Galich, Robert L.	357		1.00
	Gelsone, Frank E.	357		1.00
	Keuhl, Robert C.	357		0.50
	Kirk, Richard J.	357		1.00
	Knight, Harold I.	357		2.00
	Kubetin, William T.	357		1.00
	Lake, Joseph E.	357		1.00
	Misner, Richard F.	357		2.00
	Owens, Robert B.	357		1.00
	Patalunas, Robert J.	357		1.00
	Watkins, D. P.	357		2.00
	Weidmann, John J.	357		1.00
	Whitney, Emerson H.	357		2.00
	Dissette, Lawrence J.	358		2.00
	Lynch, William J.	358		3.00
	Marsh, Halbert G.	358		5.00
	McCollom, Francis N.	358		4.00
	Nelson, Ervin C.	358		2.00
	Plemmons, Charles E.	358		2.00
	Rowbotham, Robert C.	358		2.00
	Seeley, Grant A.	358		4.00
45-04-17	McNeil, Ray J.	357		1.00
	Gresham, Walter V. Jr.	358		1.00
45-04-20	Bille, Henry S.	357	2.00	
	Iglesias, Victor D.	357	1.00	
	Knutty, Harold P.	358	0.50	
	Parks, Robert F.	358	1.00	
	Seeley, Grant A.	358	1.00	
	Snook, Keo L.	358	0.50	
	Kinnard, Claiborne H. Jr.	HQ	2.00	

TABLE B-Awards

Pilot Name	355FG Air	355FG Ground	Other Groups Air	Other Groups Ground	Total Air	Total Ground	Total Combined
Alexander, Arthur K.	1.50	0.00			1.50	0.00	1.50
Allen, Roscoe	0.00	1.00			0.00	1.00	1.00
Austin, James P.	0.00	1.00			0.00	1.00	1.00
Baker, Ray G.	2.00	0.00			2.00	0.00	2.00
Barab, Bernard R.	1.00	0.00			1.00	0.00	1.00
Barger, Clarence R.	0.33	6.00			0.33	6.00	6.33
Barnhart, Philip W.	0.00	2.50			0.00	2.50	2.50
Beatty, Wendell W.	1.00	1.00			1.00	1.00	2.00
Beckman, Jack M.	1.00	3.00			1.00	3.00	4.00
Beeler, Glen D.	1.00	1.00			1.00	1.00	2.00
Beise, Marlin E.	0.00	1.00			0.00	1.00	1.00
Benson, Arvid E.	0.00	1.00			0.00	1.00	1.00
Bernoske, Robert	1.00	0.00			1.00	0.00	1.00
Betounes, Samuel G.	0.50	0.00			0.50	0.00	0.50
Bille, Henry S.	6.00	4.00			6.00	4.00	10.00
Blair, Charles W. Jr.	1.00	0.00			1.00	0.00	1.00
Blaylock, Donald C.	0.00	1.00			0.00	1.00	1.00
Boulet, William P.	3.00	3.00			3.00	3.00	6.00
Bradley, Robert T.	0.00	1.00			0.00	1.00	1.00
Brien, Cleveland J. Jr.	0.50	0.00			0.50	0.00	0.50
Brooks, John A. III (2SF)	2.00	0.00			2.00	0.00	2.00
Brown, Henry W.	14.20	14.50			14.20	14.50	28.70
Brown, Richard C.	0.00	3.00			0.00	3.00	3.00
Brown, Robert H.	1.00	0.00			1.00	0.00	1.00
Buckles, Clifford R.	0.50	0.00			0.50	0.00	0.50
Burnett, Willmont T.	0.00	0.50			0.00	0.50	0.50
Burroughs, Vernon A.	3.00	1.00			3.00	1.00	4.00
Butler, Reed B.	0.50	3.00			0.50	3.00	3.50
Castleberry, Marvin H. (2SF)	1.00	0.00			1.00	0.00	1.00
Cavender, James V. Jr.	0.00	1.00			0.00	1.00	1.00
Ceglarski, George W. (2SF)	1.00	2.00	0.00	2.00[1]	1.00	4.00	5.00
Chapman, John M.	1.00	0.00			1.00	0.00	1.00
Colson, Carl C.	2.00	2.00			2.00	2.00	4.00
Cooper, Randolph W.	0.00	5.50			0.00	5.50	5.50
Cotter, John A.	3.00	1.00			3.00	1.00	4.00
Covault, Vern W.	0.00	1.00			0.00	1.00	1.00
Crandell, Jack L.	1.00	2.00			1.00	2.00	3.00
Cross, Richard G. Jr.	2.00	1.50			2.00	1.50	3.50
Crossen, Morris J.	1.00	1.00			1.00	1.00	2.00
Cullerton, William J.	5.00	15.00			5.00	15.00	20.00
Culp, Harold F.	0.00	0.50			0.00	0.50	0.50
Cummings, William J. Jr.	0.00	2.00			0.00	2.00	2.00
Curran, Arthur R.	0.00	3.00			0.00	3.00	3.00
Decklar, Carl E.	3.00	0.50			3.00	0.50	3.50
DeGeorge, John J. Jr.	1.00	0.00			1.00	0.00	1.00
Delhamer, Robert W.	0.00	3.00			0.00	3.00	3.00
DeMers, Raymond	2.00	1.33			2.00	1.33	3.33
Dickson, James B.	3.00	0.00			3.00	0.00	3.00
Dillon, Richard M.	1.00	1.00			1.00	1.00	2.00
Dissette, Lawrence J.	1.00	5.00			1.00	5.00	6.00
Dix, Gerald J.	4.00	1.50			4.00	1.50	5.50
Donavan, David A.	1.50	0.00			1.50	0.00	1.50
Douglass, Ward H.	0.00	2.00			0.00	2.00	2.00
Dudley, Lawrence M. Jr.	3.00	1.00			3.00	1.00	4.00
Duffy, James E. Jr.	5.20	9.00			5.20	9.00	14.20
Dufresne, Roland J.	0.00	2.00			0.00	2.00	2.00
Duppstadt, Arthur G.	0.00	2.00			0.00	2.00	2.00
Easterly, William S.	1.00	1.00			1.00	1.00	2.00
Ekstrom, Carl F.	1.00	0.00			1.00	0.00	1.00

Pilot Name	355FG Air	355FG Ground	Other Groups Air	Other Groups Ground	Total Air	Total Ground	Total Combined
Elder, John L. Jr.	8.00	13.00			8.00	13.00	21.00
Elliot, Frank (2SF)	0.00	3.00			0.00	3.00	3.00
Ellison, James C.	0.00	2.00			0.00	2.00	2.00
Englebreit, Joseph C.	0.50	2.00			0.50	2.00	2.50
Erickson, Joel E.	0.00	4.00			0.00	4.00	4.00
Eshelman, Francis L	1.00	0.00			1.00	0.00	1.00
Falvey, Harold W.	0.00	9.50			0.00	9.50	9.50
Fees, Edwin W.	0.00	1.50			0.00	1.50	1.50
Finnesey, Robert V.	0.00	1.50			0.00	1.50	1.50
Fletcher, Jack M.	0.00	5.00			0.00	5.00	5.00
Folger, John M.	1.00	0.00			1.00	0.00	1.00
Forehand, Willard F.	1.00	1.00			1.00	1.00	2.00
Forker, George W.	0.00	4.00			0.00	4.00	4.00
Fortier, Norman J.	5.83	5.50			5.83	5.50	11.33
Foster, Thomas J.	1.00	0.00			1.00	0.00	1.00
Frost, Lionel S. (RAF)	1.00	0.00			1.00	0.00	1.00
Fuller, Leonard B.	2.50	0.00			2.50	0.00	2.50
Fussell, Roscoe J.	2.50	1.00			2.50	1.00	3.50
Gadpaille, Warren J.	0.00	1.00			0.00	1.00	1.00
Galer, Donald	0.00	5.00			0.00	5.00	5.00
Garlich, Robert L.	0.00	6.50			0.00	6.50	6.50
Gelsone, Frank E.	0.00	1.50			0.00	1.50	1.50
Gilleland, Alvah G.	0.00	1.00			0.00	1.00	1.00
Gore, Victor E.	0.00	2.50			0.00	2.50	2.50
Graham, Clarence H.	1.00	2.00			1.00	2.00	3.00
Graham, Gordon M.	7.00	9.50			7.00	9.50	16.50
Gresham, Walter V. Jr.	4.00	3.00			4.00	3.00	7.00
Griswold, Walter L. Jr.	0.00	0.50			0.00	0.50	0.50
Hardee, Sellers S.	0.00	2.00			0.00	2.00	2.00
Harrington, James C.	0.50	2.00			0.50	2.00	2.50
Hauver, Charles D.	5.00	0.00			5.00	0.00	5.00
Haviland, Fred R. Jr.	6.00	6.00			6.00	6.00	12.00
Heaton, Robert L.	0.00	2.00			0.00	2.00	2.00
Hendrickson, Edwin M.	1.00	0.00			1.00	0.00	1.00
Hill, Byron L.	1.00	3.00			1.00	3.00	4.00
Hillman, Howard K.	1.00	1.00			1.00	1.00	2.00
Hixon, Thomas R.	0.00	1.50			0.00	1.50	1.50
Hoffman, Garlyn O.	1.00	1.00			1.00	1.00	2.00
Hoffman, Harold J.	1.00	2.00			1.00	2.00	3.00
Houston, Byron G. Jr.	0.00	3.00			0.00	3.00	3.00
Hovde, William J.	10.50	2.00			10.50	2.00	12.50
Huish, Heber M.	0.50	0.00			0.50	0.00	0.50
Hulderman, Robert F.	0.00	1.50			0.00	1.50	1.50
Iglesias, Victor D.	2.00	2.00			2.00	2.00	4.00
Jabara, James	0.00	5.50	1.50	0.00[2]	1.50	5.50	7.00
Jackson, Norbert P.	0.00	1.00			0.00	1.00	1.00
Jacobson, Donald J.	0.00	2.00			0.00	2.00	2.00
James, Wayne W.	1.00	1.00			1.00	1.00	2.00
Johnston, Frederick W.	0.00	1.00			0.00	1.00	1.00
Johnston, Ben D. Jr.	4.00	3.00			4.00	3.00	7.00
Johnston, Curtis G.	0.20	4.50			0.20	4.50	4.70
Juntilla, J. O.	0.00	2.00			0.00	2.00	2.00
Kaminski, Rudolph B.	1.00	1.00			1.00	1.00	2.00
Kaplan, Albert B.	0.00	1.00			0.00	1.00	1.00
Kelley, Frederick W.	2.00	0.00			2.00	0.00	2.00
Kemper, George A. Jr.	2.00	0.00			2.00	0.00	2.00
Kenney, Paul H.	2.00	1.00			2.00	1.00	3.00
Kerch, Joseph F.	0.00	0.33			0.00	0.33	0.33
Keuhl, R. C.	0.00	0.50			0.00	0.50	0.50
King, Myles	0.00	2.00			0.00	2.00	2.00
Kinnard, Claiborne H. Jr.	7.00	15.00	1.00	2.00[3]	8.00	17.00	25.00
Kirby, Henry H. Jr.	1.00	5.00			1.00	5.00	6.00
Kirk, Richard J.	0.00	1.00			0.00	1.00	1.00
Kight, Harold I.	0.00	3.00			0.00	3.00	3.00

Pilot Name	355FG Air	355FG Ground	Other Groups Air	Other Groups Ground	Total Air	Total Ground	Total Combined
Knutty, Harold P.	1.00	2.00			1.00	2.00	3.00
Koraleski, Walter J.	5.54	0.00			5.54	0.00	5.54
Kozacka, Arthur G.	0.00	1.00			0.00	1.00	1.00
Kubetin, William T.	0.00	1.00			0.00	1.00	1.00
Kucheman, Henry J.	4.00	2.00			4.00	2.00	6.00
Kurtz, Robert G.	0.50	5.00			0.50	5.00	5.50
Lacazette, Mario	0.00	0.50			0.00	0.50	0.50
Lake, Joseph E.	0.00	1.00			0.00	1.00	1.00
Lamer, Charles W.	3.00	0.00			3.00	0.00	3.00
Langley, Donald B.	0.00	4.00			0.00	4.00	4.00
Lanius, Jonn H.	0.00	1.00			0.00	1.00	1.00
Leaf, Leroy R. Jr.	0.00	0.50			0.00	0.50	0.50
Lenfest, Charles W.	5.50	2.00			5.50	2.00	7.50
Lister, Walter B.	0.00	1.50			0.00	1.50	1.50
Long, Thurman C.	2.00	4.00			2.00	4.00	6.00
Ludeke, Edward P.	1.00	0.00			1.00	0.00	1.00
Lynch, William J.	0.00	5.00			0.00	5.00	5.00
Lyons, William S.	2.00	0.00			2.00	0.00	2.00
MacConkey, Jack S.	0.00	3.00			0.00	3.00	3.00
MacFarlane, Walter E.	1.50	2.00			1.50	2.00	3.50
Macurdy, Harold H.	2.00	0.00			2.00	0.00	2.00
Maisch, Joseph J. Jr.	2.00	1.00			2.00	1.00	3.00
Mann, Herbert R.	0.00	1.50			0.00	1.50	1.50
Marsh, Halbert G.	0.00	5.00			0.00	5.00	5.00
Marshall, Bert W. Jr.	7.00	3.00			7.00	3.00	10.00
Martin, William D.	4.00	3.00			4.00	3.00	7.00
Martyn, Donald M.	1.50	0.00			1.50	0.00	1.50
Masters, Frank R.	3.00	0.00			3.00	0.00	3.00
Max, Joseph H.	2.00	0.50			2.00	0.50	2.50
McCasland, Darwin D.	2.00	3.00			2.00	3.00	5.00
McCollom, Francis N.	0.00	5.00			0.00	5.00	5.00
McCurry, Charles R.	0.00	1.00			0.00	1.00	1.00
McElroy, James N.	5.00	6.00			5.00	6.00	11.00
McGinty, William J.	0.50	1.00			0.50	1.00	1.50
McHugh, Phillip M. N.	2.00	3.00			2.00	3.00	5.00
McLear, Robert M.	2.00	2.00			2.00	2.00	4.00
McLeod, Michael J.	0.00	2.00			0.00	2.00	2.00
McNally, Russell I.	0.00	2.00			0.00	2.00	2.00
McNeff, Edward P.	1.50	1.00			1.50	1.00	2.50
Mellen, Joseph E.	2.00	8.00			2.00	8.00	10.00
Mendenhall, Lee G.	0.50	3.00			0.50	3.00	3.50
Meteyer, Thomas O.	1.00	0.00			1.00	0.00	1.00
Michelena, Ralph L.	1.00	1.00			1.00	1.00	2.00
Michels, Kenneth M.	1.00	0.00			1.00	0.00	1.00
Mikalauskas, Kenneth E.	1.00	0.00			1.00	0.00	1.00
Miller, Kenneth J.	0.00	2.00			0.00	2.00	2.00
Mills, Newell F. Jr.	3.00	1.00			3.00	1.00	4.00
Mincemeyer, Allan J.	0.00	1.00			0.00	1.00	1.00
Minchew, Leslie D.	5.50	0.50			5.50	0.50	6.00
Misner, Richard F.	0.00	4.50			0.00	4.50	4.50
Molnar, John E.	1.00	2.00			1.00	2.00	3.00
Monahan, Harold L.	2.00	1.00			2.00	1.00	3.00
Moroney, Edward J.	3.00	2.00			3.00	2.00	5.00
Morris, Ray S.	3.50	10.00			3.50	10.00	13.50
Myers, Raymond B.	5.00	4.00			5.00	4.00	9.00
Neal, Thomas J.	4.50	0.50			4.50	0.50	5.00
Nelson, Ervin C. Jr.	0.00	2.00			0.00	2.00	2.00
Nicodemus, Ralph J.	0.00	1.00			0.00	1.00	1.00
Norman, Robert L.	1.00	0.67			1.00	0.67	1.67
Olson, Norman E.	6.00	2.00			6.00	2.00	8.00
Owens, Robert B.	0.00	1.00			0.00	1.00	1.00
Packard, Hudson F.	0.00	2.00			0.00	2.00	2.00
Pardee, Harry W. Jr.	0.00	1.00			0.00	1.00	1.00
Parks, Robert F.	0.00	4.00			0.00	4.00	4.00

	355FG		Other Groups		Total		Total
Pilot Name	Air	Ground	Air	Ground	Air	Ground	Combined
Patelunas, Robert J.	0.00	1.00			0.00	1.00	1.00
Patrinely, Costa C.	0.00	2.00			0.00	2.00	2.00
Patterson, Gilbert T.	0.00	1.00			0.00	1.00	1.00
Pearson, Richard P.	0.00	1.00			0.00	1.00	1.00
Peglar, Warren B. (RCAF)	4.00	1.00			4.00	1.00	5.00
Perry, Emil F.	2.00	3.00			2.00	3.00	5.00
Peters, Robert O.	3.00	2.00			3.00	2.00	5.00
Peterson, Noble E.	1.00	2.00			1.00	2.00	3.00
Plemmons, Charles E.	0.00	2.00			0.00	2.00	2.00
Priest, Royce W.	5.00	0.00			5.00	0.00	5.00
Ramsdell, Fred L. Jr.	1.00	0.00			1.00	0.00	1.00
Reed, Joe E.	1.00	2.00			1.00	2.00	3.00
Reedy Irving	0.50	0.00			0.50	0.00	0.50
Riffle, Elmer H.	1.00	2.00			1.00	2.00	3.00
Robinson, Allan T.	1.00	0.00			1.00	0.00	1.00
Rodebaugh, Charles R. (2SF)	1.00	0.00			1.00	0.00	1.00
Rosenblatt, Charles J.	1.00	1.00			1.00	1.00	2.00
Rouleau, Louis J. Jr.	0.00	1.00			0.00	1.00	1.00
Rowbotham, Robert C.	0.00	3.00			0.00	3.00	3.00
Salinsky, Charles J.	1.00	3.00			1.00	3.00	4.00
Sanders, Donald J.	0.00	1.00			0.00	1.00	1.00
Santos, Albert R.	2.00	0.00			2.00	0.00	2.00
Sarver, Frank A.	0.00	1.00			0.00	1.00	1.00
Scheid, Adolph J.	0.00	1.00			0.00	1.00	1.00
Schlect, Warner J.	0.00	1.50			0.00	1.50	1.50
Schmidt, George C.	0.00	1.00			0.00	1.00	1.00
Schoenfeldt, Edward E.	0.00	2.00			0.00	2.00	2.00
Shultz, Floyd W.	1.00	0.50			1.00	0.50	1.50
Schutt, Ralph C.	0.00	1.00			0.00	1.00	1.00
Schwab, Warren A.	1.00	0.00			1.00	0.00	1.00
Seeley, Grant A.	0.00	2.00			0.00	2.00	2.00
Shade, William A.	0.00	1.50			0.00	1.50	1.50
Silva, Stanley H.	1.00	6.00			1.00	6.00	7.00
Sluga, Emil L.	3.50	0.00			3.50	0.00	3.50
Snook, L. K.	0.00	1.00			0.00	1.00	1.00
Spencer, Charles H.	1.00	0.00			1.00	0.00	1.00
Spencer, Harold W.	2.00	2.00			2.00	2.00	4.00
Stanton, O. N.	0.00	1.00			0.00	1.00	1.00
Stewart, Everett W.	7.00	1.50	0.83	0.00[4]	7.83	1.50	9.33
Strachan, Robert W.	0.00	1.00			0.00	1.00	1.00
Sturm, Jack D.	1.00	2.50			1.00	2.50	3.50
Sweat. Charles H.	1.00	0.00			1.00	0.00	1.00
Szaniawski, Edward W.	3.00	4.67			3.00	4.67	7.67
Taylor, Floyd K.	0.50	0.00			0.50	0.00	0.50
Taylor, Robert G.	1.50	0.00			1.50	0.00	1.50
Thompson, Robert M.	2.00	0.00			2.00	0.00	2.00
Todd, Charles G.	0.00	3.00			0.00	3.00	3.00
Tolby, William W. Jr.	1.00	0.00			1.00	0.00	1.00
Trembarth, Floyd W.	0.00	1.00			0.00	1.00	1.00
Tuholski, David C.	0.00	1.00			0.00	1.00	1.00
Tulloch, John F. Jr.	0.00	4.00			0.00	4.00	4.00
Vickery, Duran M.	0.00	3.00			0.00	3.00	3.00
Vincent, Roland L.	1.00	0.00			1.00	0.00	1.00
Vineyard, Paul W. Jr.	1.00	1.00			1.00	1.00	2.00
Walsh, Robert J.	0.00	1.00			0.00	1.00	1.00
Watkins, D. P.	0.00	3.00			0.00	3.00	3.00
Weidmann, John J.	0.00	2.00			0.00	2.00	2.00
Westerveld, Robert	0.00	1.00			0.00	1.00	1.00
Whalen, William E. (2SF)	5.00	2.00	1.00	0.00[5]	6.00	2.00	8.00
White, Alvin S.	1.00	0.50			1.00	0.50	1.50
White, Richard M.	0.00	1.00			0.00	1.00	1.00
White, Robert M.	0.00	3.50			0.00	3.50	3.50
Whitlow, Robert V. (2SF)	1.00	0.00			1.00	0.00	1.00
Whitney, Emerson H.	0.00	1.50			0.00	1.50	1.50

Pilot Name	355FG Air	355FG Ground	Other Groups Air	Other Groups Ground	Total Air	Total Ground	Total Combined
Wilkens, John K. Jr. (2SF)	1.00	0.00			1.00	0.00	1.00
Wilkes, Henry S.	1.00	0.00			1.00	0.00	1.00
Williams, Benjamin G.	0.00	2.00			0.00	2.00	2.00
Williams, Sumner C.	0.50	2.00			0.50	2.00	2.50
Williamson, Brady C.	1.70	4.00			1.70	4.00	5.70
Wilson, John H.	3.50	3.50			3.50	3.50	7.00
Woertz, Jack R.	1.00	0.00			1.00	0.00	1.00
Wood, Thomas L.	1.00	1.00			1.00	1.00	1.00
Woody, Robert E.	7.00	2.00			7.00	2.00	9.00
Woodlard, Marion L.	1.00	0.00			1.00	0.00	1.00
Wright, Gilbert S.	2.00	0.00			2.00	0.00	2.00

Footnotes

1. Ceglarski's score with 4th FG.
2. Jabara's score with 363rd FG.
3. Kinnard's score with 4th FG.
4. Stewart's score with 352nd FG.
5. Whalen's score with 4th FG.

TABLE C-Aces

Pilot Name	355FG Air	355FG Ground	Other Groups Air	Other Groups Ground	Total Air	Total Ground	Total Combined
Brown, Henry W.	14.20	14.50			14.20	14.50	28.70
Kinnard, Claiborne H. Jr.	7.00	15.00	1.00	2.00[1]	8.00	17.00	25.00
Elder, John L. Jr.	8.00	13.00			8.00	13.00	21.00
Cullerton, William J.	5.00	15.00			5.00	15.00	20.00
Graham, Gordon M.	7.00	9.50			7.00	9.50	16.50
Duffy, James E. Jr.	5.20	9.00			5.20	9.00	14.20
Morris, Ray S.	3.50	10.00			3.50	10.00	13.50
Hovde, William J.	10.50	2.00			10.50	2.00	12.50
Haviland, Fred R. Jr.	6.00	6.00			6.00	6.00	12.00
Fortier, Norman J.	5.83	5.50			5.83	5.50	11.33
McElroy, James N.	5.00	6.00			5.00	6.00	11.00
Marshall, Bert W. Jr.	7.00	3.00			7.00	3.00	10.00
Bille, Henry S.	6.00	4.00			6.00	4.00	10.00
Mellen, Joseph	2.00	8.00			2.00	8.00	10.00
Falvey, Harold W.	0.00	9.50			0.00	9.50	9.50
Stewart, Everett W.	7.00	1.50	0.83	0.00[2]	7.83	1.50	9.33
Woody, Robert E.	7.00	2.00			7.00	2.00	9.00
Myers, Raymond B.	5.00	4.00			5.00	4.00	9.00
Olson, Norman E.	6.00	2.00			6.00	2.00	8.00
Whalen, William E.	5.00	2.00	1.00	0.00[1]	6.00	2.00	8.00
Szaniawski, Edward W.	3.00	4.67			3.00	4.67	7.67
Lenfest, Charles W.	5.50	2.00			5.50	2.00	7.50
Johnston, Ben D. Jr.	4.00	3.00			4.00	3.00	7.00
Martin, William D.	4.00	3.00			4.00	3.00	7.00
Gresham, Walter V. Jr.	4.00	3.00			4.00	3.00	7.00
Wilson, John H.	3.50	3.50			3.50	3.50	7.00
Jabara, James	0.00	5.50	1.50	0.00[3]	1.50	5.50	7.00
Silva, Stanley H.	1.00	6.00			1.00	6.00	7.00
Garlich, Robert L.	0.00	6.50			0.00	6.50	6.50
Barger, Clarence R.	0.33	6.00			0.33	6.00	6.33
Minchew, Leslie D.	5.50	0.50			5.50	0.50	6.00
Kucheman, Henry J.	4.00	2.00			4.00	2.00	6.00
Boulet, William P.	3.00	3.00			3.00	3.00	6.00
Long, Thurman C.	2.00	4.00			2.00	4.00	6.00
Kirby, Henry H. Jr.	1.00	5.00			1.00	5.00	6.00
Dissette, Lawrence J.	1.00	5.00			1.00	5.00	6.00
Williamson, Brady C.	1.70	4.00			1.70	4.00	5.70
Koraleski, Walter J.	5.54	0.00			5.54	0.00	5.54
Dix, Gerald J.	4.00	1.50			4.00	1.50	5.50
Kurtz, Robert G.	0.50	5.00			0.50	5.00	5.50
Cooper, Randolph W.	0.00	5.50			0.00	5.50	5.50
Hauver, Charles D.	5.00	0.00			5.00	0.00	5.00
Priest, Royce W.	5.00	0.00			5.00	0.00	5.00
Neal, Thomas J.	4.50	0.50			4.50	0.50	5.00
Peglar, Warren B. (RCAF)	4.00	1.00			4.00	1.00	5.00
Moroney, Edward J.	3.00	2.00			3.00	2.00	5.00
Peters, Robert O.	3.00	2.00			3.00	2.00	5.00
Perry, Emil F.	2.00	3.00			2.00	3.00	5.00
McCasland, Darwin D.	2.00	3.00			2.00	3.00	5.00
McHugh, Phillip M. N.	2.00	3.00			2.00	3.00	5.00
Ceglarski, George W.	1.00	2.00	0.00	2.00[1]	1.00	4.00	5.00
McCollom, Francis N.	0.00	5.00			0.00	5.00	5.00
Fletcher, Jack M.	0.00	5.00			0.00	5.00	5.00
Lynch, William J.	0.00	5.00			0.00	5.00	5.00
Galer, Donald	0.00	5.00			0.00	5.00	5.00
Marsh, Halbert G.	0.00	5.00			0.00	5.00	5.00

Footnotes

1. Scores with 4th FG
2. Scores with 352nd FG
3. Scores with 362nd FG

APPENDIX B

355th Fighter Group "Firstest, Fastest and Mostest"

VICTORIES - Air

Pilot	Squadron	Achievement	Date
Captain Carl Ekstrom -	358FS:	First group air victory on	10/4/43
Captain Norman Olson -	357FS:	First group pilot to shoot down two in one day on	1/29/44
Captain Henry Kucheman and Captain Robert Woody -	354FS:	(Tie) First group pilots to shoot down at least three in one day	4/24/44
Captain Robert Woody -	354FS:	First Eighth Air Force pilot to shoot down more than four in a single day (4.5) on	4/24/44
Major William Hovde -	358FS:	Only group Pilot to shoot down more than five in a single day (5.5) on	12/5/44
Captain Norman Olson -	357FS:	First group pilot to score five aerial victories	
Captain Henry Brown -	354FS:	First group pilot to score ten aerial victories	
Captain Henry Brown -	354FS:	First group pilot to score fifteen aerial victories (three shared)	
Captain Robert Woody -	354FS:	Most air victories in one month - 7 in April, 1944	
Captain Bert Marshall -	354FS:	Group ace in shortest period from start of combat operations - 60 days	
Captain Henry Bille -	357FS:	Last group air ace. Scored fifth and sixth victories on April 20, 1945	

Victories - Ground

Pilot	Squadron	Achievement	Date
Captain Charles Sweat -	354FS:	First ground victory	3/8/44
Lieutenant Clarence Barger -	354FS:	First group pilot to destroy three in one day	3/8/44
Flight Officer Henry Brown -	354FS:	First 8th Air Force pilot to destroy four(4.5) in one day	3/08/44
Lieutenant James McElroy -	358FS:	First group pilot to destroy five in one day	4/15/44
Lieutenant Henry Brown -	354FS:	First group pilot to destroy six in one day	9/10/44
Lieutenant William Cullerton -	357FS:	First 8th Air Force pilot to destroy seven in one day	9/12/44
Major Claiborne Kinnard -	354FS:	First group pilot to destroy a total of five on the ground	4/10/44
Lt.Col. Claiborne Kinnard -	355HQ:	First group pilot to destroy a total of ten on the ground	6/24/44
Captain William Cullerton -	357FS:	First group pilot to destroy a total of fifteen on the ground	3/30/45

APPENDIX C

Campaigns of the 355th

Campaigns of the 355thFG and the 355thTFW, including the 354thFS, 354thTFS, 357thFS, 357thTFS, 358thFS, 56thWS (former 358FS)

World War II
    EAME Theater
    Air Offensive, Europe
    Normandy
    Northern France
    Rhineland
    Ardennes - Alsace
    Central Europe

Korea
    First UN Counteroffensive
    CCF Spring Offensive
    UN Summer - Fall Offensive
    Second Korean Winter
    Korea Summer - Fall - 1952
    Third Korean Winter
    Korea Summer - Fall - 1953

Vietnam
    Defense Campaign - 3/2/65 to 1/30/66
    Air Campaign - 1/31/66 to 6/28/66
    Air Offensive Campaign, Phase I - 6/29/66 to 3/8/67
    Air Offensive Campaign, Phase II - 3/9/67 to 3/31/68
    Air/Ground Campaign - 1/22/68 to 7/7/68
    Air Offensive Campaign, Phase III - 4/1/68 to 10/31/68
    Air Offensive Campaign, Phase IV - 11/1/68 to 2/22/69
    TET 69/CounterOffensive Campaign - 2/23/69 to 6/8/69
    Summer- Fall, 1969, Campaign - 6/9/69 to 10/31/69
    Winter- Spring, 1970, Campaign - 11/1/69 to 4/30/70
    Sanctuary Counter Offensive Campaign - 5/1/70 to 6/30/70

APPENDIX D

Unit Citations and Awards to the 355th

World War II
  Distinguished Unit Citation, Germany
    4/5/44
Korea, Post Korea
  Air Force Outstanding Unit Award, Korea
    3/56 to 10/56
  Air Force Outstanding Unit Award, McGhee-Tyson AFB
    7/56 to 6/57
  Air Force Outstanding Unit Award, Korea
    3/60 to 2/61
  Air Force Outstanding Unit Award, George AFB
    10/62 to 12/63
Vietnam, South East Asia
  Presidential Unit Citation, Southeast Asia
    5/65 to 6/65
  Presidential Unit Citation, Southeast Asia
    6/65 to 11/65
  Presidential Unit Citation, Vietnam
    1/66 to 10/66
  Air Force Outstanding Unit Award, Combat - Vietnam
    10/66 to 4/67
  Air Force Outstanding Unit Award, Combat - Vietnam
    4/67 to 4/68
  Presidential Unit Citation, Vietnam
    8/11/67, 8/12/67, 10/24/67 and 10/28/67
  Air Force Outstanding Unit Award
    7/67 to 6/68
  Presidential Unit Citation
    4/68 to 4/69
  Air Force Outstanding Unit Award, Combat - Vietnam
    7/69 to 11/70
  Air Force Outstanding Unit Award, Southeast Asia
    1/71 to 12/71

APPENDIX E

Commanding Officers of the 355th Fighter Group
During World War II and The Occupation

Group Commanders

Major Morris C. Crossen	-11/12/42
Lieutenant Colonel William J. Cummings, Jr.	-01/16/43
Lieutenant Colonel Everett W. Stewart	-11/04/44
Lieutenant Colonel Claiborne H. Kinnard, Jr.	-02/21/45
Lieutenant Colonel William D. Gilchrist	-06/07/45
Lieutenant Colonel Bert W. Marshall, Jr.	-09/02/45
Lieutenant Colonel John L. Elder, Jr.	-10/07/45
Colonel Carroll W. McColpin	-03/14/46

Squadron Commanders

354th Fighter Squadron

Major Morris C. Crossen	-11/12/42
Lieutenant James P. Murphy	-11/22/42
Lieutenant Joe R. Williams	-02/03/43
Major Claiborne H. Kinnard, Jr.	-11/27/43
Major Henry B. Kucheman, Jr.	-06/12/44
Captain Bert W. Marshall, Jr.	-07/31/44
Major Gordon M. Graham	-10/23/44
Major Norman J. Fortier	-06/17/45
Captain James E. Duffy	-09/25/45
Major John R. Dolny	-04/29/46

357th Fighter Squadron

Major Morris C. Crossen	-11/12/42
Lieutenant John S. Poyen	-12/17/42
Lieutenant Edward S. Szaniawski	-02/02/43
Major Fred L. Ramsdell, Jr.	-05/20/44
Captain John L. Elder, Jr.	-07/26/44
Captain John F. Tullock	-09/01/45
Major William J. Hovde	-04/30/46

Commanding Officers cont'd

358th Fighter Squadron

Major Morris C. Crossen	-11/12/42
Lieutenant Theodore B. Marxson	-02/02/43
Lieutenant Raymond B. Myers	-02/08/43
Major Charles J. Rosenblatt	-06/29/44
Captain William J. Hovde	-07/11/44
Captain Emil L. Sluga	-08/02/44
Captain Walter V. Gresham	-03/22/45
Major William J. Hovde	-05/09/45
Captain Kenneth E. Mikalauskas	-08/10/45

Various Group Air Executive Officers

Lieutenant Colonel Thomas H. Hubbard
Lieutenant Colonel Gerald J. Dix
Lieutenant Colonel Everett W. Stewart
Lieutenant Colonel Claiborne H. Kinnard, Jr.
Lieutenant Colonel Bert W. Marshall, Jr.
Lieutenant Colonel William D. Gilchrist
Lieutenant Colonel John L. Elder

APPENDIX F

355th Fighter Group Pilots KIA, MIA, POW, Evaded or Rescued

Date	Unit	Type	Cause	Pilot - Circumstances
43-09-25	354	KIA	OTH.	Lieutenant James Donavan - Spun out on a training flight to Goxhill.
43-10-04	358	KIA	OTH.	Lieutenant Ralph Dean - Crash landed damaged P-47 on the English Coast rather than bail out. Hit hard by FW-109 near Eupen, at 1023, which damaged his landing gear. Died hours after the crash landing.
43-10-18	358	KIA	OTH.	Lieutenant Eugene Maben - Seen spinning down east of Cambrai. No flak or fighters seen in the area.
43-11-05	357	MIA	AIR	Lieutenant Clark Collins - Hit by Me-109s and seen in flames near West Schouwen. Chute seen near ground. Reported POW but did not show up after war.
43-11-07	357	KIA	OTH.	Lieutenant Edwin Carlson - Collided with Westphall over Holland while following Olson on a bounce.
43-11-07	357	POW	OTH.	Lieutenant James Westphall - Collided with Carlson and broke both legs on the horizontal stabilizer while bailing out.
43-11-07	358	POW	OTH.	Lieutenant William Roach - Low on fuel and made an emergency landing on the continent.
43-11-07	358	POW	OTH.	Captain Walter Kossack - Ran out of fuel over the continent and crash-landed.
43-11-07	358	MIA	OTH.	Flight Officer Chester Watson - Ran out of fuel on the way home over the Channel and bailed out near French coast. Reported POW in January 1944 by the Germans but did not turn up after the war.
43-11-13	HQ	EV	FLAK	Lieutenant Colonel Thomas Hubbard - Hit by flak while "essing" over the bombers while leading the group. Immediate heavy vibration occurred which forced Hubbard over the side. He escaped to Spain via the underground.
43-11-13	358	KIA	AIR	Lieutenant Jock Lanphier - Last seen being chased by several Me-109s over the Ems River.
43-11-15	357	KIA	OTH.	Lieutenant Lawrence McGraw - Disappeared with McNally on a weather flight. German records do not indicate either flak or fighter claims for that day in that area so the probable cause was weather or mid-air collision.
43-11-15	357	KIA	OTH.	Lieutenant Donald McNally - Lost with McGraw on the above mentioned weather flight.
43-11-29	354	MIA	OTH.	Lieutenant Alfred Del Negro - Disappeared while flying Woody's wing on penetration in clear weather. No flak or fighters encountered.
43-11-29	358	POW	OTH.	Lieutenant Charles Hecht - Ran out of gas after three encounters with German fighters and made an emergency landing on the continent.

43-11-29	358	POW	UNK.	Lieutenant Richard Peery - With Hecht during several encounters with Me-109s. Not known for certain whether or not he bellied in due to fuel problems or battle damage.
43-12-01	357	POW	FLAK	Lieutenant Jesse Williamson - Started smoking during an accurate and heavy flak barrage. Williamson bailed out over Koblenz when his P-47 started burning and filled the cockpit with smoke.
43-12-01	358	KIA	UNK.	Captain James Hull - Last seen with his flight flying into a thick cloud layer over Lierre at approximately 1200 during a flak barrage. Did not come out.
43-12-04	354	KIA	OTH.	Lieutenant Roland Vincent - Killed during RAF tactics training when the tail of his P-47 failed in a dive near Colerne.
43-12-11	358	KIA	OTH.	Lieutenant Jack Woertz - Killed when his P-47 stalled on final approach to Hastings field in bad weather.
43-12-30	354	POW	AIR	Lieutenant Raymond Murdoch - Shot down near Soissons after chasing several Me-109s down to the deck alone. Claimed one Me-109 before going over the side.
43-12-30	358	KIA	FLAK	Captain Carl Ekstrom - Last seen returning to St. Inglevert area to strafe flak targets.
43-12-30	358	KIA	AIR	Flight Officer Charles Wambier - Last seen in a head on pass with several Me-109s over Reims while flying Markin's wing.
44-01-24	357	KIA	FLAK	Lieutenant Frank Pipher - Received a hit by large coastal flak emplacements near the French coast and seen to spin into the Channel.
44-01-29	358	EV.	AIR	Lieutenant Harold Macurdy - Shot down near Koblenz by couple of Me-109s near the deck after shooting down two others. Crashed into trees but evaded capture by the Germans. Fought with the French underground until his return in late summer.
44-01-29	362FG	POW	AIR	Major J. J. Fischer - Shot down near Limburg by FW190s to become POW. Assigned to fly with the 358thFS for operational experience before returning to 362FG.
44-01-29	358	KIA	UNK.	Lieutenant Chauncy Rankin - Flying Macurdy's wing during the fight on the deck. Last seen by Macurdy making a tight chandelle with two Me-109s on his tail. Rankin was heard on the radio to say that he was hit and coming home on the deck but was never heard from again.
44-01-29	357	EV.	AIR	Captain Benjamin Martin - Hit hard by four FW-190s near Limburg. After escaping in heavy cloud cover, Martin had to bail out when his Thunderbolt became uncontrollable on the way home. Martin managed to evade capture via the underground and returned in mid May.
44-02-11	357	EV.	OTH.	Lieutenant Roland Dufresne - Experienced engine trouble during a diving bounce on several climbing FW-190s. May have been hit in the engine by the German fighters but the actual cause of the engine problem remains unknown. Dufresne bailed out and worked his way back home from Cologne by August.
44-03-08	354	KIA	FLAK	Lieutenant Charles Sweat - Hit by flak after destroying the 355th's first aircraft on the ground on Hosepe A/D and crashed near the airfield.
44-03-08	357	KIA	AIR	Lieutenant Daniel Rothenberg - Clobbered by an FW-190 during a chase while flying Norman's wing. Overran the long nose FW before Norman shot it down.
44-03-09	357	KIA	OTH.	Lieutenant William Momberger - Crashed and burned near Bassingbourne during formation assembly.
44-03-11	354	POW	FLAK	Lieutenant Lawrence Allard - Bailed out over Munster shortly after an intense flak barrage when his oil pressure dropped to zero. Approximately 1005.
44-03-11	358	POW	OTH.	Flight Officer John Chalot - Last seen in a dive over Gladsbeck. Could have been flak or an oxygen failure. No fighters encountered. Later thrown in Buchenwald but survived.
44-03-16	358	POW	AIR	Captain Donald Wright - Last seen chasing an ME-109 east of Augsburg and heading for the deck.
44-03-16	358	POW	AIR	Lieutenant Harold Carver - Last seen near Gunsburg with an ME-109 on his tail.
44-03-27	357	POW	FLAK	Lieutenant Chester Butcher - Survived a crash at high speed after getting hit by flak while

				strafing a German airfield near Bordeaux. Was in German hospital for a couple of months while recovering.
44-03-29	357	KIA	OTH.	Captain Howard Lambert - Drowned in the Channel after running out of fuel and ditching.
44-03-29	357	POW	OTH.	Captain Ben Johnston - Engine blew while chasing an FW-190 after shooting down two. Made a wheels down dead stick landing on a German airfield near Brunswick to become a guest of the Luftwaffe.
44-03-29	358	POW	FLAK	Lieutenant James McConnell - Hit by flak over Arnhem and bailed out over Rotterdam to become POW.
44-04-05	354	KIA	OTH.	Lieutenant Harold Culp - Collided with high tension power lines while strafing Landsberg airdrome.
44-04-05	357	KIA	FLAK	Lieutenant Byron Hill - Hit by flak and crashed into a parked ME-110 while strafing Dennigen A/D.
44-04-05	358	KIA	AIR	Lieutenant Edward Ondris - Last seen being chased by ME-109s over Landsberg airdrome.
44-04-08	358	KIA	AIR	Lieutenant James Dickson - Last seen bouncing several ME-109s and FW-190s alone near Emden.
44-04-08	357	KIA	FLAK	Captain Norman Olson - Mortally wounded by flak while strafing an airfield near Celle. Crashed and exploded near Hoefer.
44-04-08	357	POW	AIR	Lieutenant Irving Reedy - Shot down in a scrap while flying Szaniawski's wing west of Brunswick.
44-04-11	357	POW	FLAK	Captain William Easterly - Shot down by flak after destroying a JU-88 on Munsdorf airdrome.
44-04-11	354	POW	FLAK	Captain Curtis Johnston - Shot down by flak near Sorau after destroying three JU-88s.
44-04-15	354	POW	OTH.	Captain Walter Koraleski - Bailed out over Utrecht losing all coolant. May have been flak.
44-04-15	358	POW	FLAK	Lieutenant Paul Kenney - Hit by flak while strafing Wittstock airdrome. Spent almost six months in a German concentration camp.
44-04-15	357	POW	FLAK	Captain Joseph Kerch - Shot down by flak while strafing Wagonhof airdrome.
44-04-15	357	POW	FLAK	Lieutenant Darwin McCasland - Shot down by flak while strafing Wagonhof airdrome.
44-04-19	358	KIA	AIR	Flight Officer James MacConkey - Killed by ME-109s near Gottingen.
44-04-24	357	POW	AIR	Flight Officer Jack Sturm - Shot down over Knocke during big a fight and blown out of cockpit. Recovered consciousness in time to pull rip cord.
44-04-24	357	KIA	UNK.	Lieutenant Robert Norman - Disappeared while chasing an Me-109 through formation of B-17s. Could have been shot down by the bombers.
44-04-24	357	KIA	UNK.	Lieutenant Howard Hillman - Hillman was flying Norman's wing in the same encounter and both probably went down the same way.
44-04-24	357	KIA	FLAK	Lieutenant Raymond Demers - Shot down by flak while strafing barge after shooting down two ME-109s and sharing a third. His wing was blown off in the diving pass.
44-04-26	354	POW	OTH.	Lieutenant William Boulet - Probably shot down by top turret gunner of a B-17. No flak or fighters were in the area and Boulet's engine temperature went off the peg shortly after being shot at by a B-17.
44-04-29	354	KIA	UNK.	Captain Thomas Neal - Last seen by wingman while pulling out of a steep dive near Berlin. Neal was chasing two FW-190s at the time.
44-05-01	357	KIA	AIR	Lieutenant Rudolph Kaminski - Shot down by ME-109s near Metz in one diving pass.
44-05-04	358	KIA	AIR	Lieutenant Donald Martyn - Shot down by two ME-109s near Hanover after destroying one ME-109 and heavily damaging a second.

44-05-19	357	POW	FLAK	Lieutenant Colonel Edward Szaniawski - Shot down while strafing Diepholz or Solingen airdrome.
44-05-19	357	KIA	UNK.	Lieutenant Hudson Packard - Last seen while chasing a DO-217 over a German airfield and not heard from again.
44-05-20	354	KIA	AIR	Lieutenant Clarence Donaldson - Last seen with Jacobson just before a bounce by ME-109s.
44-05-20	354	KIA	AIR	Lieutenant David Jacobson - Disappeared with Donaldson Both probably shot down by ME-109s.
44-05-24	354	KIA	OTH.	Lieutenant Herbert Fritts - Crashed into train while strafing with Fortier. Might have been flak.
44-05-28	354	MIA	UNK.	Lieutenant Clarence Barger - Last seen on the tail of an ME-109 in a steep dive. Was heard to say he was OK and on the way home on the deck.
44-05-28	354	KIA	AIR	Lieutenant Walter Christensen - Shot down by ME-109s in a diving pass out of the sun.
44-06-03	354	POW	OTH.	Lieutenant Robert Browning - Lost coolant shortly after strafing ground targets west of Paris and bellied in near Verchoo. Could have been flak damage.
44-06-04	354	KIA	FLAK	Lieutenant Henry Davis - Had coolant problems on the way out and dropped to 4000 feet. Was hit by light flak near St. Quentin and seen to crash and burn.
44-06-06	357	KIA	FLAK	Lieutenant George Phillips - Hit by flak near La Mailleraye. Hit the tail of his Mustang when he bailed out and his chute failed to open.
44-06-06	357	POW	FLAK	Lieutenant Walter Douglass - Hit by flak near Calais and bailed out.
44-06-07	354	EV	FLAK	Lieutenant Robert Couture - Hit by flak while strafing near Nogent Le Rotrou and bailed out. Escaped capture via the French underground to return in August.
44-06-07	357	EV	FLAK	Lieutenant Harwood Harrell - Hit by flak while strafing and bellied in near Chateaudun. Evaded via the underground and returned in August.
44-06-07	357	POW	AIR	Lieutenant Walter MacFarlane - Shot down when yellow flight was bounced by 15 ME-109s near Aquigny. Bailed out OK.
44-06-07	357	KIA	AIR	Lieutenant John Guerrant - Shot down and killed near Aquigny.
44-06-07	357	KIA	AIR	Lieutenant Nils Holman - Shot down during a bounce by 15 Me-109s near Aquigny.
44-06-07	357	KIA	OTH.	Lieutenant Thomas Foster - Killed by the blast of his own bombs while flying McNeff's wing.
44-06-08	HQ	POW	FLAK	Lieutenant Colonel Gerald Dix - Bellied in near Niort after losing coolant. Probably flak related.
44-06-08	358	KIA	OTH.	Flight Officer Edward Williams - Killed while belly landing his flak damaged P-51 at Eyeworth.
44-06-19	358	KIA	UNK.	Lieutenant Ralph Coleman - Seen spinning down into the overcast with Reeves during a flak barrage. Could have been flak or a mid air collision.
44-06-19	358	KIA	UNK.	Lieutenant William Reeves - Seen spinning down with Coleman near Bordeaux.
44-06-22	357	POW	OTH.	Lieutenant Myles King - Bellied in after losing coolant near Albert.
44-06-27	354	EV	AIR	Lieutenant Thomas Ruark - Seen spinning down near Chateau Thierry when his flight was jumped by 15 Me-109s. Bailed out and evaded via the French underground.
44-07-05	354	KIA	FLAK	Lieutenant Victor Denti - Seen to crash on south edge of the Chateauroux airdrome during a strafing attack.
44-07-06	357	POW	FLAK	Lieutenant Norman Dixon - Hit by flak near Schwerin airdrome and bailed out OK.
44-07-07	354	KIA	OTH.	Lieutenant Heber Huish - Collided with debris from an exploding Me-410 near Halle after

Kinnard shot it down.

44-07-07	357	MIA	FLAK	Lieutenant Leonard Fuller - Hit by flak over Naumberg airdrome while chasing a damaged ME-109. A chute was seen to open OK but Fuller did not turn up after the war.
44-07-08	358	KIA	FLAK	Lieutenant James Lowder - Hit by flak and crashed into trees while strafing an airfield near Montmiral.
44-07-18	354	RES	OTH.	Lieutenant Fred Johnson - Bailed out over the Channel about 30 miles from Great Yarmouth. First group pilot to be rescued by Air/Sea Rescue.
44-07-19	354	POW	OTH.	Lieutenant Warren Schwab - Bailed out near Biberach after prop ran away. Seen trailing far behind Green flight just before a bounce by 15 to 20 FW-190s.
44-07-20	357	EV	FLAK	Lieutenant Walter Costello - Bailed out near front lines in France after receiving flak damage near Oschatz.
44-07-20	357	RES	OTH.	Lieutenant Robert Strachan - Rescued by Air/Sea Rescue after bailing out over the Channel.
44-07-24	354	KIA	UNK.	Lieutenant Sawchuck - Went down after strafing Lechfield airdrome. His Mustang crashed several miles away for unknown reasons.
44-07-24	358	POW	FLAK	Lieutenant Wayne Walburn - Shot down while strafing Lechfield airdrome and bellied in nearby.
44-08-01	357	RES	OTH.	Lieutenant Albert Debacker - His engine failed over the Channel on the way home. Debacker bailed out and was picked up by Air/Sea rescue.
44-08-02	357	RES	FLAK	Major John Elder - Hit by flak while strafing near Albert and collided with power lines but managed to struggle back to the Channel. Elder ditched and floated around for 45 minutes before two Frenchmen and an Englishman picked him up in a small boat and took him ashore.
44-08-02	357	EV	FLAK	Lieutenant Franklin Gowing - Hit by flak while strafing several barges near St. Poi. Bailed out at 2030 and evaded.
44-08-02	358	KIA	FLAK	Lieutenant Benjamin Orr, Jr. - Killed by flak while strafing road targets near Londimierres at 2035.
44-08-03	357	POW	FLAK	Lieutenant John Cotter - Hit by flak while shooting down an Me-109 on the deck near Mannheim. Both aircraft were seen to crash land. Cotter walked away.
44-08-03	354	POW	AIR	Captain Robert Kurtz - Hit in throttle linkage while making a head on pass on several Me-109s. Kurtz suffered a serious head injury while making a dead stick landing near a German hospital.
44-08-03	354	EV	OTH.	Lieutenant Floyd Taylor - Had engine problems and crash landed in Switzerland. Returned in September.
44-08-03	354	POW	OTH.	Lieutenant Garlyn Hoffman - Gil Patterson collied with Hoffman while turning to attack several Me-109s near Mannheim. Hoffman bailed out, broke his ankle, and still made it to the Swiss border before getting captured.
44-08-03	354	KIA	OTH.	Lieutenant Gilbert Patterson - Collided with his element leader, Hoffman, and no chute was seen to open.
44-08-06	354	KIA	UNK.	Lieutenant John Folger - Last seen chasing an Me-109 in a steep dive. Called in later to say he was OK and headed home on the deck. Never seen again.
44-08-08	357	EV	FLAK	Lieutenant Robert Bernoske - Hit by flak while strafing rail targets northeast of Vitry. Bailed out OK.
44-08-08	357	KIA	FLAK	Lieutenant Charles Lee - Mustang seen to crash and explode near St. Dizier while strafing ground targets.
44-08-11	358	KIA	FLAK	Lieutenant Frank Michela - His Mustang crashed into some trees after a strafing run near Metz.

44-08-12	357	EV	OTH.	Lieutenant Francis Eshelman - Coolant lost and bailed out near Meaux. Evaded and back in September.
44-08-14	357	EV	FLAK	Lieutenant William Shade - Hit by flak after destroying a JU-88 on Saarebourg airdrome. Managed to get out intact and evade capture.
44-08-15	358	POW	FLAK	Lieutenant Michael Graczyk - Hit by flak while strafing some marshalling yards near Vechta.
44-08-16	357	KIA	AIR	Lieutenant John Riggs - Last seen near Hildesheim with several Me-109s on his tail. Never seen again.
44-08-18	354	EV	FLAK	Captain Bert Marshall - Hit by flak while strafing a marshalling yard near the German border east of Paris. After bellying his Mustang in a nearby wheat field he was picked up by Royce Priest for the first "piggy back" rescue in the ETO. Both pilots made it back safely and Priest was awarded the DSC.
44-08-18	358	RES	FLAK	Captain Lawrence Sluga - Bailed out over the Channel after getting hit hard by flak while strafing. Picked up by Air/Sea rescue shortly afterwards. All three squadron commanders (Marshall, Elder, and Sluga) were rescued after going down for flak related reasons during August.
44-08-18	358	EV	FLAK	Lieutenant Cleveland Brien - Bellied his Mustang in near Soissons after being hit by flak. Evaded and returned to Steeple Morden in September.
44-08-26	358	KIA	OTH.	Lieutenant Richard Daves - Dove into the Channel for unknown reasons while on Air/Sea rescue patrol. No flak or fighters in the area.
44-08-28	354	EV	FLAK	Lieutenant Bert Smith - Mustang damaged by flak while strafing heavily defended marshalling yards near Metz. Bailed out on the way home just before his fighter blew up and evaded via French underground.
44-08-28	357	EV	FLAK	Lieutenant Lawrence Phillips - Bailed out near Commercy after receiving flak damage near Metz. Evaded capture via the French underground.
44-08-28	357	EV	FLAK	Lieutenant John Hurley - Bailed out near Metz. Evaded capture via the French underground.
44-08-28	358	KIA	FLAK	Lieutenant Wilson Weber - Hit hard by flak near Metz and bailed out but chute failed to open.
44-08-28	358	KIA	FLAK	Lieutenant John Gilmore - Hit hard by flak near Metz and seen to crash into power lines.
44-08-28	358	EV	FLAK	Lieutenant Kenneth Hughes - Shot down by flak near Metz and evaded capture with the help of the French underground.
44-08-28	358	EV	FLAK	Lieutenant Arthur Duppstadt - Shot down by flak while strafing near Metz. Evaded and returned shortly thereafter.
44-08-28	358	EV	UNK.	Lieutenant William Tolby - Not kown whether Tolby was hit by flak or attempting rescue of Duppstadt. Seen to land fairly close to Duppstadt's bellied Mustang. Evaded and returned.
44-09-03	354	EV	OTH.	Lieutenant Sumner Williams - Had mechanical problems while escorting 2ndSF Mustangs and bellied in near Nantes. Evaded capture and returned a few days later.
44-09-11	354	KIA	FLAK	Captain Kenneth Rafferty - Shot down while flying low over small German town on Zimmerman's wing.
44-09-11	354	KIA	FLAK	Lieutenant Charles McCurry - Shot down while strafing airdrome near Marburg. Bailed out but chute failed to open properly.
44-09-11	358	MIA	UNK.	Captain Walter Morgan - Last seen while strafing Kirchain airdrome. Heavy concentration of flak encountered in the area.
44-09-11	2SF	KIA	OTH.	Lieutenant Robert Bertleson - Lost control of group AT-6 while on a training flight and crashed near Steeple Morden.
44-09-12	354	MIA	UNK.	Lieutenant James Ellison - Last seen following FW-190 into a box of B-17's near Halle and not seen again.

44-09-12	357	POW	FLAK	Lieutenan John Chapman - Shot down by flak while strafing Schwartz airdrome.
44-09-12	358	MIA	FLAK	Lieutenant Roddy Reed - Landed in France due to engine problems after strafing. Not seen again.
44-09-18	358	KIA	OTH.	Lieutenant Robert Peters - Accidentally shot down by another 358FS pilot when he slipped in between an Me-109 and the other pursuing Mustang near Warsaw.
44-09-18	358	KIA	AIR	Lieutenant Joseph Vigna - Last seen chasing two ME-109s near Warsaw at approximately 1325. Time and location coincides with Luftwaffe claim that day.
44-10-03	354	POW	FLAK	Captain Henry Brown - Shot down by flak while destroying an Me-110 on the ground near Nordlingen. Bellied his Mustang near the airfield after losing all coolant.
44-10-03	354	POW	OTH.	Major Charles Lenfest - Landed close to Brown in Marshall's Mustang to try to rescue Brown. Got stuck in a small creek while taxiing over to meet Brown. Unknown to either pilot, Al White had also landed to try a rescue but was unable to attract either pilot's attention. Eighth AF issued a strongly worded memo following this mission strictly forbidding any future attempts of similar rescues.
44-10-05	357	POW	OTH.	Lieutenant James Juntilla - Engine failed just after turning for home over the German border. He bailed out at 1110 near the Zuider Zee.
44-10-18	357	MIA	FLAK	Lieutenant William Lonkausky - Hit by flak near Cologne and seen to bail out OK. Not known to turn up after the war.
44-10-22	354	KIA	OTH.	Captain Norman McDonald - Killed in ground accident when trailing Mustang collided with McDonald's P-51 while taxiing off main runway.
44-11-??	2SF	MIA	OTH.	Lieutenant William Hornickel - Ditched in North Sea after engine failed. Air/Sea Rescue did not find him.
44-11-02	354	MIA	OTH.	Lieutenant Albert Zimmerman - Bellied in near the German/Holland border after losing all oil pressure.
44-11-02	357	POW	FLAK	Captain Joseph Englebreit - Hit by flak while strafing Wernigerode airdrome at 1020. Seen to belly in and walk away.
44-11-09	354	POW	FLAK	Lieutenant Carl Hull - Hit by flak while strafing airdrome near Miltenburg and bellied his burning P-51 in.
44-11-16	354	POW	FLAK	Flight Officer Marion Woolard - Shot down by flak and bailed out near Barleburg at 1340 to be taken prisoner by the Germans. Woolard later escaped with Lenfest in April but mortally wounded by an artillary barrage near American front lines.
44-11-20	358	KIA	FLAK	Lieutenant Edward Haraburda - Shot down and killed by flak while strafing marshalling yards near Zulpick.
44-11-20	357	KIA	OTH.	Lieutenant Bob White - Engine failed while crossing back over the North Sea. Ditched and never seen again.
44-11-26	357	KIA	OTH.	Lieutenant Bernard Barab - Went down after mid air collision with Kelley. Both Mustangs spun out and no chutes were seen to open.
44-11-26	357	KIA	OTH.	Lieutenant Charles Kelley - Lost control of his damaged Mustang and collided with Barab west of Dummer Lake. His P-51 blew up shortly after the collision.
44-11-26	2SF	MIA	UNK.	Captain James Stauder - Last seen after the big fight near the Hannover area in which eight 2SF ships fought 75 to 100 FW-190s to score 5-1-2 for one loss. Thought to have landed in Belgium but not seen again.
44-12-05	357	POW	OTH.	Lieutenant Benjamin Williams - Bailed out west of Berlin when his oil pressure dropped to zero.
44-12-10	354	POW	OTH.	Lieutenant Maury Ivey - Lost oil pressure and bailed out near the front lines west of Bingen.
44-12-15	358	POW	OTH.	Lieutenant Arthuer - Bailed out north of Munster after losing coolant at approximately 1215.

44-12-25	357	KIA	UNK.	Lieutenant Harold Monahan - Last seen chasing an FW-190 on the deck. Vic Iglesias saw him on the FW-190's tail, looked around to clear his own tail, and lost sight of Monahan south of Koblenz.
45-01-13	358	KIA	OTH.	Leutenant Thomas Ksanzak - Spun out and crshed near Melbourne shortly after take off.
45-01-20	358	POW	FLAK	Lieutenant Frank Masters - Shot down by flak and bellied in successfully near Minden.
45-01-29	354	POW	FLAK	Lieutenant Scott Prothro - Hit by flak near Geldern at 1325 on the way home. Suffered serious burns before he bailed out and spent many months in hospitals before fully recovering.
45-02-03	358	KIA	FLAK	Lieutenant William Cummins - Nosed over and crashed from 1000 feet while strafing an armored train near Ulzen.
45-02-09	358	KIA	FLAK	Lieutenant Thomas Taylor - Died from injuries sustained during crash landing of flak crippled P-51 near Liege.
45-02-10	354	KIA	OTH.	Lieutenant Oran Stalcup - Died of exposure after ditching in the North Sea.
45-02-14	357	KIA	OTH.	Major John Wilson - Killed when his flak damaged Mustang went out of control near an emergency field in Belgium. Flak damage was sustained near Magdeburg.
45-02-21	354	KIA	FLAK	Lieutenant James Costigan - Hit by flak while strafing near Ansbach. Killed when his P-51 dove into ground.
45-02-23	354	POW	FLAK	Lieutenant George Kemper - Hit by flak near Quakenbruck at 1355 and bellied in near Dummer Lake.
45-02-23	354	POW	FLAK	Lieutenant Robert White - Hit by flak while strafing Neuburg airdrome. He bailed out just above some trees but survived to become POW.
45-02-26	357	KIA	OTH.	Lieutenant Sellers Hardee - Spun out and crashed in bad weather shortly after takeoff.
45-03-01	358	MIA	FLAK	Captain John Beckman - Hit by flak while chasing an ME-262 near the deck. Bailed out near Ingolstadt and never seen again.
45-03-15	358	EV	FLAK	Lieutenant John Long - Hit by flak near Hannover and managed to crash land near the Russian front lines. Returned to Steeple Morden in April.
45-03-15	357	EV	OTH.	Lieutenant Jack Dressler - Landed in Russian occupied territory and returned in April.
45-03-21	358	POW	FLAK	Lieutenant Colonel Lawrence Sluga - Hit by flak while strafing near Horsten airdrome, regained altitude and bailed out at 1015.
45-03-22	354	POW	FLAK	Lieutenant David Tuholski - Hit while strafing Wurzberg airdrome and bellied in close the field.
45-03-26	358	KIA	OTH.	Captain Wendell Beaty - Spun in during bad weather and crashed near Calais.
45-04-04	354	KIA	AIR	Lieutenant Robert Goth - Killed in head on pass with aggressive FW-190s over Ludwiglust airdrome.
45-04-04	354	KIA	AIR	Lieutenant Thomas Truell - Failed to pull out of a split-S at low altitude while engaging an FW-190 over Ludwiglust airdrome.
45-04-04	354	KIA	FLAK	Lieutenant Richard Gray - Hit by light flak 0900 south of Ludgwiglust and seen to spin in and explode.
45-04-05	354	KIA	FLAK	Lieutenant Robert McDonnell - Hit by German flak near Buren at 1440 hours on the way back to Steeple Morden from an emergency field.
45-04-07	354	MIA	OTH.	Lieutenant Newell Mills - Disappeared with Plowman over the North Sea while on the way home. No flak or fighters seen in the area.
45-04-07	354	MIA	OTH.	Lieutenant Gilbert Plowman - Flying Mills' wing over the North Sea when both disappeared. Could have been a mid air collision.

45-04-08 357	POW	FLAK	Captain William Cullerton - Shot down while strafing Ansbach airdrome. Hit in the fuselage tank and bailed out at low altitude. Shot in the stomach after capture by Wafeen SS and left to die. Escaped and restored to health by other Germans.
45-04-13 358	POW	FLAK	Lieutenant Warner Schelct - Hit by flak while strafing Rendsburg airdrome. Bellied in OK and captured.
45-04-16 357	KIA	FLAK	Lieutenant Joe Lake - Spun in after receiving a direct hit by flak while strafing Eferding airdrome.
45-04-16 357	POW	FLAK	Lieutenant Thurman Long - Hit hard by flak while strafing in the Linz area. Last seen flying smoking Mustang toward Russian lines.
45-04-16 358	POW	FLAK	Lieutenant William Lynch - Hit by flak at 1640 while strafing Straubing airdrome. Bellied in south of Straubing about ten minutes later, was captured and escaped.
45-04-16 358	EV	FLAK	Lieutenant John Rogers - Hit by flak over Straubing at 1642 and forced to belly his Mustang in. Evaded capture.
45-04-16 358	POW	FLAK	Lieutenant Francis McCollom - Hit by flak over Straubing at 1645 but got to Rosenburg before bellying in.
45-04-16 358	EV	FLAK	Captain Lawrence Dissette - Hit by light flak at 1650 while strafing Straubing airdrome. Bailed out ten miles northwest of the target and successfully evaded capture.

APPENDIX G

"Above and Beyond the Call of Duty"

Lieutenant James H. Howard, 354th Fighter Group-Ninth Air Force, was awarded a Congressional Medal of Honor for his courage in action on January 11, 1944, but the 354th Group was only on temporary detached service to the Eighth until more Mustang groups were available for action. It is an interesting and notable fact that no Eighth Air Force fighter pilot was awarded the Congressional Medal of Honor during World War II.

The 355 Fighter Group did have seven recipients of the Distinguished Service Cross, the nation's second highest award. Additionally, the Polish government awarded several pilots the Polish Cross of Valour, their second highest award. The group pilots receiving the awards were:

Distinguished Service Cross

April 11, 1944

Lieutenant Henry W. Brown - 354FS

Following an escort mission and a subsequent strafing attack in which Brown personally destroyed an FW-190 in the air and a JU-52 on the ground, plus damaging several others, Lieutenant Brown was separated from the rest of his flight.

While returning home alone with no ammunition, Lieutenant Brown spotted four Me-109s approaching two other Mustangs from behind. Brown warned the unsuspecting pair of their danger over the radio and immediately attacked the four German fighters, hoping to distract the Germans and bluff them away.

The German fighters and Lieutenant Brown ended up in a five ship Lufbery until, one by one, Brown managed to turn inside each German fighter and cause it to dive away. Just as the last German fighter dove away, the first one returned to attack Brown from behind. Although his aircraft was hit, Brown managed to escape and return his badly damaged ship to England.

April 24, 1944

Captain Robert E. Woody - 354FS

While leading his four ship flight of Mustangs on an escort to the Munich area, Woody spotted six Me-109s approaching B-17s in his assigned escort area. Captain Woody ordered the attack and immediately bounced the German fighters before waiting for the rest of his flight to catch up.

Woody personally destroyed four of the Me-109s with a devastating display of shooting and shared a fifth with his wingman. Woody also received credit for a probable and a damaged in another fight to become the first Eighth Air Force pilot to personally shoot down more than four German fighters in one day.

In all, his flight destroyed nine Me-109s for no losses.

July 7, 1944

Lieutenant Colonel Claiborne H. Kinnard, Jr. - 355 HQ

While leading the 355th Fighter Group on an escort mission to Leipzig, Kinnard spotted 30 to 40 twin engine German fighters, escorted by a top cover of more than 30 Me-109s, preparing to attack American heavy bombers nearby.

The German fighters attacked just as the bombers left the target. Kinnard radioed the positions of the fighters and immediately led his three ship flight into the Me-410s before the rest of the group could come to their aid. In the ensuing fight, Kinnard personally destroyed two Me-410s and one Me-109. His wingmen were also credited with the destruction of two more German fighters before the rest of the group joined the fight.

The attack was quickly broken up and unquestionably many lives were saved in the bomber force as a result of the quick and agressive action taken by Kinnard to place his small element between the German force and the bombers.

July 20, 1944

Lieutenant Robert O. Peters - 358FS

During an escort to the Oschatz, Germany area on July 20, Lieutenant Robert Peters and his wingman attacked more than 10 FW-190s and Me-109s. In a running fight from altitude to the deck, Peters destroyed two FW-190s while his wingman, Lieutenant Noble Peterson, destroyed an Me-109. After shooting down the second FW190 over a German airdrome near Leipzig, Peters spotted a DO-217 in the area and shot it down.

Peters ignored extremely heavy concentrations of 20mm flak to also destroy a He-111 and a JU-88 on the ground while damaging several others.

August 18, 1944

Lieutenant Royce W. Priest - 354FS

While on a low level sweep looking for targets of opportunity, Priest's squadron commander, Captain Bert Marshall, spotted a marshalling yard northwest of Paris and close to the German border. Marshall ordered the rest of the 354FS to orbit out of range of light flak while he personally made an attack to test the strength of the German defenses. Marshall's P-51 was immediately hit and set on fire by German flak. After ordering Priest to take command of the squadron and return home, Marshall split-S'd at low altitude and belly landed in a wheat field.

While Marshall was approaching the field, Lieutenant Priest told Marshall that he was landing in a nearby field to attempt a rescue. Marshall ordered Priest to not attempt the rescue but Priest, in willful disregard for his own personal safety, landed in a nearby field and taxied his Mustang as close to Marshall as possible to effect the pick up. Marshall arrived at the P-51's location and again ordered Priest to go home, at which time Priest threw his parachute and dingy to the ground and stepped out of the cockpit. Marshall relented and climbed in and Priest sat on his lap with his head resting against the front windshield to allow the canopy to close. The canopy opened during takeoff but the Mustang managed to clear some haystacks and take off successfully.

Priest and Marshall returned safely to Steeple Morden. The rescue was the first success by an American fighter pilot to rescue a fellow pilot behind enemy lines in Europe during World War II.

November 2, 1944

Lieutenant William J. Cullerton - 357FS

Following an escort mission to Merseburg, Germany, the 357FS spotted an airfield near Wernigerode which had a large concentration of German fighters on or above the field. In the ensuing attack, Cullerton personally destroyed an FW-190 and an Me-109 in the air before making several strafing passes on the German field.

In the face of intense anti aircraft fire, Cullerton destroyed an additional six German fighters on the ground to raise his total score to eight destroyed during the mission. Cullerton had scored the highest number of combined air and ground victories in the ETO for a single mission and became the first Eighth Air Force pilot to destroy eight in one day.

December 5, 1944

Major William J. Hovde - 358FS

While leading his squadron on an escort mission to Berlin, Major Hovde spotted a very large formation of approximately 90 German fighters forming for an attack in front of an approaching force of American heavy bombers.

With complete disregard for his personal safety, Major Hovde led his small force of Mustangs in an aggressive attack on the German fighter formation. Hovde personally destroyed five FW-190s and shared a sixth with his wingman when he ran out of ammunition. The squadron destroyed 12 total for no losses and the German attack force was completely broken up, eliminating a formidable threat to the heavy bombers approaching the target.

POLISH CROSS OF VALOR

September 18-22, 1944

Majors John L. Elder, Charles W. Lenfest, Bert W. Marshall, and Emil L. Sluga

For displaying exceptional leadership and tactical skill in the conduct of the escort of heavy bombers dropping supplies to the Polish underground in the city of Warsaw, the Polish Government presented each of the squadron commanders and the mission leader, Marshall, their second highest award for valor.

APPENDIX H

"The Last Shuttle Mission . . . a last desparate try to provide relief for the Polish Underground in Warsaw. September 18, 1944"

As told by George Shiller, Bert Marshall and Daniel Lewis.

In Memory of an Unknown Friend
by George Shiller

The day after Memorial Day, 1981 was gray at the Golden Gate National Cemetery in San Francisco. The American flags unfolded in the Pacific breeze disturbing the quietness of the white markers. I stood in silent salute. The letters, faded with time, read: "JOSEPH J. VIGNA, California 1st LIEUT. 355th AAF FIGHTER GP, World War II, May 2, 1920-September 18, 1944". I reflected on the events some 37 years ago which caused me to be here today.

September 18, 1944

"It was a sunny Monday, September 18, 1944 in Warsaw. The forty-eighth day of the Polish Uprising against the Germans was strangely very quiet. The Soviet Army had moved closer to the Vistula river few days before. The sporadic artillery fire was distant.

The combat intelligence post was on the roof of a suburban villa. I was located behind a chimney with periscope binoculars facing the enemy lines. The view was different today. The masts of the radio station were gone, the usual traffic near the Luftwaffe airfield was not there. I glanced at my watch - it was 13^{40}. In less than a half an hour my duty will be over. But not much to look forward to. The daily ration of bread was gone long time ago. Not even a cigarette!

Once again I started sweeping the horizon and paused on the bulge of an old fort hiding the Luftwaffe installation behind. And then the dull thunder of the anti- aircraft artillery started in the west and rapidly moved southward.

Something was different! The direction, intensity? I picked up a pair of field glasses and swept the sky: Twelve four-engine aircraft in flight formation. I was trying instinctively to judge the altitude. But the excitement was stronger and my hands holding the binoculars were trembling: Those are Flying Fortresses! It couldn't be. The RAF and the Poles fly Liberators from Italy - then finally the logic fell into place. Those are the Americans!

Then the parachutes appeared near the aircraft. Well, finally the Polish Parachute Brigade is coming to help us. But wait, the altitude is some 15,000 feet—something is not right. It was right, however. The parachutes were supporting containers only (with weapons and supplies).

I swept the sky again to see another group of 12 aircraft and another, crossing the cloudless sky. The multicolored parachutes slowly drifted away. The aircraft executed a turn to the east and then I spotted smaller aircraft moving like gnats among the bombers. Is the Lufwaffe attacking? No, those were the escort fighters to protect the Task Force. I looked at my watch. It was now 1345 and the show was over. The bombers disappeared in the smoke filled horizon, the multicolored parachutes bobbed gently while they drifted towards enemy lines. And then the machine gun fire started with increased intensity."

A mission ordered by the President of the United States was flown in support of the Polish Home Army (Underground) in Warsaw.

A Task Force comprised of the 95th, 100th, and 390th Bomb Groups of the 3rd Bomb Division, 8th Air Force, some 107 B-17 Flying Fortress bombers took off from the airfields of East Anglia and were escorted by the fighter planes of the 4th, 361st and finally 355th Fighter Groups. The Task Force and their escort landed at the American airfields in the Ukraine.

The aircraft of the 4th and 361st Fighter Groups returned to their bases in the United Kingdom. Some aircraft of the 355th Fighter Group engaged the Lufwaffe fighters some 30 miles NW of Warsaw. Two pilots of the Red flight of the 358th Squadron, Joseph Vigna and Robert Peters were shot down near the town of Nasielsk, 26 miles from Warsaw.

The Polish Forces in Warsaw received less than 100 containers with supplies, while the rest of the 1100 containers were lost or went to the enemy.

The isolated southern sector of Warsaw, a suburb known as Mokotow, fell into enemy hands only seven days after the American drop, and the rest of the city stopped the fight on October 2, 1944.

George Shiller
November, 1983

The Warsaw Mission and Last Shuttle

Bert W. Marshall, Jr.

The last Shuttle Mission was almost anti-climatic as we had started to go several times before but came back for a variety of reasons.

As I recall, a Major Franklin from the 4th Group helped us on the briefing on the night of September 12. Apparently the situation for the Poles was very critical in Warsaw and the Russians were not doing anything to help them. We were to escort bombers from the Third Division whose responsibility was to drop containers of food, ammo and medicine to the Polish Underground in Warsaw. Wing was pretty emphatic about appearances so we were instructed to leave our sidearms at home, not to discuss politics and, in general, just stay the hell out of trouble. A monumental task for most fighter pilots! If any pilot had to make an emergency landing on Russian soil, he was instructed to stay in his '51 and not wander off.

Our job was to pick up the bombers on the other side of Berlin and escort them all the way to Russia and back, by way of Italy. Stewart was to lead at the head of my 354th Squadron, Elder had the 357th and Sluga had the 358th. I led the "bastard" Borax Squadron as mission deputy and had Chuck Hauver flying my wing along with Peglar and Hulderman to round out Red flight. Henry Brown led Yellow while Gresham and Crandell had Blue and Green flights. Borax was a collection of pilots from all three of our squadrons, plus P-51s from the 4th, the 361st and our group, the 355th. Really pretty colorful with the assorted white, red and yellow noses and tail markings. As you might imagine, the hardest part of the mission was telling a lot of pilots that they couldn't go. We had around 100 pilots in the group at this point in the war and only 64 could go. Danny Lewis, our group I.O. and the engineering officer, McMillan, from the 358th went with the bombers to lend a helping hand if we needed it.

We scrubbed on the 13th, on the 14th and made it as far as Bremen before getting recalled on the 15th. The bombers were having trouble punching through a front so the deal was called off. The mission was set for the 18th and we lifted about 72 birds, including spares, away from the base somewhere near 0800. Stewart aborted as we made landfall on the other side of the channel, so I took the lead while my Squadron Ops, Chuck Lenfest picked up the lead of the 354th. Our route was straight across Germany while the bombers, escorted on the penetration by the 4th and the 361st, took the northern route along the Baltic. The only real concerns we had were related to fuel.

We had instructed everybody to lean the mixtures way back, stick with the bombers and stay away from extended chases of the Lufwaffe if they made an appearance. It's ironic that we had been bitching for months about the lack of activity from German fighters and now an early appearance could have screwed up the whole deal! Somewhere near Steinhuder Lake, we got a call from the bombers on C-channel alerting us that they were running about 15 minutes late so I proceeded to make a mistake. Rather than stooge around the R/V point and attract unwelcome attention, I ordered the group to slow down a little more. About 20 minutes later the bombers called us up to let us know that they were now about 15 minutes early! I spent a busy couple of minutes re-plotting a new R/V, took a heading of 145 and prayed that the weather wouldn't get much worse.

We lucked out and picked up the Forts on the other side of Torun at about 14,000 feet, in between two solid layers of clouds. Northwest of Warsaw, Brown called in some 109s about six o'clock to the bombers and asked if he could give 'em a go. He took his flight back and got one in the air, plus another couple of damaged. I didn't see him again for some time so I was a little worried, but Henry showed up just before we broke escort. Fortunately, because of our fuel situation, the German didn't challenge us very hard, but I believe we got four and lost a couple from the 358th. I found out after the war that the Germans only claimed one, so I don't know what happened but neither Peters nor Vigna made it to Russia.

Over Warsaw, we could see the city through some breaks in the clouds. The flak wasn't as bad as Berlin or Misburg but we were pretty low and we lost a couple of bombers by the time we left escort. Orbiting at 14,000 feet above heavy German AA is not a lot of fun. Somewhere near Brest Litovsk we left the bombers and set course for Piryatin. The B-17s flew to Mirgorod and Poltava while we milled around looking for our planked needle in a wheat field haystack. We were very close but it took us 30 minutes to get everybody on the ground. I was the last one down after seven hours and 30 minutes of flying time.

I spent about an hour on the ground counting noses and checking out the damage. Thanks to my little "short cut", we had to skirt a little too close to Stettin and Germans really put up a heavy concentration. Hoffman took a hit in the arm and his canopy was pretty badly dinged, as well as several other ships with some flak damage, but all in all we were pretty lucky. My fault for slowing down when we got the word that the Heavies were late!

I then took off and flew to Poltava and Mirgorad to plan the next day's mission with Colonel Truesdell, the bomber commander. After completing the mission plan for the 19th, Colonel Lancaster took me under his wing and fed me my first hamburger since I left the states. Lancaster escorted me around the base perimeter for an inspection of the base. It was pretty cold at the time and I remember that several Russian guards had consumed quite a bit of vodka.

We had a party that night at Poltava, with a lot of toasts, and I kept thinking that we had a trip the next day over unfamiliar territory, so I took it pretty easy. The two impressions I had the next morning were how cold it was crawling out of that sleeping bag, and how sore my fanny was after seven hours in the saddle the day before.

After breakfast, I carried the operations order to Mirgorod and then back to Piryatin to brief my group. Sluga's bird was down so Hovde took over the 358th for the rest of the trip. Several other ships were also down for various mechanical reasons so we left Piryatin with only 56 P-51s. We took off early, made rendezvous with the bombers and bombed some marshalling yards in Szolnok, Hungary. We saw no German fighters and proceeded to the Foggia area to land at three separate airfields.

We were detained in Italy for a couple of days and I really don't recall why. At any rate, we left Italy on the morning of the 22nd to return home via southern France. The weather was truly miserable over Steeple Morden. We could see the airfield from above but had zilch forward visibility. How we got everyone down with no mid-airs will always remain a mystery to me.

A couple of days later, after coming back from a mission, I was ordered to Wing headquarters by Kepner where the Polish Chief of Staff awarded several of us for our small part in the mission. I was deeply honored to have received the Polish Cross of Valor, even more than my Silver Star, and the mission was one of the most memorable of the war to me."

Bert Marshall
January, 1978

MISSION TO RUSSIA AND ITALY
Daniel M. Lewis-Group Intelligence Officer

The city of Warsaw, on the western banks of the coiling Vistula River, was visable for perhaps twenty minutes before we reached it. The surrounding country from our altitude of 16,000 feet appeared flat and rather unproductive like some of the wastelands of our own far west. A thick layer of dust and smoke hung over the city . . . the sick breath of the war in its streets. As we began our run to drop the supplies of guns, ammunition, food and medicine to the Polish patriots below, the lead group had already entered the range of the German heavy flak defenses. (The Germans held parts of the city while the patriots held others.) We slid into our appointed dropping position in the force. The few black puffs of fire had multiplied a hundred fold and the next few seconds reminded me of the final approach to the top slope of the roller coaster at State Fair Park. For the next four or five minutes we were in the thick of it, slightly altering our course and altitude constantly to evade the bursting shells of anti-aircraft fire. When the bomb bay doors opened, I thought for an instant of the hope in the invisible faces looking up from below. What manna from heaven, these bundles from Fortresses. I recalled the recent quotations in the British press, 'Hang on, relief is on the way.' I glanced down at the city and instead of seeing the expected flash of guns, tank maneuvers, troop concentrations and all that one associates with a street fight, all seemed strangely deserted. We turned eastward, back over the Vistula and set course for our base beyond Poland, deep in the Russian Ukraine. It was then about 1300 hours. We had been flying since 0530 in the morning and still there remained some four hours to go. But I looked forward to every minute of it and it was a relief to get out of the gun fire and the enemy fighters which had also been attacking during the bombing run. I had not seen them, but I did notice the red bursts of flak which often signals them to enter the fray.

There were hundreds of evergreen forests dotting the Polish and western Russian landscape. Most of the groves appeared to be forestation projects because there was a symmetry to the rows and heights of the trees. As we flew further into Russia, the same flat terrain existed but the country became less wooded and the spots of wasteland grew farther and farther apart. Vast wheat and rye fields took their place until that was all that could be seen in any direction for fifty miles. From the air, the country looked much like our own grain producing states of the middle and far west. It was comforting to think that the Russians had won back their breadbasket. What a prize for the Germans to lose! We drew near the winding Dnieper and were soon passing over the city of Kiev on the banks of the river. The gutted buildings could be plainly seen, buildings which seemed to be of the same architecture as those in cities at home. Other structures seemed intact and in the smaller communites surrounding there were only isolated signs of war damage. Scattered around the countryside, in almost any direction one looked, artillery and bomb craters could be seen. The trench systems and their relation to water holes, woods and gentle slopes had us wondering about the ground battles that occured within the last year; The casualties for each mile taken and retaken. The small communities that dot the land scape are numerous and fairly close together - say four or five miles apart. One could see how the Russians, by advancing ten or fifteen miles on a thirty mile front, liberated 50 to a 100 "places" a day. Ten hours and forty-five minutes after takeoff we landed at our base. There was a long landing strip of steel matting and a short strip of concrete blocks. The latter, so we learned, has been constructed by the Germans when they held the territory. We dropped out of the nose hatch of the bomber. It was a thrill to land on the russian soil, the focal point of so much contemporary history - on the ground that produced one of the most terrific military machines of all time.

We walked to the far end of the field for interrogation. A Russian guard stood at the entrance of the tent, the first Soviet soldier I had seen. He wore a long great coat of thick material held tightly about him by a thick, wide leather belt . . . no buttons. On his head was a visored style cap, on his feet black boots. He appeared smartly clad for a soldier and certainly warm. But over all his uniform blended well with the dusty, war faded, land. . . as though he were spewed up by the military earthworks that were everywhere about the drome. His fixed bayonet glistened red in the setting sun. His right arm was bent behind his back. He stood with his feet spread and firmly set, toes straightened. It was a solid loooking pose and we turned to the other Russians around, and the stance was characteristic. We recalled the words of those who had been in Russia on previous shuttle trips - when a Russian guard says, "Stoy" (stop) it's smart to do nothing but just that. After interrogation all crews were taken in G.I. trucks driven by Russian soldiers through the village to a brick barracks some two miles from the field. It was quite dark and we were unable to see as much of the buildings, people and just everything we wished to see. Only in the headlights of the trucks were the peasants visable trudging in the dust beside the road. Some walked while others rode in crude two wheel carts or wagons. All probably coming home from working all the daylight hours in the fields. The barracks was once a Russian school, then a Russian cavalry post, later a German barracks and now an American quarters. Each person was assigned a camp cot and issued four G.I. blankets. At the mess we were served with typical C rations including carrots, peas and dehydrated potatoes plus some Russian black bread which was very coarse and rather sour tasting. The mess was run by Americans but the food was served by buxom Russian girls clothed in G.I. fatigues. The patter behind the counter was a mixture of English and Russian with each nationality speaking both.

Near the mess area was a restaurant, the only place to go in the village for recreation. It was run by the Soviets through a representative of the government. All the personnel attached to the place were from Moscow. The representative also administered the affairs of the entire community. It was a one story, square, bungalow type house apparently built of bricks or cement as were all the buildings surrounding. It contained a small snack bar where wines, vodka and champagne could also be had. Two rooms, possibly the living room and the dining room of the house, had perhaps thirty tables where food was served. Black and red caviar, eggs, fish each served in a variety of ways, were some of the dishes listed on the menu. We had black caviar just so we could say we had had the real thing. The sea food came from the White Sea. We also had a glass of vodka - potent stuff with a water-innocent appearance. Although the prices were high, with caviar a dollar for a small portion and the vodka about three dollars per glass, there was no chiselling on prices, no tipping, and the Russian government vouched for the purity of everything.

Though the general atmosphere in the place was one of plainness and want, still a spirit of comraderie and even gaity prevailed. American officers and enlisted men and Russian officers only were allowed. There has been some talk about the friendliness of the governments of Russia and her allies. Perhaps I missed something, certainly the time spent in Russia was too short to adequately judge, but what little was seen and in numerous conversations with the men who had been stationed there for five months, the people as individuals are most friendly and hospitable and the Yanks return the feeling.

Through a twenty year old chap who spoke quite good English we talked with the overseer, the high potentate from Moscow who runs everything. The latter was about thirty years old and had lots of bushy hair, thick lensed spectacles with intense alert eyes behind. In appearance, a very intelligent fellow. He seemed to want to talk with us as much as we did with him and regretted as much as we that the evening was late, near to closing time of eleven o'clock. We did learn, however, that the grain crops had been good, that the Jerry soldier makes good fertilizer for the grain. They laughed heartily when we asked if the enemy remains might not stunt the growth of their crops. Through the two Russians we became acquainted with a third, a captain in the infantry. The latter gladly exchanged his three stars denoting rank for a Second Lieutenant's bar and a pair of wings then searched his pockets for something additional since he thought he had bettered us. We asked them why we hadn't heard any singing in the cafe that night for we had heard that when any two Russians go together some close harmony is bound to ensue. Although two or three of the waitresses had entertained us at the piano with many Russian songs during the evening, they explained that time was too short for a song fest. The overseer promised that the next day they would open the place at two o'clock in the afternoon instead of evening and that we'd have a party . . . song, dances and all.

We left the restaurant for our quarters with much regret but looked forward to the morrow's festivities hoping that any mission scheduled could be completed by the two o'clock appointment time, or not long after. I intended to arise early and arrange for transportation to the base where the escorting fighters of my group had landed some 60 miles away.

Shortly after dawn in the morning we were awakened and told that previous plans had been cancelled and we were to take off about 0830 on the next lap of our journey - Italy. All were disappointed since we wished to stay in Russia at least a few days more.

Very few of the boys visited the cafe on the previous night since all were tired after the long trip from England. They had no opportunity to look around. Of course the new arrangements made it impossible for me to get to my fighter base since the bombers would take off before I could get to Piryatin, assist in planning the mission and still return to the bomber base in time for take off.

At briefing we found the day's target to be a marshalling yard at Szolnok, Hungary, some 60 miles southeast of Budapest. The yard was important since its rail lines served the enemy forces on the southern Russian front. Between briefing and start engine time we had a couple hours to again talk with the men who had been serving in the Eastern Command since its activation. They told us about the cemetery in the village with its 1500 graves of townspeople who had been machine gunned by the Germans at the time the latter retreated. The Russian soldier who had a partial denture made from the steel of German bayonet. There were stories of discipline in the Russia army like that of the girl at the dance who seemed a little too inquisitive to the Yanks who danced with her. Their suspicions were reported to one of the Russian officers present, who promptly took her outside and shot her. A three year old boy was knocked down by a jeep and suffered a fractured arm as the result. The station doctor set the limb and is now called pop by the little fellow. The child's father was killed at Stalingrad, his brother and sister shot by the Germans and his mother carried off to the Fatherland.

A railroad, consisting of fourteeen passenger coaches, passed near the airdrome as we stood talking. It was a train of wounded from the front, the only kind of passenger train seen in this section. Four to six of these trains come through the village each day. When the Yanks have time, they go down to the station and give the Russian soldiers cigarettes and candy. On their days off, some go into the fields with the farmers they have become friendly with and help harvest the crops.

Some of the boys told about dung stamping parties. The peasants pile up the manure from the stables and barns and, when a sufficient amount has been built, a load of straw is dumped on top. Then the whole is worked together by trodding. After the mixing, the mass is cut into cakes, or bricks as you prefer, and used for fuel during the cold months.

After a day's work in the fields, the soldiers report they are given a feast such as any threshing crew at home would expect. All in all, the people are very similar to the stalwart farmers who migratred to various parts of the United States from Poland, Russia and other Western European nations. They worked from the crack of dawn to sunset, everyone in the family who is able. They are hearty and rugged.

I forgot to mention that on the way back to the field from the barracks the ride was quite brisk. I was wearing long, G.I. underwear (very handy at high altitude) woolen trousers and shirt, summer flying suit, and a winter flying jacket and I was just comfortable. Among the natives who were going about their daily tasks was a barefooted old woman. I imagine, however, that the soles of her feet were as thick as those of my army boots. One of the earlier shuttle raids received quite a bombing from the Jerries after the Fortresses had landed in Russia. Among the weapons dropped were land mines. When clearing up the mines from the airfield area, the Russki soldiers determined the duds from the good ones by simply kicking the mines. They lost 17 men that way. It seemed a paradox to me, that they can have such a lust for life - the songs, the dances, the love of companionship and a good time - and still consider life so cheaply.

The mission to Italy was rather uneventful. As we neared the foothills of the Carpathians, the broad fields of the Ukraine changed to the smaller, truck gardening type landscape of the Balkans. Again we could see no semblance of a front line in the hills below. As we flew over the Carpathians we left Russia, entered Romania, then Poland and Czechoslovakia, Romania again and then Hungary.

The fighters made R/V perfectly, and I felt relieved. By this time I had fully adopted the sentiment of the bomber crews that there isn't a more beautiful sight in the world than three or four flights of friendly fighters weaving back and forth around the formation of Big Friends. At the target I saw only four bursts of flak. My only uneasiness arose from the thick weather we entered a few minutes later and milled around in for some minutes, but we were soon out of it.

During the afternoon we crossed the plains of Hungary and the winding Danube River. What a beautiful waterway with its many rivulets and tributaries. Passing over Brod, in Yugoslavia, the low group encountered some flak that was really reading their mail for altitude, range, and speed. Seventy black bursts marred the sky in about the time it takes to say it. Luckily, no bomber was brought down though one received some forty holes.

The mountains bordering the west coast of Yugoslavia are rugged and steep and it was obvious why no large scale invasion landings had been attempted. The Adriatic Sea was crossed in an hour and by late afternoon we were circling our base near Foggia, located close to the spur of the Italian boot.

We were interrogated in a stable which was part of a Foggia lawyer's estate taken over by the Air Force. The room was an attractive briefing room - the field was actually the base of a Fifteenth Air Force Fortress group. Our quarters were G.I. pyramidal tents and bunks again were camp cots with two blankets which proved inadequate for the Italian nights. Some of the permanent personnel at the base had built stone and cement houses with the aid of the Italian masons and black market mortar. We were amazed that the attractive cottages which were erected for as little as $25.00. Complete with fire place!

The following day I visited two of the three fields where our fighters landed, covering about 80 miles to do it. A mission was not scheduled so the pilots were touring the surrounding country. I learned from the fighter base S-2 and S-3 that all arrangements had been made for briefing and navigation computation. It was a relief for I was wondering how I could help at three different bases at the same time.

The Italian towns are a combination of the sublime and the ridiculous. It astounded us to see such indescribable filth, poverty, squalor amid beautiful works of architecture and statuary.

The second day we traveled by army truck to Melfredonia for a swim. Incidentally, the Italian roads were a mass of chuck holes except for the Roman highways. No road is rougher and no travel is dustier. On the way to the beach through Foggia, we saw the destruction wrought by allied bombing prior to the capture of the city. Little wonder that many of the local citizens looked the other way when Yanks with wings met them of the street.

The ride from Italy back to England was uneventful operationally . . . we carried no bombs, saw no flak. The Mediterranean Sea, and its islands of Elba and Corsica, when viewed from 16,000 feet was like a huge jewel of blue green emerald with rich cameo settings on the surface. Of all the places I should most like to visit on a peace time tour . . . basing the desire on my view from the air . . the islands west of Italy and the southern coast of France, extending 150 miles inland, would get my money.

Late in the afternoon we passed Paris and made landfall out east of Le Havre. A dusky thick haze grew hazier and dustier as we crossed the channel toward Selsey Bill and through it we could hardly make out the coast line. The weather conditions proved, if nothing else, that it was England. Our route to home base took us around Dover, across the Thames estuary and up towards the Wash. Though we passed through fog, rain, high low and middle cloud, the England we know, it was good to be back for we realized we had the best wartime conditions of all the places we recently visited or flew over.

The entire trip totaled four days and we logged 27 hours operation time, not counting 5 hours and 45 minutes on an earlier attempt to Russia which was recalled because of weather.

APPENDIX I

A profile of a typical fighter mission in 1945

"One Mission"

by
Daniel M. Lewis
Major, Air Corps,
Group Intelligence Officer
Group Historical Officer
355th Fighter Group

The bell clangs on the teletype machine. The operator drops the book with which he has been whiling away the hours and watches the keys of the soulless nerve center of this station. It rattles on . . . yes, it's a warning order, "Expect to use all groups in support of heavies, normal effort, external tanks, zero hour 0800." A glance at the clock shows 2200 hours.

The duty intelligence officer has just turned off the light and settled back in his bunk wondering if he'll be undisturbed until morning, or for only ten minutes. It's only for ten minutes, because the teletype operator is turning on the light, warning order in his hand. "Good evening, sir; looks like we're going to be busy!"

Signing for the warning order, the I.O. says, "Corporal, don't be so nonchalant about wishing me a good evening when you know darn well, based on almost two years experience, that that little missive you are bearing means that I can expect practically no sleep this night. There is only one message you can announce in that lilting tone . . . the one that says, 'the war in Europe is over, cease fire, organized resistance has ended,' or whatever it's going to say."

The corporal laughs. "Give me another month and I'll have it for you and a carbon copy for my own memoirs." He returns to his office, picks up his book, cocks his feet on the desk and the clock loudly tick-tocks the minutes away. At 0210 the bells ring again and the machine starts that sudden staccato noise as the operator, miles away orders, "stand by mates, here comes the field order at you." Letter after letter, word after word, sentence after sentence, paragraph after paragraph comes the story of another impending day of destruction for Nazi Germany.

Field Order 1683A comes off the machine, completed, at 0236 hours and is immediately delivered to the duty intelligence officer who groggily fumbles through its five and a half feet of length from top to bottom and back to top again. Ah, here it is . . . "Third force, four boxes of 80, 60, 70, 90 aircraft each, 2nd Division B-24s, flying boxes in trail, bomb GO1516 and GH6088. Escort 4 AB, 56 AB, 479 AB, 355 AB (that's us). Now down to paragraph two to check the zero hour. Yep, it's still 0800 hours. Then to paragraph three C-Charlie, "355 AB group (P-51) from 5238-0700E on 3rd box."

"Route and Timings" . . . the main spring in the mechanism that heaves USAAF Station F-122(Steeple Morden) from its sack this morning of March 2, 1945, is listed at the bottom of the field order. The 2nd Air Division will be at the rendezvous point (5237-0700E) at zero plus 92 minutes - at 0932 in other words. But the I.O. has just arrived at this calculation when his corporal friend trots in with Amendment number one to F.O. 1683A. "Add ten (10) minutes, repeat add ten (10) minutes to all 2nd Division timings. O.K., that will make R/V time 0942. Well, we might as well face it; we must leave the warm office and trek into the frigid operations office to the 1:500,000 map, plot the course to the R/V point and determine a tentative Start Engine time.

Without considering winds and temperature it will take the group roughly one hour to reach rendezvous, a point on an arc 140 miles from the base, at an altitude of 20,000 feet. This one hour period includes start engines, eight minutes to taxi out for take-off, 15 minutes from take-off to formation assembly and setting course over the field at an altitude of 3000 feet. Once 20,000 feet of altitude is reached our ground speed, not considering winds or temperature, will be roughly 270 miles per hour. Taking the 270 mph speed rule we calculate the additional minutes to the rendezvous point and find that we get 34 minutes flying time from the altitude point to R/V. The hour plus 34 minutes is subtracted from the R/V time of 0942 giving us a start-engine time of 0808 hours.

True, start-engine time is tentative since no allowance has been made for the effect of wind and temperature, but experience has proved that on only two or three occasions has the actual start engine time been as much as twenty minutes early or late and, in most instances, the actual time is missed by approximately five minutes. Note that on this day's mission the tentative time and the actual time of start engine, after the complete navigational flight plan has been calculated, are the same 0808 hours.

Briefing time is next and it is the policy of the group to allow an hour and 15 minutes from briefing to start-engines. We'll make briefing time 0645, which allows an hour and 23 minutes till start-engines, but that's O.K. and keeps briefing time in round, easily remembered figures. It is now three o'clock (0300) and the first phone calls are to be made at 0445. "Operator, give me a buzz at 0430 unless something comes in in the meantime." And once again we hit the bunk for a few fretful moments.

At 0345 the station weather office calls, beating us to the punch, and asks if we have anything cooking for the day and if so what time briefing is to be. We give them the ungarbled word and conclude that they must have already been tipped off and are already working on the forecast for the Scouting Force which is also stationed at this base. This force usually begins its activity an hour or so before the fighter group since it receives the bomber field order which comes in an hour before that of the fighter group. The 2nd Scouting Force also takes off ahead of us for their duties require them to be in the target areas 20 minutes before target time.

At the specified time, the intelligence officer gets up once and for all to begin the day's work. First he wakes the duty enlisted man, who stokes the fires, helps gather necessary maps and target material, serves as a driver for those who will come to the line to work on the show, and, duties permitting, assists in displaying the field order on the briefing map. An assistant operations officer with only a few days experience is to help with the work of the flight plan today, so he's called at 0430 to give an extra 25 minutes for his calculations, in addition to the standard two hours ordinarily allowed. Until it is time for the 0445 calls we look up the targets for the day . . . synthetic oil plants, an airdrome, and a marshalling yard.

With the attached call sheet (Figure 1) as a guide let's observe the activity resulting from each call. Notice that all calls are made either two hours before or one hour before briefing. First, then, the two-hour calls:

Group S-2

One of the three headquarters intelligence officers briefs each day. The schedule is set by a monthly roster. However, if one of the three group I.O.s is serving his tour as duty intelligence officer (also a monthly schedule based on a roster of the nine intelligence officers assigned to a fighter group) it is understood that he will carry through with the briefing.

His first task is to display all routes of all forces on the briefing map using yarn and pins to show the courses. At the appropriate geographical coordinates are placed silhouettes of the fighter groups assigned to escort. These side view cut-outs of fighter aircraft show the distinctive nose markings of the each fighter groups. Hence, the pilots know where and which groups they can expect to see throughout the mission. For instance, on this day's mission, the 4th, 56th, 479th, 361st and ourselves (355th FG) all make rendezvous at 5237-0700E at zero plus 102 minutes.

The geographical check points (used for mutual reference between the aircraft and the ground controller) are also pinned at the proper place. Today there are seven such places and the code letters spell the word "w-h-i-s-p-e-r." Next the I.O. posts, on a blackboard at the front of the briefing room, the time schedule for each task force showing the relative times of landfall in, target time, break escort time, landfall out time—and/or any other times that portray clearly and significantly the positions of the respective forces at any moment. These timings suggest the "hottest" spots on the mission to the squadron and flight commanders . . . where the enemy is most likely to attempt an attack.

As a further aid in identifying the bomber groups to be escorted by the 355th Fighter Group, miniature replicas showing the tail markings on the vertical stabilizers and rudders of each group we are specifically assigned to escort are displayed on the map. These markings have proved valuable in identifying and sticking with the assigned task force. Every pilot at every briefing is impressed with the appearance of the bomb unit he is to protect since it has been demonstrated on a number of occasions that the Luftwaffe can take advantage of even a short gap in escort to knock down as many as 22 out of 35 bombers in one group.

If this group planned to strafe airdromes or dive-bomb targets in assigned areas; the intelligence officer has work more similar to his counterpart in the bombardment outfits. All photographs, night-flying charts, and information sheets are taken from the files and posted in the briefing room. The enemy order of battle is checked for the latest dope on the number of aircraft observed or photographed within the assigned area. Flak maps with latest postings are studied and, in addition, the wing flak section is called for their latest detailed posting of flak positions surrounding possible targets. No stone is left unturned to get every whit of material possible, since light flak is the greatest single source of casualties to a fighter unit.

Small scale maps—1:100,000 and 1:50,000—are displayed on the ops table and briefing map for minute study by the leaders who must make their target identification and navigating decisions as accurately and quickly as possible. These maps are a further benefit in determining the best possible approaches to the target considering defenses, wooded areas, and terrain.

When the show itself has been posted in all detail, the duty intelligence officer checks the "to be briefed" file for information to be brought to the attention of all pilots. He assists the operations officer in routing the group around restricted areas and inner artillery zones. When the group and squadron leaders arrive, he stands by to get any additional information they may request.

Group S-3

It is the policy of the officers in group operations to have those pilots not scheduled to fly the day's mission take care of all activity associated with their sections. Accordingly he arrives at the line along with the Group S-2. He first draws the entire route of the group on the ops table, including of course, the route of the bombers we are to escort. The table is covered with the usual 1:500,000 map, showing the flak areas in red. The group weather officer supplies the latest winds and temperature.

Recently a navigator was assigned to the group to assist in flight plan computation . . . a navigator who had completed his tour with the 'Big Friends.' This valuable new man allows the operations officer more time for administering the numerous other duties required before a mission.

All true courses are determined with a protractor. Using the current winds and considering the magnetic variation, each true course is transposed into compass heading by the use of the usual computers and standard methods. In evolving the time and distance section of the flight plan all climbing indicated air speeds, with two 108 gallon wing tanks, are taken as 180 miles per hour. Cruising indicated air speeds, with wing tanks . . . 195 mph; without tanks 210 mph; let down 230 mph. All escort timings are based on the bomber indicated air speed of 155 mph for B-17s and 160 mph for Liberators.

A word of explanation about determining start engine time: notice that on the flight plan for the mission that rendezvous time is 0942 and that each lap of the course up to that point, in terms of minutes, is subtracted including 15 minutes from takeoff to set course and eight minutes from start engine to take off.

While those computations are being made, the usual interruptions occur; The group operations officer, who has been checking the navigator's course calculations and times, turns to the telephone.

We happen to be short of aircraft at this time because many of the planes on yesterday's mission had to remain overnight at emergency bases on the continent. The 354th Squadron has only fourteen planes available, the 357th eleven, and the 358th nine . . . a total of 34 planes. For a normal effort with A and B groups, as required in the warning order, we should have at least 60 aircraft. A call is made to higher headquarters requesting permission to fly one group of 34 ships which, logically, is granted. Fighter Wing calls us to see if we can furnish four ships for PRU escort. We remind them that we have only 34 planes available. One of the squadrons asks if we are escorting the Second Division, since they require special communication installations. (explained later) Another squadron calls to inquire about detonators in the wing tanks. There will be no detonators since we have been ordered not to strafe and don't need that capability.

Group Communications

These two headquarters officers are responsible for the proper presentation of paragraph five in the order and arrive at the briefing room in ample time to study the field order for proper call signs and frequencies of bombers and fighters. Our task force this day is the third, the First and Third Divisions between Task Forces One and Two, respectively. Our assigned group for escort is the third in the string. Hence, the call-sign Vinegrove 3-3 is chalked up on the communications board in the briefing room. We are the seventh group to make rendezvous so our bomber-fighter call sign on C-channel is Balance 3-7 which is also chalked up, along with the fighter recall code word "Mazola" and the recognition signals for the period. An explanation of the balance of the communications board will be further described as we more fully cover the briefing.

After posting the information on the communications board, the officer checks with the three squadrons to make doubly sure they have sufficient crystals for communication with the Second Division bombers and then pays a visit to the Second Scouting Force. After determining that they are prepared to install radio crystals for each of the bomb groups in the Second Division, he calls the service group intelligence officer to tell him the briefing time and target time. Thus the telephone monitoring system is set in motion.

Group Weather Officer

The weather officer, "Fog" as he is nicknamed, is the last of the headquarters officers to receive the call two hours before briefing. He catches the S-2 jeep to the line along with those mentioned previously. All headquarters officers who work with field orders are quartered in the same barracks.

"Fog's" first job, upon arrival at the line, is checking the area in which the group will be operating; then to his office on the ground floor of the control tower where he buries himself in maps and charts and scientific instruments and reams of teletype reports in an effort to discover a fact or two about the English weather for the next eight or ten hours. But let's let him explain his method of supplying S-3 with the necessary information preparatory to flight plan computations.

"Basically, the ops forecast for weather and winds originates at higher command and is made with all the skill and knowledge available. However, the group officer develops more up to date information from available maps, charts and reccos, and works up the ops forecast. The weather officer must first determine the targets, routes, and rough timings for this mission. Next, winds are calculated and preliminary clouds and visibility forecasts are developed for the local area to assist in assembly and climb estimates. The winds are then checked against the 10,000 and 20,000 foot pressure patterns and against the latest winds reported from other observing stations. Particular care is used in forecasting the movements of troughs and wedges aloft and the wind shifts these involve. This done, the way is clear for the weather forecast. Basically, the forecast starts with the ops forecast. Against the ops forecast, frontal movements involved in the mission, the latest available reports and trends of fronts, pressure systems, and hourly weather reports are checked. The reccos are considered as detached and not absolutely reliable reports, since they are usually made at night, but we work them over to explain any discrepancies they may show from the forecast." For the immediate use of the S-3 officers computing the flight plan, the winds and temperatures are supplied in the form of wind and temperature charts and graphs.

As the S-2 officer balances precariously on his ladder attempting to spot a pin at a coordinate just out of reach, as the operations section turns the discs and slides the cards of the computers, as the weather man chases the clouds over his maps, and as the communications officer makes sure that the right people can talk to the right people during the coming mission, the first angry bursts from the 12 cylinders of a Mustang riddle the stillness of the early morning. We momentarily picture the ever faithful crew chief huddled in the cockpit. His fur-lined jacket has a tear here and there. His grassy overalls offer scant protection from the frosty metal of the seat. He huddles beneath the windscreen to escape the icy slipstream. Surely... evenly he goes through the pre-flight procedure checking the luminous figures on the instrument panel.

All group officers having been called, we now get on with the two-hour calls.

Squadron Intelligence Officers

The general procedure of these three in getting their units underway is fundamentally the same although each has some slight variations dictated largely by relative distances from the line, living facilities in their respective areas (some snack bars are at the line, others in the barracks areas) and the desires of the squadron commander, engineering officer and various section chiefs. After the call from the duty intelligence officer, the squadron I.O. calls his engineering officers and passes on the information: "Briefing 0645, 108 gallon wing tanks, escorting the Second Division, normal effort."

Either the engineering officer or the I.O. also calls the Charge of Quarters. The CQ puts on his hat, picks up his flashlight and wends his way through the night from Nissen hut to hut, announcing the time of day, the time of briefing and passing the information that we are escorting the Second Division along to the flight line and section chiefs. Amidst yawns, growls, and various profanities, the men ease from their bunks, draw on their coveralls and leather suits. Once the chill of the typical English morning hits them, the dressing is done with alacrity. The inevitable one-each-mess-cup is fastened to the rear pocket and in twos, thress and gaggles, on bicycles and on foot, they head for the line.

One by one, with increasing crescendo from all parts of the airdrome, the fighters snarl out their wrath at the Luftwaffe. First comes the servicing with fuel, oxygen, coolant and hydraulic fluid if necessary. A visual inspection of the airplane is made to make certain that the landing and tail gear struts are OK and tires are properly inflated, and that no damage has occurred to the ship during the night.

After pulling the propeller through a few revolutions, the crew chief is ready to start pre-flighting. During the pre-flight, the controls are checked for freedom of movement, the operation of the flaps are checked, and the lights are switched on and off. The engine is started and allowed to run until the oil and coolant temperatures are within the desired range. Immediately after starting, the oil pressure is monitored. After the desired operating temperature is reached, the oil and coolant scoops are operated manually and the propeller control is tested at each range. The RPM drop is noted and all instruments are read. The electrical system and magnetos are checked and rechecked. Strict attention is paid to the reading of the ammeter and operation of the gyro instruments. Those assemblies are of the utmost importance and demand the closest inspection during preflight. After the engine run-up, the cowling is removed from sections of the airplane and a visual search is made for oil, coolant, and fuel leaks. All accessible fuel cocks are drained.

The crew chief is lucky if everything checks satisfactorily on the pre-flight. Generally he is kept busy for an hour or so after the pre-flight changing spark plugs, cleaning magneto points, repairing a tachometer, replacing leaking wing tanks, replacing instruments, or stopping coolant and fuel leaks.

When the ship is in A-1 condition, its status is phoned into squadron engineering as a re-check on the status of the previous evening. Squadron operations makes any necessary adjustments to their schedule of available planes.

From now until the pilot arrives at the plane, the crew chief makes sure the cockpit is spotless, that the safety harness is properly adjusted and he polishes the canopy and wind screen. The final gesture of complete readiness occurs when he whips the rag from his pocket to wipe that ever-present last drop of oil from the underside of the engine cowling, then lies down to absorb the first warm rays of the rising sun. Simultaneously, the soldier in charge of the Mustang's communications checks the radio set for transmission and reception. Those planes flying the Yellow two position are re-equipped with a complete radio set carrying the proper frequency to contact the Vinegrove 3-3 bombers on C-channel.

The men inspecting armament check the firing mechanism of the guns, the operation of the gun sight, particularly making sure that the lens is spotless, and that the gun camera is in perfect order.

Each of the squadron intelligence officers has a flight plan listing the pilots who are to fly the day's mission. Between an hour and a quarter to one hour before briefing, the fliers are awakened. Those who have many missions under their belts are wide-eyed at the first tap, while the new ones require a shout and a night-stick to arouse them. A weapon carrier, (one is assigned to each unit) dispatched by the CQ, arrives in the squadron officers barracks area an hour before briefing to transport the pilots to their respective dispersal huts on the line. Here they get breakfast at the snack bars and then go to the briefing room . . .

But it is only 0545 and we are skipping a gear or two in the machinery.

Sergeant of the Guard

The Guard House is called two hours before briefing and told that the crews will begin arriving at the line in about a half hour. This permits the military police to relieve the posts around the airdromes and aircraft efficiently and with a minimum of time spent in halting and identifying personnel.

Mess Sergeant, Enlisted Mess

With the coming of the longer spring days, the men are up and about their duties long before the usual breakfast hour. To assist the mess in having food ready, the mess sergeant is also called two hours before briefing.

Group Armament

On the few occasions when the group carries bombs, the group armament officer is notified two hours before briefing. He notes the weight and type of bombs and the fuses to be used, then makes his request to the station ordnance unit who deliver the weapons to the airplanes. The respective squadron armament and ordnance personnel fuse and hang the bombs.

The intelligence officer steps down from the area of Denmark which is just beneath the peak of the roof on his 1:250,000 briefing map. It is one hour until briefing time, and hence, the one hour calls should be made:

Group Commander and Air Executive Officer

"Good morning, this the Jiffy Intelligence Service." "Yeah. Why can't you do business at a reasonable hour?" "Well, early bird gets the worm . . . and all guff like that there."

(Everyone's humor is functioning in the same dull way.) "Briefing at 0645—it is now 0545. We have a fair spot in the show. Weather will be pretty good. We're escorting the lead boxes." "O.K., be right up . . . and send your jeep down for me."

Flight Surgeon

Next, the flight surgeon for the medics makes it a policy to attend briefings and note the overall psychology of the pilots - also pick out the ones who are hoping to be put on the flight schedule at the last minute, even though they may have colds or other ailments that preclude safe and efficient flying.

Chaplain

He never misses a briefing if he's on the station. It is a comfort to the pilots to have his blessing after briefing . . . the final touch to the picture of their needs as they face the flight ahead.

Flying Control

Every day, before flying begins, a physical inspection of the entire airdrome is made by the flying control personnel to be sure that all facilities are in proper order for operations. The radio communications system, consisting of two homers, two transmitters, two receivers and the battery powered stand-by equipment in the tower are all tested. In addition, the six VHF channels, two of which are used only by the Scouting Force, are given the once over. The tower switchboard, tie lines and both operational and administrative telephones are re-checked prior to the day's work. Crash trucks, and fire fighting equipment, lighting facilities — all must be in readiness.

When flying control gets the one hour call, each squadron is called for the personnel flying schedule. Each pilot is posted, using the numbered pin method, on a board which shows the individual's position in the fight and in the squadron. It is a "know the players by their numbers" system that gives the control officer instant check on the entire group launching procedure from start-engines to the time that all planes are back in their hardstands or otherwise accounted for.

Station Photographic Department

Each of the three squadrons have two planes with camera installations. It is the policy of the group to carry the cameras even though no special task be assigned for their use in the field order. It is felt that any and all pictures taken of target damage and potential future targets — either for strafing or bombing — enhances the coverage desired by headquarters and also gives the group material from which to work on possible airdrome strafing missions. The photo department supervises the camera installations and are responsible, of course, for developing and printing and sending forward any pictures that may have been taken. After the one-hour phone calls, and up to briefing time, the "wheels" begin drifting in to study the field order, watch the computation of the flight plan, and inevitably discuss the possibilities of knocking down a few German fighters. Flight, squadron, and group leading experience gives all the older pilots a sixth sense... that ability to assimilate their past experience, relative routes and timings, escort position, proximity to German operational stations, priority of targets and Luftwaffe capabilities... assimilate it all into a picture that suggest possibilities for raising the group score. When the "feel" suggests a milk run, the brass gives lead positions to junior pilots to gain experience. During this period, the leaders also discuss which units are to be close escort, which are to range out on the free-lance search for the Hun, who is to fly high and low, over the lead boxes or the rear boxes. When strafing is permissible and intended, all the available material gathered by the intelligence officer is studied and possible methods of attack reviewed.

About five minutes before briefing time, most of the flying personnel have arrived and are seated in their usual squadron sections. Each and every one is busy copying down the flight plan... place, compass heading, minutes to run and estimated time of arrival (ETA). Who knows when he might become separated from his squadron or flight leader and left to rely solely upon himself to continue the mission or return home by himself?

All geographical checkpoints are copied down for later notation on the flight maps. It is these points which mean so much when it comes to achieving a proper rendezvous and intercepting enemy fighters... the mutual reference between pilot and ground controller that was mentioned earlier.

Squadron intelligence officers, at least one from each, always attends the briefing, taking all pertinent information so they can transfer the group's part in the show to their own squadron wall maps and supply the pilots with any details, later, that they may have missed at the group briefing.

Now let's check the communications board. Able channel, an operational channel and for local homings (used only by this fighter group), call signs "Colgate" (figher wing controller) and "Tworoom" (local base control). Baker channel is still used for Air Sea Rescue and the proper procedure is to give the "Mayday" three times followed by the individual's call sign. Charlie channel is strictly a fighter-bomber communication channel and the bombers we escort today are, as we determined earlier, Vinegrove 3-3 while we are Balance 3-7. Dog channel will be used only for D/F fixing and pip squeak. Colors of the day from 0700 to 1300 are green-green and from 1300 to 1900, red-red. The fighter recall word is "Mazola".

Special Assignments: The pilot flying Yellow two position in each squadron (wingman to the leader of the second flight in the squadron formation) stands by on Charlie channel to maintain watch on fighter-bomber communications. The ship flying Green-two in each squadron (wingman to the leader of the fourth flight) stands by on Charlie channel to maintain radio contact with the Second Division bombers only. These are the ships in the group, you will recall, that carry the radios with the special frequency crystals. By way of explanation, those pilots who must stand by on channels other than Able channel, the group operating frequency, are given what is deemed the safest position within the squadron formations since their ability to defend themselves is lessened when they cannot hear warnings which may come from other members of the group.

Next, in order down the board, are a few special instructions. Green-green flares fired by the bombers is a request for fighter aid and yellow-yellow flares denote identification. Finally, and quite important, are listed four stations equipped to give emergency homings and fixes and four which also provide servicing facilities for airplanes which may be forced to land there.

FIGURE 1.

CALL SHEET

DUTY INTELLIGENCE OFFICER

DATE _____ Mar 2 1945 _____

Information given to Squadron Intelligence Officers:

    Strength of effort _____ Normal _____

    Wing Tank _____ 108 _____

    2nd Division escort _____ Yes _____

B.T. minus 2 hrs.	Group S-2	10 & 9	Duty 10
	Group Operations	" "	0430
	Group Communications	9	0430
	Weather Office	19	0345
	354th Sqdn.	17	0445
	357th Sqdn.	15	0445
	358th Sqdn.	20-1	0445
	Sgt. of the Guard	A-11	0445
	Enlisted Men's Mess	A-40	0445
	*Group Armament	9	
B.T. minus 1 hr.	Group C.O. & Group Exec.	32	0545
	Flight Surgeon	A-8	
	Chaplain	A-28 & 41	0545
	Flying Control	11	0545
	**Station Photo (Lt. Dumas)	A-4 before 8 a.m.	
		A-60 before 8 a.m.	

I hereby certify that I notified the above officers at times stated.

                                                        Duty Intelligence Officer

BRIEFING

The pilots are still busy writing on their wrists, or slips of paper, or on plexi-glass covered knee boards, the gen on navigation, etc. The weather officer inserts his panoramic view in the epidiascope and switches the unit on momentarily to see if it is working properly. A few words about the group's policy in conducting the briefing is appropriate.

Three officers regularly participate in the briefing: the intelligence officer, weather officer and the tactical commander, in that order on the platform. The communications officer and flying control officer are always present should there be any questions involving their work or to explain any special instructions peculiar to the day's mission.

The need for a smooth running performance cannot be stressed too much. We strive to make each "act" of the show polished and accomplished since a shoddy presentation can produce a shoddy psychological attitude in the pilot, resulting in a similar frame of mind during the entire mission. Following are a few examples which tend to make a briefing amateurish: miscalculations of tentative rendezvous time which is the basis for all activity previous to take-off. A hurry-up show is never conducive to facing the flight with confidence. When a field order has not been thoroughly studied by those conducting the briefing, the ensuing questions and even arguments, relative to who, what, when and where, among the assembly of pilots causes doubts, naturally, as to the ability of those in charge. All material presented, whether it's the show on the map or a picture on the epidiascope, must be completely set up and ready for explanation at the moment planned. Fumbling and indecision is poor form; showmanship has a definite role. Every attempt is made to capitalize on layout or display artistry that is available from the personnel assigned to the unit.

Now to the briefing: Since the group intelligence officer is responsible for, and has arranged the show on the map, he is familiar with the task of each force, and the route and timings. He explains the field order to the pilots, force by force, giving the number of aircraft in each division, the target each force is hitting along with all material supplied as to the target's importance to the German war effort, the number of groups escorting, the places of rendezvous, the times that each force can be expected at crucial points along the route, the call signs and tail markings of the particular bomb groups we are to escort and the altitudes at which the Big Friends will be flying.

All special instructions are read, "Groups will not, repeat will not strafe and will remain with the bombers. Groups will stay above 8000 feet when returning through restricted coastal area. Reference base altitude is 25,000 feet."

It is not the policy of the group intelligence officers to gaze into the crystal ball so far as enemy intentions are concerned. However, all enemy capabilities are constantly reviewed with the multitudinous material available on the subject. The tactical commanders do make an attempt to anticipate the tactics and strategy of the enemy.

Other items, not necessarily concerned with the day's mission, but which are to be brought to the attention of all pilots are briefed: "The practice of firing on navigational buoys in the North Sea will cease immediately. Commendation from the command on the good work done during the previous weeks' missions. It is now permissible to carry. 45 cal. service pistols on operational flights."

"Are there any questions?"

"What did you say was the reference base altitude?"

"RBA is 25000 feet; any other questions?" Silence. "O.K. weather."

The weather is unreasonably good today for England so the weather officer starts off with, "It just cain't be! There's a weak cold front to the south of the route, but all it has been able to squeeze out is some drizzle. This will be clear of the route with a possibility of the target area having more clouds remaining than forecast. Behind the front is good weather ... no problems. Watch to the south along the front coming out for heavy cumulus developing" with the customary warning that clear ice and turbulence is characteristic of these clouds.

"Lights off please," and the briefing room becomes inky dark. The beam of the epidiascope shines to weather picture on the portable screen. Cigaret smoke drifts through the night.

England will be clear with no assembly problems. The coastal areas and Channel will have four to six tenths stratocumulus based at 4000 feet with tops at 6000 feet. The northwest wind along the center of the coast can easily form a belt of heavier cumulus so watch for it and keep out. On the continent four to six tenths stratocumulous and cumulus with tops at six to seven thousand feet breaking inland to from three to six tenths.

On the route out, the clouds experienced over the continent will have increased to four to six tenths and towering up to 8000 feet over the channel. Back over England the cover again drops to three to five tenths, based at four thousand feet, tops at 8000 feet. There is no middle cloud and only nil to scattered high cirrus at 25000 feet along the entire route. Don't let the sunshine throw you. Visibility at take-off will be two to three miles in light haze, lowering from present value for one hour after sunrise. Visibility over the continent, four to six miles going and coming. Aloft visibility, air to air, is excellent, air to ground thirty to fifty miles. Freezing level this morning is 1000 feet at take-off time, lifting to three thousand feet by return. There may be nil to light rime ice in the low clouds although you have no icing worries as long as you stay out of the heavier cumulus.

"Winds are from the northwest and, a warning; they increase sharply at altitude over the continent. Over the base, from 330 degrees at forty miles an hour at ten thousand feet. From 330 at seventy five miles per hour at 20,000 feet. From 330 at eighty five mph at 30,000 feet. The southeast winds, as altitude increases over the continent, to 100 mph from 320 degrees at 20,000 feet and 125 mph at 30000 feet from the same direction.

"Contrails will be nil to light and non-persistent at 25,000 feet.

"One more warning. Our jeep iced up coming up here this morning so check your plane for frost before taking off. Any questions?"

The lights are flicked back on. The tactical commander for the day takes the platform. The squadron commander of the 354th is leading the group today.

"OK boys, it looks like a pretty simple mission with good flying weather. The Jerries could be up easily and, judging from recent experience, we are most likely to see their jet jobs. I can't think our division is in a likely spot to get the attack, if it does come, but keep your eyes open just the same. I'll take off first. The 358th will be next and the 357th last. I'll fly high over the center of our force. I want the 358th on the front and the 357th covering the rear. If the ground controller gives us any vectors I'll go after them and if necessary tell the 358th to come also. The 357th will remain as close escort since it is their turn for that tiresome duty today.

"Remember, if we get into a scrap, I want the flights to hang together as long as possible and always in at least elements of two. The Hun lately has been making most of his attacks from the rear and out of the clouds and contrails. I'm going to stay at least 3000 feet above the bombers and I'd suggest that the other two squadrons do the same since we need all the altitude we can get for diving attacks on the jets. That's the only way we have a chance with them. Even though we may not shoot many down, remember that we have been pretty successful in keeping them away from the bombers and that is our job.

"And say, you guys that are standing by on the Scouting Force channel! I want you listening out on that channel all the time. Recently they have seen quite a number of enemy formations which they reported back to us and no one received the information. Speaking of the radio... stay off the air unless you have something important to say. You are fighter pilots and the only man in the airplane that can make a decision. No one can help you. If your engine is running hot or cold or about to fall out... make up your mind whether or not to continue on the mission and act accordingly. Don't discuss the matter with everybody in the group. Just do what your training and common sense tell you to do. Are there any questions?"

"At what altitude are you going to set course?"

"Three thousand feet. If that's all, time check please."

The Group communications officer, who checks his fancy clock with higher headquarters each morning, says, "It will be 0710 in 30 seconds... 15 seconds... 10 seconds... 5, 4, 3, 2, hack. 0710."

They burst from the briefing room like it was eighth grade recess. The Protestant and Catholic chaplains are soon surrounded with a congregation outside the door where a brief prayer and blessing is given. Then, on trucks, or bicycles or on foot, the pilots go to their respective squadron dispersals.

The next half hour is devoted to donning the flying equipment: G-suits, flying coveralls, Mae Wests, parachutes, helmets, oxygen masks, maps, escape and evasion equipment, extra socks, cigarettes, ad infinitum.

We'll walk up to the control tower where we can watch the take-off better. The flying control officer has his two motorcycle M.P.s standing by. They are responsible for keeping all traffic, pedestrian and vehicular, off the airdrome. Every runway in use has a guard posted at either end. The checkered wagon of the airfield controller is stationed at the end of the runway. All radio checks have ceased and the silence will be observed until the mission is over. The ambulance and crash trucks are standing by at the tower and at the end of the runway. The runway in use takes the aircraft over a highway as soon as airborne, so all civilian and military traffic is re-routed by the guards.

The second hand in the tower clock moves to straight up—0808. We scan the field. Props are turning in all corners. In a moment, the place sounds like the inside of a beehive. The planes waddle from their hardstands on to the perimeter track and join the flow of traffic to the take-off position. At assembly point at the end of the runway all engines revved up for the final check. A guard leans into the prop wash, his coat flying in the wind. The noise dies down and at 0816, the first element move down the runway. As they clear the end, the next element has begun its take-off . . . and so on until all 34 planes in the group are airborne. The group leader and squadron is now approaching the field again at an altitude of 1500 feet. All ships have assumed the usual four ship flight formation at the finish of the 180 degree turn.

When the circle is completed, all flights will be tucked nicely together into a squadron. Over the radio we hear the group leader announce that he will set course in another minute. All three squadrons are now in view over the field. The leader heads into the rising sun. Twelve minutes have elapsed since the first ships took off.

The group won't be back until 1330. Let's discuss interrogating and reporting for a minute. Interrogation is accomplished by the respective squadron intelligence officers and, in the event that group officers are flying, by group S-2 personnel. The style of the interrogation is first of all a chronological resume of the mission as it was flown: information supplied largely by group, squadron and flight commanders. It has been found, incidentally, that the most comprehensive and coherent reporting is given by a handful of pilots, almost invariably the best pilots. It is on these people, logically, that the interrogator depends.

With experience, the ability of flying personnel to give good information naturally increases and an interrogation discipline becomes apparent. The thoughtless pilot, who may in his early hours figure his words not worth much, or that reports are just another tiresome addition to the paper war, soon finds that a good mission summary report reads like Diamond Dick and that he is responsible for the information given. When he has become impressed with the fact that the future safety of himself and mates, the victory score of the group, and the success of the bombing is an integral part of the picture he brings back, he queues up to give his bit and phones dope in later that may have slipped his mind at the interrogation. They like to see their stuff in print . . . evidenced by the squawk raised if some bit of information they gave is omitted.

The experience of the intelligence officers in this fighter group show that airdrome strafing missions present the greatest difficulty to the interrogator. The problems arise in determining the number of targets on the field, the number of passes made by flights, the number of planes fired at and the total fires observed as the last plane leaves the area. The difficulties are trebled when all three squadron shoot up the same airdrome. Best results are obtained when the entire group is interrogated at one time taking each flight in order of their appearance over the enemy field. Using all pictures, target maps, and blackboard drawings, the tactical commander orients himself and the fliers and then proceeds to lead in outlining what each one did.
Thus, the story of each individual pass helps to complete the picture of who, what, when, where and how.

Escort missions are comparatively simple even though many air battles may have occurred. A good interrogator soon gets a picture in his mind of the number of enemy formations seen, location, direction, altitude, tactics and the part his unit played in the fight. The best check on the thoroughness of the interrogation is made at the mess in the evening. How much additional information about the mission does one hear that he didn't get immediately afterwards!

Emphasis on S-2/pilot buddyship pays its dividends in the interrogation. The closer an intelligence officer comes to being the father (or mother) of his flock, the more outstanding is his success. It means the difference between a sketchy account of the mission given to a bookkeeper and a complete story given to an ardent friend-listener.

When one thinks of the mission summary report as the sole written communication between the day's air war over Europe and the outside world, that the information given in the report is a direct reflection on the ability of the group to operate, then one can visualize that how the story is told directly affects the reputation of the organization both among other groups and with higher echelons. The group S-2 officer wishes that each of his intelligence officers had worked for ten years with the New York Times and that he, himself, had been managing editor. Not that military reports permit glowing accounts in fine words of description! Facts speak for themselves. But the way they are spoken and written—well, the old adage about the pen and sword has merit.

A fine discipline between group and squadron S-2 officers must be maintained in the reporting procedure. As in all human activity the natural tendency is to relax the vigil, and as report after report is passed from squadron to group, a decline in the amount of essential information and the speed with which it is transmitted may be noted. Taking that part of the report that concerns enemy air activity as an example . . . time, place, altitude, how many enemy aircraft, type of formation, direction flying, position relative to friendly forces—all are elements in setting the stage. Each fact is essential to the big picture. If a squadron officer fails to get one of the points—and it can be obtained simply by asking—and even though the Group I.O. may already have the information from one of the other squadrons, it is important, purely for discipline purposes, to demand the complete story from all. Of course the report from each serves as a check on the accuracy of the other.

On 2 March 1945, the entire group had landed by 1350 hours. As the pilots drift into their dispersals to hang up their equipment and as they eat a sandwich and drink a cup of coffee, they begin to tell their stories to the squadron I.O. on duty. As usual, they "hangar fly" among themselves while the interrogation of squadron and flight leaders is in session. About 15 minutes after they have landed, the I.O. has the sketchy account (chronological and outstanding observations) required for the flash report to group S-2. Within an hour, all squadron flash reports have been compiled into the group flash to wing. As the squadrons deliver their written mission summary reports to group headquarters, the I.O. in the latter echelon is already pounding out on the typewriter the preliminary paragraphs of his final report. The group summary of the mission report is compiled from the squadron reports, and at 1545 the story is on the teletype.

Attached are copies of the actual reports received and sent forward by the group for the mission of March 2, 1945.

We have now arrived at the spot where one mission ends and another begins. One squadron has a critique (all do periodically) in which all aspects of this and a few past missions are discussed, pulled apart, views expounded, criticisms made, suggestions forwarded. New rules are made and old ones discarded. One pilot is fined a pound for unnecessary use of the radio. Another is praised for "flying a good wing." Take-off, form-up, formation, rate of climb, tactics, strategy, flak, enemy aircraft, blunders,... an endless procession of observations, facts and conclusions are struck together to make the squadron and the group a better organization.

The group engineering section has the following work ahead after this mission: three ships are due for 25 hour inspections, three more are due for 50 hour inspections. The following parts were used to place aircraft back "in" on the status boards: four engines, one wing, ten brake assemblies, one carburetor, one generator, one fuel pump, one after-cooler pump, one fuel cell, one selector valve, one pump primer, one airspeed tube, one stabilizer, one wing tip, one shock strut. Gasoline consumed: 1,920 gallons. Oil consumed: 102 gallons.

We take a jeep ride around the perimeter track and see the following activity by the ground crews: spark plugs are being changed, valves adjusted, oil screens cleaned, daily inspections performed, ammunition removed, guns cleaned, gun camera film being removed, fuel tanks filled, tires checked. A couple of enlisted men from the photographic department are removing film showing target damage. In four hours the prints will be sent to the fighter wing via motorcycle courier.

In group operations, we learn that one pilot has completed his second tour of 180 hours. Six pilots are eligible for clusters to their Air Medals. Of the 34 planes dispatched, 29 flew effective sorties after five returned early for mechanical reasons.

On 2 March 1945, at 1800 hours, another duty intelligence officer starts his tour along with the next enlisted man on the roster. Another teletype operator has already begun a night of interrupted reading. At 2312 hours it begins again... "expect to use all groups in support of heavies."

-END-

354th FIGHTER SQUADRON
355th FIGHTER GROUP
APO 558

2 March 1945.

MISSION SUMMARY REPORT

Red Flight		Blue Flight	
Lt. Col. Graham	F	Lt. Mills	L
Lt. Mincemeyer	B	Lt. Walsh	E
Lt. Goth	N	Lt. Galer	Y
Lt. Vickery	C	Lt. Beeler	Q
Yellow Flight		Spares	
Capt. A.S. White	I	Lt. Gadpaille	Z
F/O Hixson	T	Lt. Barnhart	H
F/O Falvey	E		
Lt. Fletcher	D		

1. 354th Fighter Squadron: Lt. Col. Graham leading Group w/354.
2. 14 up at 0817; landed at 1350.
3. Nil.
4. Ramrod, Field Order No. 1683A, 2nd Div.
5. - 8. Nil.
9. L/F in at 0925, Ijmuiden 23,000 ft. R/V at 0930 Zuider Zee 24,000 ft, 3rd Box B-24's, black on yellow; target time 1040 bombing thru 9/10s cloud cover. On withdrawal our squadron swept Hannover-Bremen-Dummer Lake area at 12,000 ft. Left B/F at 1235 Zuider Zee 12,000 ft., making L/F out at 1250 Ijmuiden 10,000 ft.
10. Nil.
11. Many trains obsvd but because of altitude direction not determined. Two obsvd E of Brunswick; two N of Magdeburg; one SE of Bremen; and three NE of Dummer Lake. No strafing - no fun.
12. Nil.
13. Heavy, intense, accurate at target 24 to 27,000.
14. 8/10s with large breaks; tops 12,000.
15. Nil.

MYRON J. GLANTZ
Capt., A.C.,
Int. O.

357th FIGHTER SQUADRON
355th FIGHTER GROUP
APO 558
2 March 1945.

MISSION SUMMARY REPORT

1. 357th, Capt. McNeff leading.
2. 11 off 0816, down 1345.
3. Two early returns.
4. Bomber escort, penetration, target and withdrawal, VIII A.F., F.O. 1683A.
5. - 8. Nil.
9. R/V with 2nd Div. B-24, yellow tails and black stripes, east of Zwolle, 0940, 20,000ft. Escorted at 25,000ft, right side, same level. Observed bombings on PFF from 23,000', 1030. Broke escort east of Meppel, 1230, 23,000ft. L/F out north Ijmuiden, 1250, 20,000'.
10. Nil.
11. 1 B-24 down near Lingen, 1200, no chutes.
12. Nil.
13. Heavy, accurate and intense at target and Brunswick.
14. 9/10s cumulous in target area up to 8,000' making bombing necessary on PFF. 15. Nil.

JOHN S. POYEN,
Capt., A.C.,
Int. O.

358th FIGHTER SQUADRON
355th FIGHTER GROUP
APO 558

2 March 1945.

MISSION SUMMARY REPORT

Red   **Yellow**   **Blue**

H   Fussell   Q   Dissette   G   Blair
A   Lister   F   Curran   U   McCollom
K   Tolby (ER)   I   Allen (ER)
J   Roberts (ER)

1. 358th Fighter Squadron, Capt. Fussell leading.
2. 9 P-51's. Up: 0816 Down: 1345.
3. Three.
4. Ramrod. VIII A.F. F.O. 1683A. 2nd Div. Target - Magdesburg M/Y and Synthetic oil. 5. Nil.
6. Nil.
7. Nil.
8. 5-2-0 ME-109's (Air)
9. R/V 0930, N. of Zwolle, 24,000', bombers 20,000'. Target 1040, 26,000'. Left bombers 1236, 20 miles E of Zuider Zee at 18,000', bombers 17,000' to 21,000'. L/F out 1255, 13,000'.
10. Nil.
11. Bomber smoking and in spiral 1152, E. of Steinhuder 15,000', 3 or 4 chutes. Rocket 1202 same area.
12. Nil.
13. Flak: target - heavy, intense, inacc.
14. 8/10 top 8,000'.
15. Nil.
16. 5 ME-109's Destroyed - Air - Lt. Roscoe R. Allen. 2 ME-109's Probably Destroyed - Air. Lt. Allen aborted 1010, E. of Dummer Lake, because of lack of oxygen. At 1020, 21,000' in the Dummer Lake area, he saw 15 ME-109's with bombs, flying at 13,000' on a heading of approximately 195 degrees. They were directly beneath Lt. Allen, flying in two groups, one above the other about 700'. Eight in the top group and seven in the lower. Both gruops were echeloned to the left out of the sun. Their wing tips and elevator tips were painted a very light blue so that from a distance they looked like P-51's. Three had red yellow dragon like insignia. They never did drop their bombs, and seemed reluctant to break formation. On his first pass from above and behind, Lt. Allen blew up the plane on the left of the top group. Pulled over to the next, getting in a burst. The plane started to smoke and the pilot bailed out. A third rolled over on his back after taking a few hits. Lt. Allen then saw the lower group breaking up. He made another pass on one of the remaining five who had stayed somewhat together. Good hits caused the pilot to bail out. Lt. Allen followed another through three-fourths of a turn. This one blew up. Seein one going for the clouds, he caught him and set him on fire. A long flame came from this plane. A 109 was coming in fast from 7 o'clock, Lt. Allen made three or four turns with this E/A. They lost altitude and dropped below the clouds. The E/A broke and hit the deck. Lt. Allen chased him among tree tops for 15 minutes. During the chase Lt. Allen got many hits. Lt. Allen last saw E/A as the 109 went under Lt. Allen who was forced to pull up from 50' because of engine trouble, and he was low on ammunition. The E/A was less than 50'. The chase broke off NE. of Koblenz at 1045.

CHARLES E. BARTLETT,
1st Lt., A.C.,
Int. O.

HEADQUARTERS
THREE HUNDRED FIFTY-FIFTH FIGHTER GROUP
APO 558   AAF STATION F-122

2 March 1945.

MISSION SUMMARY REPORT

1. 355th Fighter Group - Lt. Col. Graham leading.
2. 34 P-51's (14-354th; 11-357th; 9-358th) Up: 0816 Down: 1350.
3. Five.
4. F.O. 1683-A, Ramrod, B-24's, Second Division to Magdeburg.
5. Nil.
6. Nil.
7. Nil.
8. 5-2-0 / Air.
9. R/V 0930, Zuider Zee, 24,000 ft. with third box, B-24's, Second Division, 18/20,000 ft. Target, 1040. Broke escort, 1236, Zuider Zee, 18,000 ft. bombers 17/21,000 ft. One squadron swept Hannover-Bremen-Dummer Lake area on withdrawal at 12,000 ft. without incident, rejoined bombers, and broke escort at Zuider Zee.
10. Nil.
11. (a) Many trains observed but because of altitude, direction not determined. Two obsvd. east of Brunswick, two north Magdeburg, one southeast Bremen, three northeast Dummer Lake. (b) One B-24 down near Lingen, 1200, no chutes. Bomber smoking and in spiral, 1152, north Steinhuder Lake, 15,000 ft. Three or four chutes.
12. Lt. Allen, 358th sqdn., aborted, 1010, east Dummer Lake because of lack of oxygen. At 1020, flying at 21,000 ft. in the Dummer Lake area he saw 15 ME-109's with bombs flying at 13,000 ft. on a heading of approx. 195 degrees. The E/A's were directly below Lt. Allen, flying in two groups, one above the other about 700 ft., eight in the top group, and seven in the bottom. Both groups were echeloned to the left out of the sun. Their wing tips and elevator tips were painted a very light blue. At a distance they looked like P-51's. Three had dragon-like insignia on fuselage. They did not drop their bombs when attacked by Lt. Allen and seemed reluctant to break formation. He believes he destroyed seven E/A's but pending assessment claims five destroyed and two probably destroyed. The chase broke off northeast of Koblenz, at 1045.
13. Target - heavy, intense, accurate; Brunswick - same.
14. 8-9/10 in target area up to 8,000 ft.
15. Nil.
16. 5-2-0
    Five ME-109's Destroyed - Lt. Roscoe Allen, 358th Sqdn. Two ME-109's Probably Destroyed - Lt. Roscoe Alen, 358th Sqdn.

/s/Kenneth W. Mason
KENNETH H. MASON
Captain, Air Corps
Assistant Group I.O.

ABOUT THE AUTHOR

Bill Marshall is all Air Force. He reckons he was conceived at Randolph Field, Texas in December 1944, and he arrived on schedule nine months later at his mother's home in Atlanta, Georgia. His father, Lt. Col. Bert Marshall, Jr., was CO of the 355th Fighter Group on occupation duty at Gablingen, Germany by then. Bill was named for Bert's brother James William, killed in an AT-6 accident in 1944.

Bill's education includes bachelor and masters degrees in aerospace engineering at the University of Texas in Arlington. He is senior executive of a high-technology research and development company in Dallas, where he makes his home with Dawn, his wife of 17 years, and their children Kimberley, Amanda and Bert II. His hobbies include skiing, hunting and custom gunsmithing.

This volume marks a unique event in U.S. publishing. It is the first aviation unit history written by an offspring of a fighter ace. As such, it is a loving tribute not only to Bert Marshall, Jr., but to all the friends of his youth.

ABOUT THE ARTIST

Having an interest in aviation illustrations since he was old enough to pick up a pencil, Harley Copic picked up a book in his high school library titled *"How To Draw Planes"* by Frank Wooton. Overcoming his disbelief that the pictures therein were actually drawings rather than photos, Harley has never altered his objectives to someday be one of today's finest aviation artists, an objective he feels he's only accomplished with an abundance of devine guidance.

With over a dozen paintings in the USAF art collection, numerous rides in USAF aircraft, many trips to USAF bases, including a tour of U.S. bases in Thailand during the Vietnam conflict, Harley still remains inspired by aviation artists such as Frank Wooton, Keith Ferris, and R.G. Smith.

Many of Harley's paintings reside in private collections and a number of his works have been reproduced on dust jackets of various aviation books. His greatest satisfaction is that his hobby of aviation art supports his other hobby of collecting performance cars of the '60's and '70's an enjoyment he could not otherwise afford.

THE CHAMPLIN FIGHTER MUSEUM

The Champlin Fighter Museum ranks as one of the world's unique historical institutions. Unlike most museums, it is privately operated, owing its origin to Douglas L. Champlin, a long-time collector of vintage aircraft. Champlin began acquiring WW II fighters in 1969 and opened his museum in Mesa, Arizona (25 miles east of Phoenix) in January 1981. With addition of original and reproduction WW I aircraft, the collection includes some 30 historic airplanes representing five nations. Most are maintained in airworthy condition.

Designated official home of the American Fighter Aces Association in 1982, the museum has added jet aircraft of Korean and Vietnam War vintage. CFM Press has begun a series of volumes which will cover the history of the men and machines which have made fighter aviation a subject of enduring fascination.

Other CFM books in print:

Big Friend, Little Friend	Lt. Col. Richard E. Turner, USAF (Ret)
The Champlin Fighter Museum Coloring Book	Bob Stevens, artist
America's First Eagles	Lt. Lucien H. Thayer (co-published with Bender Publishing, San Jose, California)
Fox Two	Randy Cunningham with Jeff Ethell

Forthcoming titles include:

The Austro-Hungrian Aces of WW I	Dr. Martin O'Connor
Winged Samurai: Saburo Sakai Japanese Navy Aces	Henry Sakaida
Fighting Mustang: Chronicle of the P-51	William N. Hess

Champlin Fighter Museum
Falcon Field
4636 Fighter Aces Drive
Mesa, Arizona 85205

(602) 830-4540